Famous Speeches in American History

Glenn R. Capp

FAMOUS SPEECHES IN AMERICAN HISTORY

FAMOUS

PEECHES IN
AMERICAN HISTORY

13 44

LENN R. CAPP
ylor University

 THE **BOBBS-MERRILL** COMPANY, INC.
A SUBSIDIARY OF **HOWARD W. SAMS & CO., INC.**
Publishers • INDIANAPOLIS • NEW YORK

To College Students—past, present, and future—May this anthology inspire you to seek inclusion in future volumes of famous speeches.

PREFACE

FAMOUS SPEECHES IN AMERICAN HISTORY is intended primarily for beginning courses in oral communication as a supplement to any good textbook. It includes well-known speeches because the compiler believes that the beginning student should acquaint himself first with speeches of greatest historical significance. If he later takes advanced courses, he will perhaps desire to study lesser-known American speeches and speakers and speeches of other countries. The introductory material on how to analyze speeches is elementary and nontechnical because the beginning student is not yet ready for the finer points of rhetorical criticism.

The decision to compile this anthology grew out of a series of meetings with college administrators about whether speech should be made a required course. The administrators recommended that any required course in oral communication should contain a liberal arts content—that the student should become acquainted with the significant speakers and speeches of history and with the issues and circumstances surrounding them. Furthermore, they expressed belief that such knowledge could be taught without sacrificing classroom time devoted to the acquisition of skills in speechmaking.

The study of great speeches should be made in addition to the study and practice of rhetorical principles. This anthology provides a means for carrying out the recommendations of these educators.

Teachers of public address raised three practical questions about the volume: (1) Upon what basis should speeches be selected for analysis and how can a practical number be selected from the many significant speeches of history? (2) Can an anthology be prepared that presents a representative and practical number of speeches to avoid the necessity of using several volumes? (3) Can a volume be published that will not be too expensive, considering the fact that the student must also buy a textbook and other materials?

This anthology attempts to meet all three of these problems. Perhaps no entirely satisfactory answer can be given as to which speeches comprise the most significant in history, but the consensus of leading teachers of public address in American colleges and universities gives a basis for decision. The eighteen speeches included in this volume were selected by vote of the professors of public address listed in the directory of the Speech Association of America. The ballot instructed the professors to list the most significant speeches in American history (1) prior to 1900, and (2) since 1900. Although no specific standards were given for judging the significance of the speeches, the teachers were asked to consider the relationship of the speeches to the prevailing times: "(1) What effect did they have on the issues with which they dealt? (2) How well did they conform to the prevailing rhetorical standards?" In brief, the speeches were chosen more on the basis of their historical significance than upon their rhetorical excellence, more on the basis of the rhetorical standards prevailing at the time the speeches were given than upon present-day standards. The speeches are presented in chronological order together with introductory materials concerning the speaker, the occasion, and the speech. If the majority opinion of these leading educators be accepted, this anthology meets the requirements for a collection of representative speeches in a single, inexpensive volume.

Best results for use of the anthology can perhaps be attained by assigning one speech each week for the eighteen weeks of a semester. For schools on the quarter plan, three speeches may be assigned for each two-week period. By having the students analyze the speeches by the plan explained in the introduction and answer the questions listed after each speech, a minimum of classroom time will be required for the assignment. By this procedure, the analysis of these famous speeches should add to the liberal arts content without detracting from the skills-acquiring function of the beginning course in speech.

Grateful acknowledgment is made to the following: to the copyright holders for permission to reprint copyrighted materials; to the Baylor Research Committee for a financial grant which facilitated the completion of the anthology; to George A. Schell, Jr., Professors Edna Haney, Gladys Beckwith, and Mary Booras for reading and criticizing parts of the manuscript; and to my wife, Thelma Robuck Capp, for her valuable counsel and assistance.

GLENN R. CAPP
Waco, Texas

CONTENTS

Part II: CONTEMPORARY SPEECHES

FAMOUS SPEECHES IN AMERICAN HISTORY

INTRODUCTION

THE STUDY OF FAMOUS SPEECHES

Why Should You Study Famous Speeches?

Students of oral communication can learn about the principles of public address by studying significant speeches of history. Who determines what constitutes effective oral communication? The principles come from two sources: (1) the rhetoricians—those teachers and writers of oral communication beginning with the Classical Period who have set forth their findings and practices; and (2) outstanding speakers—those men in history who have used speech effectively. The traditional methods of instruction in our schools stress a study of the rhetoricians. Such instruction can be supplemented by a study of the methods of famous speakers who used speech effectively to help shape history. Although few men included in this anthology wrote about their theories of speechmaking, all of them employed the principles effectively and thereby helped to establish standards by usage. What they did should concern all serious students of speech. Did they do what modern rhetoricians say should be done? How well do their practices conform to the rhetorical principles of the times? What changes in rhetorical principles can be noted with the changing times?

By a study of great speakers and their speeches, the present-day student of oral communication can derive several benefits: (1) He can gain ideas for his background of knowledge. Since great speeches deal with significant ideas, one acquires information by reading and analyzing speeches. A background of information and ideas constitutes the most important prerequisite for successful communication. (2) He can learn how great speakers utilized communicative skills. Skills of presentation cannot be studied by means of printed speeches, but skills of composition and style can. Thus, one learns how famous speakers arranged their speeches, supported their points, used psychological appeals, and put their ideas into colorful and forcible language. (3) He can gain appreciation of speaking and thus enhance his enthusiasm for improving his own skills. Many modern-day speakers date the beginning of their interest in speechmaking from the reading of famous masterpieces of eloquence. Thus, by analyzing the significant speeches of history, a student can add to his storehouse of ideas, learn new communicative skills, and acquire enthusiasm for self-improvement.

Students of history can also profit from studying famous speakers and speeches. Almost all great speeches deal with significant issues, movements which affect history. New crises bring forth great speeches which often profoundly affect the outcome of the crises. A study of speeches gives new insight into these events and varying concepts concerning them. Knowledge of the speaker, the occasion, and the speech brings about understanding and appreciation of historical events and thus constitutes one method of studying history.

Persons without specialized interests in oral communication and history should also be interested in these famous speeches. Many of the speeches deal with the most dramatic events in history and were given by some of the nation's most distinguished statesmen. To study the speeches and the circumstances surrounding them adds to a person's background of information and provides interesting reading. Thus the benefits derived from reading famous speeches may be both utilitarian and aesthetic.

Which Speeches Are the Most Famous in American History?

Perhaps no two people would agree completely on the eighteen most significant speeches in American history. As explained in the preface, however, the speeches included in this collection represent a consensus among leading professors. The speeches are arranged in chronological order in this volume, but they are listed below in the order of their rank.

SPEECHES BEFORE 1900

1st: Abraham Lincoln—"Gettysburg Address"
2nd: Patrick Henry—"Liberty or Death"
3rd: Daniel Webster—"Reply to Hayne"
4th: William Jennings Bryan—"Cross of Gold"
5th: Henry W. Grady—"The New South"
6th: Abraham Lincoln—"Second Inaugural Address"
7th: George Washington—"Farewell Address"
8th: Booker T. Washington—"Atlanta Exposition Speech"
9th: Ralph Waldo Emerson—"The American Scholar"

SPEECHES AFTER 1900

1st: Franklin D. Roosevelt—"First Inaugural Address"
2nd: Franklin D. Roosevelt—"Declaration of War Against Japan"
3rd: Woodrow Wilson—"For the League of Nations"
4th: Woodrow Wilson—"Declaration of War"
5th: Douglas MacArthur—"Address before Congress"
6th: Adlai E. Stevenson—"Acceptance Speech, 1952"
7th: Theodore Roosevelt—"The Man with the Muck Rake"
8th: Woodrow Wilson—"Fourteen Points"
    John F. Kennedy—"Inaugural Address"*

The fourteen speakers represented in this volume include six Presidents of the United States, four other men known primarily for their political activities, one minister-educator, one educator, one newspaper editor, and one military leader. Woodrow Wilson is represented by three speeches, Franklin D. Roosevelt by two, Abraham Lincoln by two, and the remaining eleven men by one each. Fifteen of the eighteen speeches deal primarily with political issues, and two with educational

---

* Added by the editor as a representative recent speech after the vote was taken.

problems. One is a brief speech of dedication. Perhaps the preponderance of political speeches indicates that speeches involving public policy make the greatest historical impact; they become the most famous.

How Should a Speech Be Analyzed?

If a speech is to become famous, the right man must say the right thing at the right time. Daniel Webster put the matter a little differently: "True eloquence . . . consists in the man, in the subject, and in the occasion." A speech cannot be appraised properly without knowledge of the man who spoke it and of the issues, the circumstances, and the occasion which called it forth. In brief, any speaking situation consists of (1) the speaker, (2) the occasion—including the audience, and (3) the speech.

THE SPEAKER

Rhetoricians beginning with the Classical Period have written about the importance of the character of the speaker to the total speaking situation. Aristotle stressed three means of persuasion: ethos—the character of the speaker; pathos—the appeal to the basic drives and desires of man; and argument—the logical appeal or the use of evidence and reason. A good speech contains elements of all three types of appeal, but it must originate with an able man—a man of character, knowledge, and good will.

When a man speaks he mirrors what he knows, the type of person he has become, and the skills he has acquired in organizing and presenting his ideas. He is a product of his environment, training, and experience. To understand a speaker's ideas one must understand what he knows, thinks, and feels. To understand a particular speech fully, one must study the biography of the speaker. What factors in his early environment influenced his interest in speechmaking and in the subject of his historically famous speech? What factors in his training had bearing on his development as a speaker? How did he prepare his speeches for delivery? What accounts for his interest in, and how fundamental was his knowledge of, the subject of his speech? The answers to these questions serve as the basis for analyzing a speech.

To illustrate, one may compare Woodrow Wilson with George Washington. Wilson was well educated, a dreamer, and a man of ideas. Washington was poorly educated, a pragmatist, and a man of action. Wilson insisted on writing his own speeches. He first wrote an outline in shorthand, then wrote the speech in shorthand, and finally typed it himself. When pressed for time, he dictated the speech to a stenographer from his shorthand outline and corrected the manuscript. Washington discussed his ideas with members of his staff and trusted them to put his speeches into final form. For example, Hamilton, Jay, and Madison helped prepare Washington's Farewell Address and Hamilton wrote the final draft. Wilson engaged in activities in college that contributed to his speaking skills. He participated in the speech activities of the literary societies, served as editor of his college newspaper, and engaged in school politics. He enjoyed speaking. Washington had only an elementary education with no formal training in speechmaking. He avoided making speeches whenever possible. Each was a great man but in different ways. Their early environment, training, and interests are reflected in their speeches. Wilson's speeches reveal a noble spirit dedicated to a great cause. Washington's speeches fail to reveal his greatness because he made his contributions in acts and deeds, not words. Knowledge of these differences is prerequisite to a proper analysis and evaluation of their speeches.

During Adlai Stevenson's campaigns for the Presidency, the criticism was often heard that he spoke above the level of his audiences, that his speeches were too literary and too profound. A study of his speeches fails to validate these claims. Perhaps the fact that he failed to conform to the popular concept of a politician gave rise to this belief. He dared to say what he thought should be said rather than what the people wanted to hear. He used the campaign to inform the people on the issues as well as to get votes. Perhaps he did these things because his early environment, training, and exposure to high ethical standards made him incapable of stooping to sophistic devices solely to gain votes. These principles permeate his life. One must understand the man, Stevenson, in order to appraise his speeches accurately.

Franklin D. Roosevelt's two speeches received the largest number of votes of the contemporary period in the poll taken to determine what speeches were chosen for this anthology. Since Roosevelt spoke so often and so effectively, many people believed that speaking came easily to him and that his speeches required little preparation. A study of his methods of preparation reveals that he prepared his speeches with great care. His important speeches went through as many as ten revisions. His superior speeches resulted from his thorough background knowledge, his skills in composition and delivery, and his maturity of judgment. Knowledge about the life of Roosevelt aids in appraising his speeches, as is true for all the speakers in this volume.

THE OCCASION

For proper evaluation, a speech must be analyzed in its setting. It must be considered in relation to the issue with which it dealt, to the climate of opinion on the issue at the time, and to the attitudes and feelings of the audience who heard it. A significant speech is never given in a vacuum; it treats vital issues for interested people on important occasions. The ultimate test of a speech may well be the effect it had on the issue with which it dealt. The immediate effect depends largely on the adaptation the speaker makes to the occasion and to his audience. For example, Adlai Stevenson made several statements about not seeking the presidential nomination in his acceptance speech at the Democratic National Convention in Chicago, Illinois, on July 26, 1952. A reader unfamiliar with what transpired at the convention might conclude that Mr. Stevenson belabored this point. In fact, a concerted "draft Stevenson" movement preceded his nomination, a movement which he at first opposed. The interest which generated from Mr. Stevenson's reluctance permeated the entire convention, a factor which needs to be understood for proper evaluation of the speech. Furthermore, the brevity and lively style show how effectively he adapted to the 3:00 A.M. hour and to the fatigue of the audience.

To evaluate properly the effective psychological appeal made by Henry W. Grady in his speech "The New South," one must understand the circumstances that confronted Grady when he spoke to the New England Society of New York City during the reconstruction period following the Civil War. Here we find a young Southerner, a liberal newspaper editor, advancing a point of view hostile to the beliefs of his conservative, Northern audience. How well he succeeded with a hostile audience cannot be appreciated without knowledge of the intense feelings of his audience toward the South.

Almost all the speeches in this volume show speakers rising to the occasion to meet specific situations. How could one understand fully General Douglas MacArthur's address before Congress without knowledge of the strong emotional feelings occasioned when President Harry Truman relieved MacArthur of his command in Japan? To understand Patrick Henry's "Liberty or Death" speech advocating military readiness by Virginia, one must know about the people's feelings of oppression in this country just before the Revolutionary War. William Jennings Bryan received the Democratic nomination for President in 1896 because he spoke so eloquently at the convention on the troublesome issue of bimetallism versus the gold standard. His dominant personality, commanding delivery, and intense enthusiasm carried the issue for bimetallism. Without knowledge of the importance of the bimetallic issue to the period, one could not understand or evaluate his speech properly.

Knowledge of the occasion and the prevailing circumstances is essential to an accurate evaluation of any speech; it serves as the background for proper analysis.

THE SPEECH

A study of the speech itself is the most important factor in analyzing a written speech. Since only three of the fourteen speakers discussed in this volume are still living, present-day students have little opportunity to observe the speakers' presentation skills. Skills of composition and style can be studied, however, from their printed speeches. For proper appraisal, the following three limiting factors must be considered.

First, who was responsible for the text of the speech? Almost all the speakers included in this volume were important governmental officials who had staffs at their command for research and writing.

Some relied heavily on their assistants, others very little. As already explained, many of George Washington's speeches were put into final form by others. The only known text of Patrick Henry's speech "Liberty or Death" was written by William Wirt from notes and newspaper accounts almost forty years after Henry's death. Conversely, Adlai Stevenson, Woodrow Wilson, Booker T. Washington, and Ralph Waldo Emerson are known to have written their speeches themselves, although they often sought criticisms by others before presenting them. Franklin D. Roosevelt's speeches were sometimes a cooperative endeavor between him and his staff. He made the original plans for his speeches, but others assisted with the research and writing. Obviously, the importance of studying the speaker's life and the circumstances under which he spoke apply only if the speaker prepared his own speeches. With the exceptions already noted, however, the speeches included in this volume are primarily the work of the speakers.

A second limiting factor is whether the printed text represents accurately what the speaker said on the occasion. In some instances, a speaker may speak extemporaneously and later write or dictate his speech for publication. This method was often used by William Jennings Bryan. Others may use a prepared manuscript and later edit the manuscript for publication. Ralph Waldo Emerson used this method for the original publication of the "The American Scholar." Other speakers may have their speeches recorded in shorthand as they speak and later edit the transcription. This method was used by Daniel Webster for his "Reply to Hayne." For proper evaluation of the speaker's oral-communication skills from a printed speech, the text analyzed should conform to the speech as presented. The texts included in this anthology were taken from the sources of their original publication but, as already noted, some deviations may exist between the printed text and the speech as presented.

A third limiting factor relates to the standards for evaluating a printed speech. Standards change with the times. For example, although a direct, communicative style prevails today, an elaborate, ornate style characterized the period of elocution of the late nineteenth century. The rhetorical standards should be analyzed for an understanding of varying concepts, not as principles to be emulated. Furthermore, the standards which prevailed when the speeches were given must be considered, not present-day standards. With these limiting factors in mind, consider the following suggestions as aids to analysis.

Plan of Analysis

A printed speech may be studied for an understanding of the ideas and information which it contains and as a basis for rhetorical criticism. One adds to his storehouse of knowledge by studying historically significant speeches. The primary purpose of speech is to communicate ideas. By reading speeches, one develops his facility in comprehending the ideas which they contain. First, one should read the speech in its entirety with emphasis on comprehension; then he should attempt to reproduce the main ideas of the speech from memory. The ability to comprehend the fully developed idea of a speech can be improved with practice; therefore, this exercise should become easier as one proceeds with the study.

A speech may also be analyzed as a means for acquiring information about rhetorical skills—how to organize a speech, how to support one's points, how to utilize methods of proof, and how to express one's ideas in acceptable language. These factors are explained in almost all text-books* for beginning speech courses; only the salient factors will be covered here as an overview before the student studies the principles in detail from his textbook.

SPEECH ORGANIZATION

In analyzing the arrangement of a speech, attempt first to isolate the central idea—the philosophy and principles underlying the speech. For example, in his inaugural address President John F. Kennedy spoke first of our heritage of liberty and contrasted our beliefs with those of our forebears. He made a pledge of cooperation to our old allies, to our new allies, to those struggling against mass misery, to the South American republics, and to the United Nations. Finally, he made

* See Glenn R. Capp, *How to Communicate Orally* (Englewood Cliffs, N.J.: Prentice-Hall, Inc., 1961).

a plea that our adversaries renew the quest for peace, and concluded by showing how the peoples of the world can contribute to the cause of freedom. Permeating all these points was a central idea—through looking to the future and by a united effort, we can win in the struggle against tyranny, poverty, and war.

The organizational pattern is the order in which a speech is arranged into main points, subpoints, and supporting data to bring out the central idea. Almost all speeches are divided into an introduction, a body, and a conclusion.

The introduction attempts to create a favorable atmosphere by putting the audience into the proper attitude to listen, stimulates interest by making the first reference to the topic compelling and provocative, and clarifies the topic by dividing it into its logical divisions and by defining necessary terms.

Not all introductions are clearly distinguishable from the body of the speech, and some omit one or more of the functions listed above. In some situations the proper atmosphere may already have been created by a previous speaker, the procedure for the occasion, or the interest in the topic. For example, Franklin D. Roosevelt referred immediately to his topic in the opening statement of his speech declaring war against Japan because the proper atmosphere already existed—the interest of the nation was focused on his speech. Adlai Stevenson began his acceptance speech at the 1952 Democratic National Convention with "I accept your nomination—and your program." His audience had waited until three o'clock in the morning for his nomination; no technique for getting interest was needed. Ralph Waldo Emerson performed all three functions in the introduction of "The American Scholar" because he had a heterogeneous audience and no momentous event gave rise to his speech. In his speech "The New South," Henry W. Grady used almost half his time on his introduction because he needed to create a receptive attitude among his hostile listeners. The nature of the speech and the occasion determines how detailed the introduction should be.

The body of a speech normally discloses the central idea, divides it into main and subordinate points, and arranges the points into an organizational pattern. The body may be organized by several methods, depending upon the adaptation of the material to the occasion and the purpose of the speech. The general organizational pattern can usually be recognized as deductive or inductive in form. The deductive method states the points first and develops them by various forms of support. The inductive method presents the details first and states the conclusion as a climax to the point. William Jennings Bryan utilized the deductive method in his speech "Cross of Gold" because it consisted largely of refutation of points made by previous speakers. He first stated the points and then answered them. Conversely, Lincoln's "Gettysburg Address" is inductive in form. He started by reviewing the circumstances that gave rise to the occasion and concluded by showing the significance of these circumstances to the American people.

The conclusion usually summarizes the main points, amplifies the central idea, and emphasizes the desired action. Not all speeches perform all these functions; the purpose of the speech and the circumstances of the occasion determine the extent of the conclusion. For example, Booker T. Washington used all three steps in his Atlanta Exposition speech as follows: (1) he summarized his ideas by a paraphrase of his points; (2) he emphasized his central idea by a pledge to his audience; and (3) he predicted that his proposed action would bring about better understanding and trust among the races. Franklin D. Roosevelt concluded his speech for declaring war against Japan without a summary; he simply spelled out the action desired—that Congress declare war on Japan.

FORMS OF SUPPORT

The forms of support are used to clarify, amplify, and prove the points in a speech; they give support to the ideas and contentions, much as evidence does in law cases. Without the expanding process of supporting material, the organizational pattern would be a mere skeleton and the ideas would remain undeveloped. The principal forms of support consist of statistics, examples, analogies, and quotations from authority.

Statistics consist of figures that signify relationships, the relative number of occurrences of facts. In his speech before Congress, General Douglas MacArthur used statistics to show that Asia had become a new force in the world, as follows: "Mustering half of the earth's population, and sixty per cent of its natural resources, these people are rapidly consolidating a new force. . . ." Booker T. Washington used statistics to show the impact of the Negro in the South in his "Atlanta Exposition" speech when he said, "Nearly sixteen millions of hands will aid you in pulling the load upward; or they will pull against you the load downward. We will constitute one-third and more of the ignorance and crime of the South, or one-third its intelligence and progress. . . ." Numbers become statistics when they indicate the proportion of instances of a specific fact. They prove valuable in explaining or in supporting ideas, but their use may be easily abused. Accuracy can be attained by careful definition of the units upon which the statistics are based, by comparing only those statistics that use the same unit, and by giving up-to-date facts. Statistics may also prove dull and uninteresting. Effective speakers ensure interest by making statistics vivid and graphic and by relating them to matters familiar to the audience.

Examples consist of real or hypothetical situations, instances, or past happenings. Examples may be used to amplify explanations or as a basis for inferences. They may consist either of specific instances or of detailed illustrations. For example, Franklin D. Roosevelt used specific instances in his speech declaring war against Japan by making reference to several countries that Japan had attacked the previous evening. He merely referred to the instances without developing them. Booker T. Washington used a detailed illustration effectively in his "Atlanta Exposition" speech in his example of a ship lost at sea. He developed the illustration in detail. It pertained aptly to the central idea of his speech and served as a unifying force for his points. Accuracy in the use of examples is attained by choosing representative cases, by giving the details accurately, and by giving a variety of cases. Effective examples make clear the point to be gained, show vividness and timeliness, relate to matters close to the listeners, and include active material.

An analogy compares two or more objects for the purpose of pointing out similarities and differences. In explanation, an unfamiliar object may be compared to a familiar one to clarify the unfamiliar. In reasoning, one may infer that if two things are alike in pertinent known respects, then they will probably be alike in respects not known. William Jennings Bryan concluded his "Cross of Gold" speech with an analogy: "You shall not press down upon the brow of labor this crown of thorns. . . ." He compared imposition of the gold standard on labor to pressing down a crown of thorns on a person's head. The analogy is used effectively when it compares cases familiar to the audience and uses vivid and colorful comparisons.

Quotations from authority consist of statements of opinion of others used to corroborate one's own conclusions. When used as testimony, quotations probably have more persuasive than logical effect. On most questions of policy, the experts disagree; equally able authorities can be quoted on either side of controversial issues. Testimony may have strong persuasive effect, however, by lending prestige to the speaker's conclusions, especially if the authority is highly regarded by the audience. Testimony should come from unprejudiced persons who are qualified by training, experience, and ability to render expert judgments. The quotation should represent the author's statement accurately and should not be lifted from its context. If quotations are unusual, interesting, and acceptable to an audience, they aid the speaker in getting his ideas accepted. Henry W. Grady used a quotation from Benjamin H. Hill effectively in beginning his speech "The New South" because Mr. Hill was revered by his audience. The quotation from an acceptable authority tended to lessen the hostility of the audience toward Mr. Grady's point of view. Adlai E. Stevenson added the weight of authority to his "Acceptance Speech" when speaking of corruption in office, as follows: "If the fear is corruption in official position, do you believe with Charles Evans Hughes that guilt is personal and knows no party?" The quotation helped clinch his point.

The Methods of Proof

The methods of proof mean the types of appeal used to get one's point accepted. They consist of ethical, emotional, and logical appeals.

Ethical appeal pertains to the ethos of the speaker—impressions that the audience forms of the speaker as a result of his reputation, his actions, and his comments. A large part of a speaker's ethical appeal comes from his reputation and his manner of presentation, but what he talks about also gives impressions of his character, ability, and attitudes. A speaker who expresses intelligent ideas and makes mature judgments will be regarded as an able man by his audience. He may also make statements about, or refer to matters highly regarded by, his listeners and thus create favorable impressions. Such ethos-evincing statements may include references to sources consulted, special studies made, honors held, positions attained, or places visited that bear on one's ability to appraise his topic accurately. Fittingly, Franklin D. Roosevelt created ethical appeal in the conclusion of his "First Inaugural Address" by asking for divine guidance: "In this dedication of a nation we humbly ask the blessings of God. May He protect each and every one of us! May He guide me in the days to come." Henry W. Grady created ethical appeal in his speech "The New South" by requesting a fair hearing: "I ask an indulgent hearing from you. I beg that you will bring your full faith in American fairness and frankness to judgment upon what I shall say."

Emotional appeals consist of statements that affect the basic motives, desires, and needs of man. Judicially used, they aid a speaker in getting his ideas accepted. If a speaker can show his listeners that his proposal will result in material gain, increased prestige, greater authority, or preservation of ideals, they will accept his ideas partly for emotional reasons. When Woodrow Wilson spoke of making "the world safe for Democracy" in his war message, he appealed to patriotism and self-preservation—the desire to protect that which we hold dear. Patrick Henry's concluding statement in his "Liberty or Death" speech is a strong appeal to the emotions: "Is life so dear, or peace so sweet, as to be purchased at the price of chains and slavery? Forbid it, Almighty God! I know not what course others may take; but as for me, give me liberty, or give me death!" General Douglas MacArthur's concluding statement in his "Address Before Congress" also shows emotional appeal: "The world has turned over many times since I took the oath at West Point, and the hopes and dreams have all since vanished, but I still remember the refrain of one of the most popular barracks ballads of that day which proclaimed most proudly that old soldiers never die; they just fade away. And, like the old soldier of that ballad, I now close my military career and just fade away, an old soldier who tried to do his duty as God gave him the light to see that duty. Good-by."

Logical appeal depends primarily upon evidence and reasoning. Evidence consists of the facts and opinions used to support one's contentions. Facts consist of the circumstances and conditions of a situation, tangible findings; opinions encompass statements of belief and conjecture. Factual evidence normally has more probative effect than opinion evidence, but each applies to logical proof. Reasoning is the process of showing proper relationships between evidence and the conclusions drawn from it. It consists of drawing inferences from evidence. It appeals to understanding in order to influence belief. Logic tests the thinking processes to determine if they conform to established rules; it distinguishes between good and fallacious reasoning. To illustrate, Daniel Webster made effective use of logical reasoning in his "Reply to Hayne" by refuting the arguments of Senator Hayne. He balanced each of his arguments with those of his opponent and supported them by evidence and reasoning. Woodrow Wilson's speech "For the League of Nations" affords another excellent example of logical appeal.

THE USE OF LANGUAGE

Style relates to the speaker's choice and arrangement of words, his use of language. Present-day rhetoricians stress that speakers should use language to communicate clearly and precisely, not to display their skills—language is for communication, not exhibition. Yet many of the older speeches in this volume were delivered at a period when ornate style predominated. Patrick Henry's speech "Liberty or Death" illustrates the ornate style of that period. The speech is almost poetic in style. To illustrate further, compare the direct and communicative style of John F. Kennedy's "Inaugural Address" with the elaborate style of William Jennings Bryan's "Cross of Gold" speech. Language should be analyzed with the understanding that style varies with changing times.

Consider also that oral style differs from written style; it is more informal, repetitious, and direct. The writer uses titles and subtitles as well as paragraphs and summaries and makes transitions to his next point. The reader can turn back the page and reread ideas not originally understood; the listener must comprehend instantaneously. These differences should be understood for proper analysis of speaking style.

Oral style should be unambiguous so as to express precision in meaning. To achieve precise meaning, style should be specific rather than general, simple rather than complex; it avoids wordiness and technical language and uses repetition and restatement judiciously. An effective speaker chooses from the many ways of expressing an idea that way which enables him to convey his thoughts with greatest precision.

Oral style should be appropriate to the occasion, audience, and type of speech. Persuasion calls for more forceful language than does the informative speech. For formal occasions, style should show more restraint than for informal occasions. Appropriate language avoids triteness, vulgarisms, name-calling, and euphemisms as well as the overuse of slang and foreign phrases. Language, properly employed, aids a speaker in communicating his ideas; it does not call attention to itself.

Oral style should aid the speaker in maintaining interest. It should be adapted to a specific audience, not to general readers. It should be vivid and graphic. The language of oral communication should be direct and personal so that listeners will recall their life experiences. By using colorful words, figurative language, and action words, the speaker helps maintain interest.

EVALUATION OF THE SPEECH

As a final step, briefly evaluate the speech on the basis of your analysis. Were you able to understand the speaker's ideas upon first reading the speech? Was the central idea or philosophy of the speech clearly discernible? Was the speech well organized? Were the forms of support used accurately and effectively? Was there a balance among ethical, emotional, and logical proof? Was the language clear, appropriate, and interesting? What were the strong points and weaknesses of the speech? The questions and exercises following each speech will help you make a more detailed analysis.

PART I
HISTORICAL SPEECHES
before 1900

I *LIBERTY OR DEATH*

PATRICK HENRY
(1736-1799)

The Speaker

Patrick Henry was born in Hanover County, Virginia, but spent most of his boyhood at Mount Brilliant, later known as The Retreat. Although Henry's parents were middle-class folk, they were respected for their cultural and intellectual attainments. After attending country schools until he was ten, Henry was tutored by his father. He early demonstrated an aptitude for mathematics and history and later became proficient in the use of words and in the mechanics of writing. After failing in business twice, Henry studied law and passed the law examination at Williamsburg in 1760.

On December 1, 1763, Henry achieved prominence by speaking in favor of the Parsons' Cause, or in opposition to an act by the Assembly of Virginia which would have the effect of decreasing the salaries of ministers of the Church of England. He was elected to the House of Burgesses in 1765 and later became a member of the First Continental Congress. He was elected the first Governor of the State of Virginia in 1776 and was re-elected three times, although he declined a fourth term. After leading an unsuccessful opposition to the Federal Constitution, he was elected to the Virginia Assembly as a Federalist in 1799. He died soon thereafter on June 6, 1799.

Henry was not the fiery, backwoodsman orator of obscure background popular tradition describes. Although his appearance and manners created a poor first impression, his conversation revealed a keen intellect. He was a shrewd and pragmatic political leader, but not a great social thinker. As a speaker, he depended largely on delivery. His voice was clear and powerful, but his speaking was uneven, ranging from ineffective, overemotional delivery and fallacious reasoning to electrifying brilliance. He is widely recognized as the outstanding spokesman of the American Revolution in spite of his shortcomings.

The Occasion

The high point of Patrick Henry's career was his "Liberty or Death" speech, sometimes called the "Call to Arms" speech. On March 20, 1775, the second Virginia Convention assembled in St. John's Church, Richmond, Virginia. Peyton Randolph, the conservative leader, was elected president. On March 23, the Convention considered a petition and memorial of the Assembly of the Island of Jamaica, addressed to the king, dated December 28, 1774. It defended the rights of the Colonists, but stated all powers were independent of the people and were derived exclusively from the king. The Virginia Convention resolved that acknowledgment and thanks be sent to the speaker of the Jamaica Assembly. The democratic leaders opposed this action, and Henry submitted three resolutions for putting Virginia in a state of military preparedness by raising and training a militia. During the ensuing debate Henry delivered the speech which ended with the now immortal phrase, ". . . give me liberty, or give me death."

His immediate audience consisted of political leaders of some prominence and attainment who were delegates to the convention. There was a sharp division between conservatives and the democratic liberals whose cause Henry championed. The bitter debates which ensued ended in a narrow victory of five votes in favor of Henry's resolutions.

The Speech

The only known text of the speech was originally published in 1817 in William Wirt's *Life and Character of Patrick Henry*, the first biography of Henry's life. The text, based on accounts of witnesses, is apparently incomplete. Wirt took the high points, changed some of the language, and left the impression that the speech was printed in its entirety. Although Henry's basic ideas are preserved, the rhetorical style appears superior to that of others of his reported speeches.

In the introduction to the speech, Henry paid tribute to his opponents but emphasized his right to disagree. He created a sense of urgency, stating that "liberty or slavery" depended upon military readiness. He subtly accused his opponents of failure to face facts. The body of the speech consists largely of a description of the plight of the colonies under British control—an intolerable situation which Henry proclaimed justified a resort to arms. The organizational pattern takes the problem-solution form. Throughout the speech much use is made of rhetorical questions, emotion-filled words, and appeals to fight for liberty. The conclusion is a ringing declaration of the alternatives confronting Henry—liberty or death. The text is taken from: William Wirt, *Life and Character of Patrick Henry* (Philadelphia: Claxton and Co., 25th ed., 1881), pp. 38-42.

MR. PRESIDENT: No man thinks more highly than I do of the patriotism, as well as abilities, of the very worthy gentlemen who have just addressed the House. But different men often see the same subjects in different lights; and, therefore, I hope that it will not be thought disrespectful to those gentlemen, if, entertaining as I do, opinions of a character very opposite to theirs, I shall speak forth my sentiments freely and without reserve. This is no time for ceremony. The question before the House is one of awful moment to this country. For my own part I consider it as nothing less than a question of freedom or slavery; and in proportion to the magnitude of the subject ought to be the freedom of the debate. It is only in this way that we can hope to arrive at truth, and fulfill the great responsibility which we hold to God and our country. Should I keep back my opinions at such a time, through fear of giving offense, I should consider myself as guilty of treason toward my country, and of an act of disloyalty toward the majesty of heaven, which I revere above all earthly kings.

Mr. President, it is natural to man to indulge in the illusions of hope. We are apt to shut our eyes against a painful truth, and listen to the song of that siren, till she transforms us into beasts. Is this the part of wise men, engaged in a great and arduous struggle for liberty? Are we disposed to be of the number of those who, having eyes, see not, and having ears, hear not, the things which so nearly concern their temporal salvation? For my part, whatever anguish of spirit it may cost, I am willing to know the whole truth; to know the worst and to provide for it.

I have but one lamp by which my feet are guided; and that is the lamp of experience. I know of no way of judging of the future but by the past. And judging by the past, I wish to know what there has been in the conduct of the British ministry for the last ten years to justify those hopes with which gentlemen have been pleased to solace themselves and the House? Is it that insidious smile with which our petition has been lately received? Trust it not, sir; it will prove a snare to your feet. Suffer not yourselves to be betrayed with a kiss. Ask yourselves how this gracious reception of our petition comports with these warlike preparations which cover our waters and darken our land. Are fleets and armies necessary to a work of love and reconciliation? Have we shown ourselves so unwilling to be reconciled, that force must be called in to win back our love? Let us not deceive ourselves, sir. These are the implements of war and subjugation; the last arguments to which kings resort. I ask gentlemen, sir, what means this martial array, if its purpose be not to force us to submission? Can gentlemen assign any other possible motives for it? Has Great Britain any enemy, in this quarter of the world, to call for all this accumulation of navies and armies? No, sir, she has none. They are meant for us; they can be meant for no other. They are sent over to bind and rivet upon us those chains which the British ministry have been so long forging. And what have we to oppose to them? Shall we try argument? Sir, we have been trying that for the last ten years. Have we anything new to offer on the subject? Nothing. We have held the subject up in every light of which it is capable; but it has been all in vain. Shall we resort to entreaty and humble supplication? What terms shall we find which have not been already exhausted? Let us not, I beseech you, sir, deceive ourselves longer. Sir, we have done everything that could be done to avert the storm which is now coming on. We have petitioned; we have remonstrated; we have supplicated; we have prostrated ourselves before the tyrannical hands of the ministry and parliament. Our petitions have been slighted; our remonstrances have produced additional violence and insult; our supplications have been disregarded; and we have been spurned, with contempt, from the foot of the throne. In vain, after these things, may we indulge the fond hope of peace and reconciliation. There is no longer any room for hope. If we wish to be free—if we mean to preserve inviolate those inestimable privileges for which we have been so long contending—if we mean not basely to abandon the noble struggle in which we have been so long engaged, and which we have pledged ourselves never to abandon until the glorious object of our contest shall be obtained, we must fight! I repeat it, sir, we must fight! An appeal to arms and to the God of Hosts is all that is left us!

They tell us, sir, that we are weak; unable to cope with so formidable an adversary. But when shall we be stronger? Will it be the next week, or the next year? Will it be when we are totally disarmed, and when a British guard shall be stationed in every house? Shall we gather strength by irresolution and inaction? Shall we acquire the means of effectual resistance by lying supinely on our backs, and hugging the delusive phantom of hope, until our enemies shall have bound us hand and foot? Sir, we are not weak, if we make a proper use of the means which the God of nature hath placed in our power. Three millions of people, armed in the holy cause of liberty, and in such a country as that which we possess, are invincible by any force which our enemy can send against us. Besides, sir, we shall not fight our battles alone. There is a just God who presides over the destinies of nations; and who will raise friends to fight our battles for us. The battle, sir, is not to the strong alone; it is to the vigilant, the active, the brave. Besides, sir, we have no election. If we were base enough to desire it, it is now too late to retire from the contest. There is no retreat but in submission and slavery! Our chains are forged! Their clanking may be heard on the plains of Boston! The war is inevitable—and let it come! I repeat it, sir, let it come!

It is in vain, sir, to extenuate the matter. Gentlemen may cry peace, peace—but there is no peace. The war is actually begun! The next gale that sweeps from the North will bring to our ears the clash of resounding arms! Our brethren are already in the field! Why stand we here idle? What is it that gentlemen wish? What would they have? Is life so dear, or peace so sweet, as to be purchased at the price of chains and slavery? Forbid it, Almighty God! I know not what course others may take; but as for me, give me liberty, or give me death!

Questions and Exercises

1. Where was Patrick Henry born?_____
   What was his childhood environment?_____
2. Where did he receive his elementary education?_____
   _____ His law training?_____
3. What was the highest political office that he held in Virginia?___
   _____
4. Where did he give his "Liberty or Death" speech?_____
   _____ When?_____
5. With what principal issue did the speech deal?_____
   _____
   _____
6. What was the central idea of the speech?_____
   _____
   _____
7. Give an example of emotional proof._____
   _____
   _____
8. Record the number of times that the following forms of support
   were used: _____examples; _____analogies; _____statistics;
   _____quotations.
9. What was the basic organizational pattern? _____inductive;
   _____deductive.
10. Find a sentence that illustrates the style of the speech._____
    _____
    _____

II *FAREWELL ADDRESS*

GEORGE WASHINGTON
(1732-1799)

The Speaker

All nations have popular heroes about whom many myths are form-
ulated. George Washington is perhaps our greatest national hero.
What school child has not heard the cherry-tree myth which Parson
Weems originated? Although not the saint that popular legend depicts
him, George Washington was unquestionably a great man. He was
largely a man of action rather than words. It is something of a paradox
that Washington was chosen as a famous speaker in American history,
because he did not like public speaking and went to great lengths to
avoid it. Yet his influence affected public policy perhaps more than
many of the outstanding orators of his day. For example, as presiding
officer of the Constitutional Convention, he did not take part in the
debates. The knowledge of Washington's desire for a strong central
government, however, had great influence on the formulation of the
Constitution. The effect of Washington's pronouncements on public
policy accounts more for the significance of his speeches than do his
style and skills in oral communication. The majority of Washington's
speeches were written by others but the ideas with which they dealt
were his own.

Washington was born in Westmoreland County, Virginia, on February 22, 1732. He distinguished himself as a military and governmental leader, not as an orator or literary figure. He received little formal education and left school at the age of fifteen with only a limited knowledge of arithmetic, reading, and writing. The foundation of Washington's greatness lies not so much in knowledge acquired from books as from his wide range of worldly experience. In 1749, he became official surveyor of Culpepper County, Virginia. In 1752, he received an appointment as major in the Virginia Militia. He served later as aide-de-camp to General Braddock and became commander in chief of the Virginia forces. Washington won election to the House of Burgesses in 1758. After several terms as a burgess he was elected to the First Continental Congress in 1774 and to the Second Continental Congress in 1775. In that same year Washington assumed the command of the Army of the United Colonies. Washington served as president of the Constitutional Convention in 1787 and became the first President of the United States by unanimous election in 1789. In 1792 he won unanimous re-election.

As a public speaker, Washington was far from dynamic. Slow in expression, his delivery lacked fluency. A strong champion of republicanism, Washington adhered to the rule of reason and justice. Despite his aristocratic background and manners, the thought of autocratic or monarchical government repelled him. After he refused a third term as President, his successor, President Adams, appointed him Commander in Chief of the armies. He died at Mount Vernon on December 14, 1799, from an attack of acute tonsillitis. He was buried in the family tomb on the grounds of Mount Vernon. Harry Lee's statement about Washington constitutes an almost perfect tribute: "First in war, first in peace, first in the hearts of his countrymen."

The Occasion

Washington had planned originally to retire at the end of his first term. In 1792, James Madison wrote the first draft of what later became the "Farewell Address."* Feeling a great responsibility for his

---

* Marcus Cunliffe, *George Washington: Man and Monument* (Boston: Little, Brown and Co., 1958), p. 157.

country's future, Washington desired a carefully prepared address. The basic ideas were Washington's, but he had the helpful assistance of Madison, Jay, and Hamilton. Hamilton was responsible for the final draft as we know it today. The literary style of the "Farewell Address" is considered beyond Washington's ability as a writer. In May, 1796, Washington instructed Hamilton of his desires for the speech: "My wish is that the whole may appear in a plain style, and be handed to the public in an honest, unaffected, simple part."†

The address was read before Congress from a written manuscript in September of 1796 and was published in the *American Daily Advertiser* of Philadelphia.

The Speech

Although many Americans in discussing the "Farewell Address" refer to Washington's warning against "entangling alliances," the phrase was never used. No doubt such an inference may be drawn from the section on foreign policy relating to world alliances, the most controversial section in the speech.

In the introduction Washington states his intention to retire from office at the end of the second term and thus to end the movement that he accept a third term. He imparts advice to his fellow countrymen and implores them to maintain a unified government. He argues against political parties and urges all individuals to be staunch Americans. He concludes with a brief résumé of his administration and states the desires that motivated him as President.

The style is vigorous, although many sentences may appear tedious and the language ornate by contemporary standards. Little direct evidence is cited in support of many of his ideas; the authority and prestige of Washington and the office of the Presidency make detailed support unnecessary. The first part of the speech is largely narrative and explanatory in form. Later he enumerates and develops several suggestions for future development of the country. The concluding résumé of his administration deals with factors arranged in chronological

---

† Norman Hapgood, *George Washington* (New York: The Macmillan Co., 1915), p. 392 (Letter from Washington to Hamilton quoted).

order. Several statements tend to increase the prestige of the speaker but the speech contains a minimum of emotional appeal. For text of speech, see: John C. Fitzpatrick, Ed., *The Writings of George Washington* (Washington, D.C.: United States Government Printing Office, 1940), Vol. 35, pp. 214-238.

FRIENDS AND FELLOW-CITIZENS: The period for a new election of a citizen, to administer the executive government of the United States, being not far distant, and the time actually arrived when your thoughts must be employed in designating the person who is to be clothed with that important trust, it appears to me proper, especially as it may conduce to a more distinct expression of the public voice, that I should now apprise you of the resolution I have formed, to decline being considered among the number of those out of whom a choice is to be made.

I beg you, at the same time, to do me the justice to be assured that this resolution has not been taken without a strict regard to all the considerations appertaining to the relation which binds a dutiful citizen to his country; and that in withdrawing the tender of service which silence, in my situation, might imply, I am influenced by no diminution of zeal for your future interest, no deficiency of grateful respect for your past kindness, but am supported by a full conviction that the step is compatible with both.

The acceptance of, and continuance hitherto, in the office to which your suffrages have twice called me, have been a uniform sacrifice of inclination to the opinion of duty, and to a deference for what appeared to be your desire. I constantly hoped that it would have been much earlier in my power, consistently with motives which I was not at liberty to disregard, to return to that retirement from which I had been reluctantly drawn. The strength of my inclination to do this, previous to the last election, had even led to the preparation of an address, to declare it to you; but mature reflection on the then perplexed and critical posture of our affairs with foreign nations, and the unanimous advice of persons entitled to my confidence, impelled me to abandon the idea.

I rejoice that the state of your concerns, external as well as internal, no longer renders the pursuit of inclination incompatible with the sentiment of duty or propriety, and am persuaded, whatever partiality may be retained for my services, that in the present circumstances of our country, you will not disapprove of my determination to retire.

The impressions with which I first undertook the arduous trust were explained on the proper occasion. In the discharge of this trust I will only say, that I have with good intentions contributed towards the organization and administration of the government, the best exertions of which a very fallible judgment was capable. Not unconscious, in the outset, of the inferiority of my qualifications, experience, in my own eyes, perhaps still more in the eyes of others, has strengthened the motives to diffidence of myself; and every day the increasing weight of years admonishes me more and more that the shade of retirement is as necessary to me as it will be welcome. Satisfied that if any circumstances have given peculiar value to my services they were temporary, I have the consolation to believe, that while choice and prudence invite me to quit the political scene, patriotism does not forbid it.

In looking forward to the moment which is intended to terminate the career of my public life, my feelings do not permit me to suspend the deep acknowledgment of that debt of gratitude which I owe to my beloved country for the many honors it has conferred upon me; still more for the steadfast confidence with which it has supported me; and for the opportunities I have thence enjoyed of manifesting my inviolable attachment, by services, faithful and persevering, though in usefulness unequal to my zeal. If benefits have resulted to our country from these services, let it always be remembered to your praise, and as an instructive example in our annals, that under circumstances in which the passions, agitated in every direction, were liable to mislead, amidst appearances sometimes dubious, vicissitudes of fortune often discouraging, in situations in which not unfrequently want of success has countenanced the spirit of criticism, the constancy of your support was the essential prop of the efforts, and a guarantee of the plans by which they were effected. Profoundly penetrated with this idea, I shall carry it with me to my grave, as a strong incitement to unceasing wishes that heaven may continue to you the choicest tokens of its beneficence; that your union and brotherly affection may be perpetual; that the free constitution, which is the work of your hands, may be sacredly maintained; that its administration, in every department, may be stamped with wisdom and virtue; that, in fine, the happiness of the people of these States, under the auspices of liberty, may be made complete by so careful a preservation and so prudent a use of this blessing as will acquire to them the glory of recommending it to the applause, the affection, and adoption of every nation which is yet a stranger to it.

Here, perhaps, I ought to stop. But a solicitude for your welfare, which cannot end but with my life, and the apprehension of danger, natural to that solicitude, urge me, on an occasion like the present, to offer to your solemn contemplation, and to recommend to your frequent review, some sentiments, which are the result of much reflection, of no inconsiderable observation, and which appear to me all-important to the permanency of your felicity as a people. These will be offered to you with the more freedom, as you can only see in them the disinterested warnings of a parting friend, who can possibly have no personal motive to bias his counsel. Nor can I forget, as an encouragement to it, your indulgent reception of my sentiments on a former and not dissimilar occasion.

The unity of government which constitutes you one people is also now dear to you. It is justly so, for it is a main pillar in the edifice of your real independence, the support of your tranquillity at home, your peace abroad, of your safety, of your prosperity, of that very liberty which you so highly prize. But as it is easy to foresee, that from different causes and from different quarters, much pains will be taken, many artifices employed, to weaken in your minds the conviction of this truth; as this is the point in your political fortress against which the batteries of internal and external enemies will be most constantly and actively (though often covertly and insidiously) directed, it is of infinite moment that you should properly estimate the immense value of your national union, to your collective and individual happiness; that you should cherish a cordial, habitual, and immovable attachment to it; accustoming yourselves to think and speak of it as of the palladium of your political safety and prosperity, watching for its preservation with jealous anxiety; discountenancing whatever may suggest even a suspicion that it can in any event be abandoned; and indignantly frowning upon the first dawning of every attempt to alienate any portion of our country from the rest, or to enfeeble the sacred ties which now link together the various parts.

For this you have every inducement of sympathy and interest. Citizens, by birth or choice, of a common country, that country has a right to concentrate your affections. The name of American, which belongs to you in your national capacity, must always exalt the just pride of patriotism more than any appellation derived from local discriminations. With slight shades of difference, you have the same religion, manners, habits, and political principles. You have, in a common cause, fought and triumphed together; the independence and liberty you possess are the work of joint councils and joint efforts, of common dangers, sufferings, and successes.

But these considerations, however powerfully they address themselves to your sensibility, are greatly outweighed by those which apply more immediately to your interest. Here every portion of our country finds the most commanding motives for carefully guarding and preserving the union of the whole.

The North, in an unrestrained intercourse with the South, protected by the equal laws of a common government, finds, in the productions of the latter, great additional resources of maritime and commercial enterprise, and precious materials of manufacturing industry. The South, in the same intercourse, benefiting by the agency of the North, sees its agriculture grow and its commerce expand. Turning partly into its own channels the seamen of the North, it finds its particular navigation invigorated; and while it contributes, in different ways, to nourish and increase the general mass of the national navigation, it looks forward to the protection of a maritime strength, to which itself is unequally adapted. The East, in like intercourse with the West, already finds, and in the progressive improvement of interior communications, by land and water, will more and more find a valuable vent for the commodities which it brings from abroad or manufactures at home. The West derives from the East supplies requisite to its growth and comfort, and what is perhaps of still greater consequence, it must of necessity owe the secure enjoyment of indispensable outlets for its own productions to the weight, influence, and the future maritime strength of the Atlantic side of the Union, directed by an indissoluble community of interest as one nation. Any other tenure, by which the West can hold this essential advantage, whether derived from its own separate strength, or from an apostate and unnatural connection with any foreign power, must be intrinsically precarious.

While, then, every part of our country thus feels an immediate and particular interest in union, all the parts combined cannot fail to find, in the united mass of means and efforts, greater strength, greater resource, proportionably greater security, from external danger, a less frequent interruption of their peace by foreign nations; and what is of inestimable value, they must derive from union an exemption from those broils and wars between themselves which so frequently afflict neighboring countries, not tied together by the same government, which their own rivalships alone would be sufficient to produce, but which opposite foreign alliances, attachments, and intrigues, would stimulate and embitter. Hence, likewise, they will avoid the necessity of those overgrown military establishments, which, under any form of government, are inauspicious to liberty, and which are to be regarded as particularly hostile to republican liberty. In this sense it is that your union ought to be considered as a main prop of your liberty, and that the love of the one ought to endear to you the preservation of the other.

These considerations speak a persuasive language to every reflecting and virtuous mind, and exhibit the continuance of the union as a primary object of patriotic desire. Is there a doubt whether a common government can embrace so large a sphere? Let experience solve it. To listen to mere speculation, in such a case, were criminal. We are authorized to hope that a proper organization of the whole, with the auxiliary agency of governments for the respective subdivisions, will afford a happy issue to the experiment. 'Tis well worth a fair and full experiment. With such powerful and obvious motives to union, affecting all parts of our country, while experience shall not have demonstrated its impracticability, there will always be reason to distrust the patriotism of those who, in any quarter, may endeavor to weaken its bands.

In contemplating the causes which may disturb our union, it occurs, as a matter of serious concern, that any ground should have been furnished for characterizing parties by geographical discriminations—Northern and Southern, Atlantic and Western—whence designing men may endeavor to excite a belief that there is a real difference of local interests and views. One of the expedients of party to acquire influence within particular districts is to misrepresent the opinions and aims of other districts. You cannot shield yourselves too much against the jealousies and heart-burnings which spring from these misrepresentations; they tend to render alien to each other those who ought to be bound together by fraternal affection. The inhabitants of our western country have lately had a useful lesson on this head. They have seen, in the negotiation by the executive, and in the unanimous ratification by the Senate, of the treaty with Spain, and in the universal satisfaction of that event throughout the United States, a decisive proof how unfounded were the suspicions propagated among them of a policy in the general government and in the Atlantic States, unfriendly to their interests in regard to the Mississippi; they have been witnesses to the formation of two treaties—that with Great Britain and that with Spain—which secure to them everything they could desire, in respect to our foreign relations, towards confirming their prosperity. Will it not be their wisdom to rely, for the preservation of these advantages, on the union by which they were procured? Will they not henceforth be deaf to those advisers, if such there are, who would sever them from their brethren, and connect them with aliens?

To the efficacy and permanency of your union, a government for the whole is indispensable. No alliances, however strict, between the parts, can be an adequate substitute; they must inevitably experience the infractions and interruptions, which alliances, in all times, have experienced. Sensible of this momentous truth, you have improved upon your first essay by the adoption of a constitution of government better calculated than your former for an intimate union, and for the efficacious management of your common concerns. This government, the offspring of our own choice, uninfluenced and unawed, adopted upon full investigation and mature deliberation, completely free in its principles, in the distribution of its powers, uniting security with energy, and containing within itself a provision for its own amendment, has a just claim to your confidence and your support. Respect for its authority, compliance with its laws, acquiescence in its measures, are duties enjoined by the fundamental maxims of true liberty. The basis of our political systems is the right of the people to make and to alter the constitutions of government. But the constitution, which at any time exists, until changed by an explicit and authentic act of the whole people, is sacredly obligatory upon all. The very idea of the power and the right of the people to establish a government presupposes the duty of every individual to obey the established government.

All obstructions to the execution of the laws, all combinations and associations, under whatever plausible character, with the real design to direct, control, counteract, or awe the regular deliberation and action of the constituted authorities, are destructive of this fundamental principle, and of fatal tendency. They serve to organize faction, to give it an artificial and extraordinary force, to put in the place of the delegated will of the nation, the will of a party, often a small, but artful and enterprising minority of the community; and according to the alternate triumphs of different parties, to make the public administration the mirror of the ill-concerted and incongruous projects of faction, rather than the organ of consistent and wholesome plans, digested by common councils, and modified by mutual interests.

However combinations or associations of the above description may now and then answer popular ends, they are likely, in the course of time and things, to become potent engines, by which cunning, ambitious, and unprincipled men will be enabled to subvert the power of the people, and to usurp for themselves the reins of government; destroying afterward the very engines which have lifted them to unjust dominion.

Toward the preservation of your government and the permanency of your present happy state, it is requisite, not only that you speedily discountenance irregular opposition to its acknowledged authority, but also that you resist with care the spirit of innovation upon its principles, however specious the pretexts. One method of assault may be to effect, in the forms of the constitution, alterations which will impair the energy of the system, and thus to undermine what cannot be directly overthrown. In all the changes to which you may be invited, remember that time and habit are at least as necessary to fix the true character of governments as of other human institutions; that experience is the surest standard by which to test the real tendency of the existing constitution of a country; that facility in changes, upon the credit of mere hypothesis and opinion, exposes to perpetual change, from the endless variety of hypothesis and opinion. And remember especially, that for the efficient management of your common interests, in a country so extensive as ours, a government of as much vigor as is consistent with the perfect security of liberty, is indispensable. Liberty itself will find in such a government, with powers properly distributed and adjusted, its surest guardian. It is, indeed, little else than a name, where the government is too feeble to withstand the enterprises of faction; to confine each member of society within the limits prescribed by the laws, and to maintain all in the secure and tranquil enjoyment of the rights of person and property.

I have already intimated to you the danger of parties in the State, with particular reference to the founding of them on geographical discrimination. Let me now take a more comprehensive view, and warn you, in the most solemn manner, against the baneful effects of the spirit of party, generally.

This spirit, unfortunately, is inseparable from our nature, having its root in the strongest passions of the human mind. It exists under different shapes, in all governments, more or less stifled, controlled, or repressed. But in those of the popular form, it is seen in its greatest rankness, and is truly their worst enemy.

The alternate domination of one faction over another, sharpened by the spirit of revenge, natural to party dissensions, which, in different ages and countries, has perpetrated the most horrid enormities, is itself a frightful despotism. But this leads, at length, to a more formal and permanent despotism. The disorders and miseries, which result, gradually incline the minds of men to seek security and repose in the absolute power of an individual; and sooner or later, the chief of some prevailing faction, more able or more fortunate than his competitors, turns this disposition to the purposes of his own elevation on the ruins of public liberty.

Without looking forward to an extremity of this kind, (which, nevertheless, ought not to be entirely out of sight), the common and continual mischiefs of the spirit of party are sufficient to make it the interest and duty of a wise people to discourage and restrain it.

It serves always to distract the public councils, and enfeeble the public administration. It agitates the community with ill-founded jealousies and false alarms; kindles the animosity of one part against another; foments occasionally riot and insurrection. It opens the door to foreign influence and corruption, which find a facilitated access to the government itself, through the channels of party passion. Thus the policy and the will of one country are subjected to the policy and will of another.

There is an opinion, that parties, in free countries, are useful checks upon the administration of the government, and serve to keep alive the spirit of liberty. This, within certain limits, is probably true; and, in governments of a monarchical cast, patriotism may look with indulgence, if not with favor, upon the spirit of party. But in those of popular character, in governments purely elective, it is a spirit not to be encouraged. From their natural tendency, it is certain there will always be enough of that spirit for every salutary purpose. And there being constant danger of excess, the effort ought to be, by force of public opinion, to mitigate and assuage it. A fire not to be quenched, it demands a uniform vigilance to prevent its bursting into a flame, lest, instead of warming, it should consume.

It is important, likewise, that the habits of thinking, in a free country, should inspire caution in those entrusted with its administration, to confine themselves within their respective constitutional spheres, avoiding, in the exercise of the powers of one department, to encroach upon another. The spirit of encroachment tends to consolidate the powers of all the departments in one, and thus to create, whatever the form of government, a real despotism. A just estimate of that love of power, and proneness to abuse it, which predominate in the human heart, is sufficient to satisfy us of the truth of this position. The necessity of reciprocal checks in the exercise of political power, by dividing and distributing it into different depositaries, and constituting each the guardian of the public weal against invasion by the other, has been evinced by experiments ancient and modern: some of them in our country, and under our own eyes. To preserve them must be as necessary as to institute them. If, in the opinion of the people, the distribution or modification of the constitutional powers, be, in any particular, wrong, let it be corrected by an amendment in the way which the constitution designates. But let there be no change by usurpation; for though this, in one instance, may be the instrument of good, it is the customary weapon by which free governments are destroyed. The precedent must always greatly overbalance, in permanent evil, any partial or transient benefit which the use can at any time yield.

Of all the dispositions and habits, which lead to political prosperity, religion and morality are indispensable supports. In vain would that man claim the tribute of patriotism, who should labor to subvert these great pillars of human happiness, these firmest props of the destinies of men and citizens. The mere politician, equally with the pious man, ought to respect and to cherish them. A volume could not trace all their connection with private and public felicity. Let it simply be asked, where is the security for property, for reputation, for life, if the sense of religious obligation desert the oaths, which are the instruments of investigation in courts of justice? And let us with caution indulge the supposition that morality can be maintained without religion. Whatever may be conceded to the influence of refined education on minds of peculiar structure, reason and experience both forbid us to expect, that national morality can prevail in exclusion of religious principles.

It is substantially true, that virtue or morality is a necessary spring of popular government. The rule, indeed, extends with more or less force to every species of free government. Who, that is a sincere friend to it, can look with indifference upon attempts to shake the foundation of the fabric?

Promote, then, as an object of primary importance, institutions for the general diffusion of knowledge. In proportion as the structure of a government gives force to public opinion, it is essential that public opinion should be enlightened.

As a very important source of strength and security, cherish public credit. One method of preserving it is to use it as sparingly as possible; avoiding occasions of expense by cultivating peace, but remembering also that timely disbursements to prepare for danger frequently prevent much greater disbursements to repel it; avoiding likewise the accumulation of debt, not only by shunning occasions of expense, but by vigorous exertions in time of peace to discharge the debts which unavoidable wars may have occasioned, not ungenerously throwing upon posterity the burden which we ourselves ought to bear. The execution of these maxims belongs to your representatives, but it is necessary that public opinion should co-operate. To facilitate to them the performance of their duty, it is essential that you should practically bear in mind, that towards the payment of debts there must be revenue; that to have revenue there must be taxes; that no taxes can be devised which are not more or less inconvenient and unpleasant; that the intrinsic embarrassment, inseparable from the selection of the proper objects (which is always the choice of difficulties) ought to be a decisive motive for a candid construction of the conduct of the government in making it, and for a spirit of acquiescence in the measures for obtaining revenue which the public exigencies may at any time dictate.

Observe good faith and justice towards all nations; cultivate peace and harmony with all; religion and morality enjoin this conduct; and can it be that good policy does not equally enjoin it? It will be worthy of a free, enlightened, and, at no distant period, a great nation, to give to mankind the magnanimous and too novel example of a people always guided by an exalted justice and benevolence. Who can doubt that, in the course of time and things, the fruits of such a plan would richly repay any temporary advantages that might be lost by a steady adherence to it? Can it be, that Providence has not connected the permanent felicity of a nation with its virtue? The experiment, at least, is recommended by every sentiment which ennobles human nature. Alas! is it rendered impossible by its vices?

In the execution of such a plan, nothing is more essential than that permanent, inveterate antipathies against particular nations, and passionate attachments for others, should be excluded; and that in place of them, just and amicable feelings towards all should be cultivated. The nation, which indulges towards another an habitual hatred, or an habitual fondness, is in some degree a slave. It is a slave to its animosity or to its affection, either of which is sufficient to lead it astray from its duty and its interest. Antipathy in one nation against another, disposes each more readily to offer insult and injury, to lay hold of slight causes of umbrage, and to be haughty and intractable, when accidental or trifling occasions of dispute occur.

Hence frequent collisions, obstinate, envenomed, and bloody contests. The nation, prompted by ill-will and resentment, sometimes impels to war the government, contrary to the best calculations of policy. The government sometimes participates in the national propensity, and adopts through passion what reason would reject; at other times, it makes the animosity of the nation subservient to projects of hostility instigated by pride, ambition and other sinister and pernicious motives. The peace often, and sometimes, perhaps, the liberty of nations, has been the victim.

So, likewise, a passionate attachment of one nation for another produces a variety of evils. Sympathy for the favorite nation facilitating the illusion of an imaginary common interest in cases where no real common interest exists, and infusing into one the enmities of the other, betrays the former into a participation in the quarrels and wars of the latter, without adequate inducement or justification. It leads also to concessions to the favorite nation of privileges denied to others, which is apt doubly to injure the nation making the concessions; by unnecessarily parting with what ought to have been retained; and by exciting jealousy, ill-will, and a disposition to retaliate, in the parties from whom equal privileges are withheld; and it gives to ambitious, corrupted, or deluded citizens (who devote themselves to the favorite nation) facility to betray, or sacrifice the interests of their own country, without odium, sometimes even with popularity; gilding, with the appearances of a virtuous sense of obligation, a commendable deference for public opinion, or laudable zeal for public good, the base or foolish compliances of ambition, corruption, or infatuation.

As avenues to foreign influence, in innumerable ways, such attachments are particularly alarming to the truly enlightened and independent patriot. How many opportunities do they afford to tamper with domestic factions; to practise the arts of seduction; to mislead public opinion; to influence or awe the public councils! Such an attachment of a small or weak nation, toward a great and powerful one, dooms the former to be the satellite of the latter.

Against the insidious wiles of foreign influence (I conjure you to believe me, fellow-citizens), the jealousy of a free people ought to be constantly awake; since history and experience prove, that foreign influence is one of the most baneful foes of republican government. But that jealousy, to be useful, must be impartial; else it becomes the instrument of the very influence to be avoided, instead of a defence against it. Excessive partiality for one foreign nation, and excessive dislike of another, cause those whom they actuate, to see danger only on one side; and serve to veil and even second the arts of influence on the other. Real patriots, who may resist the intrigues of the favorite, are liable to become suspected and odious; while its tools and dupes usurp the applause and confidence of the people, to surrender their interests.

The great rule of conduct for us, in regard to foreign nations is, in extending our commercial relations, to have with them as little political connection as possible. So far as we have already formed engagements, let them be fulfilled with perfect good faith. Here let us stop.

Europe has a set of primary interests, which to us have none, or a very remote relation. Hence she must be engaged in frequent controversies, the causes of which are essentially foreign to our concerns. Hence, therefore, it must be unwise in us to implicate ourselves, by artificial ties, in the ordinary vicissitudes of her politics, or the ordinary combinations and collisions of her friendships and enmities.

Our detached and distant situation invites and enables us to pursue a different course. If we remain one people, under an efficient government, the period is not far off when we may defy material injury from external annoyance; when we may take such an attitude as will cause the neutrality we may at any time resolve upon, to be scrupulously respected; when belligerent nations, under the impossibility of making acquisitions upon us, will not lightly hazard the giving us provocation; when we may choose peace or war, as our interest, guided by justice, shall counsel.

Why forego the advantages of so peculiar a situation? Why quit our own, to stand upon foreign ground? Why, by interweaving our destiny with that of any part of Europe, entangle our peace and prosperity in the toils of European ambition, rivalship, interest, humor, or caprice?

'Tis our true policy to steer clear of permanent alliances with any portion of the foreign world; so far, I mean, as we are now at liberty to do it; for let me not be understood as capable of patronizing infidelity to existing engagements. I hold the maxim no less applicable to public than to private affairs, that honesty is always the best policy. I repeat it, therefore, let those engagements be observed in their genuine sense. But, in my opinion, it is unnecessary, and would be unwise, to extend them.

Taking care always to keep ourselves, by suitable establishments, in a respectable defensive posture, we may safely trust to temporary alliances for extraordinary emergencies.

Harmony, and a liberal intercourse with all nations, are recommended by policy, humanity, and interest. But even our commercial policy should hold an equal and impartial hand; neither seeking nor granting exclusive favors or preferences; consulting the natural course of things; diffusing and diversifying, by gentle means, the streams of commerce, but forcing nothing; establishing, with powers so disposed, in order to give trade a stable course, to define the rights of our merchants, and to enable the government to support them, conventional rules of intercourse, the best that present circumstances and mutual opinion will permit, but temporary, and liable to be, from time to time, abandoned or varied, as experience and circumstances shall dictate; constantly keeping in view, that it is folly in one nation to look for disinterested favors from another; that it must pay, with a portion of its independence, for whatever it may accept under that character; that, by such acceptance, it may place itself in the condition of having given equivalents for nominal favors, and yet of being reproached with ingratitude for not giving more. There can be no greater error than to expect to calculate upon real favors from nation to nation. It is an illusion, which experience must cure, which a just pride ought to discard.

In offering to you, my countrymen, these counsels of an old and affectionate friend, I dare not hope they will make the strong and lasting impression I could wish; that they will control the usual current of the passions, or prevent our nation from running the course which has hitherto marked the destiny of nations. But, if I may even flatter myself, that they may be productive of some partial benefit, some occasional good; that they may now and then recur to moderate the fury of party spirit; to warn against the mischiefs of foreign intrigues; to guard against the impostures of pretended patriotism; this hope will be a full recompense for the solicitude for your welfare, by which they have been dictated.

How far, in the discharge of my official duties, I have been guided by the principles which have been delineated, the public records and other evidences of my conduct must witness to you and to the world. To myself the assurance of my own conscience is, that I have at least believed myself to be guided by them.

In relation to the still subsisting war in Europe, my proclamation of April 22, 1793, is the index to my plan. Sanctioned by your approving voice, and by that of your representatives in both Houses of Congress, the spirit of that measure has continually governed me, uninfluenced by any attempts to deter or divert me from it.

After deliberate examination, with the aid of the best lights I could obtain, I was well satisfied that our country, under all the circumstances of the case, had a right to take, and was bound in duty and interest to take, a neutral position. Having taken it, I determined, as far as should depend upon me, to maintain it with moderation, perseverance, and firmness.

The considerations which respect the right to hold this conduct, it is not necessary, on this occasion, to detail. I will only observe, that, according to my understanding of the matter, that right, so far from being denied by any of the belligerent powers, has been virtually admitted by all.

The duty of holding a neutral conduct may be inferred, without anything more, from obligation which justice and humanity impose on every nation, in cases in which it is free to act, to maintain inviolate the relations of peace and amity towards other nations.

The inducements of interest for observing that conduct will best be referred to your own reflection and experience. With me, a predominant motive has been to endeavor to gain time to our country to settle and mature its yet recent institutions, and to progress, without interruption, to that degree of strength and consistency which is necessary to give it, humanly speaking, the command of its own fortunes.

Though, in reviewing the incidents of my administration, I am unconscious of intentional error, I am, nevertheless, too sensible of my defects, not to think it probable that I may have committed many errors. Whatever they may be, I fervently beseech the Almighty to avert or mitigate the evils to which they may tend. I shall also carry with me the hope that my country will never cease to view them with indulgence, and that after forty-five years of my life dedicated to its service, with an upright zeal, the faults of incompetent abilities will be consigned to oblivion, as myself must soon be to the mansions of rest.

Relying on its kindness in this, as in other things, and actuated by the fervent love toward it, which is so natural to a man who views in it the native soil of himself and his progenitors for several generations, I anticipate, with pleasing expectations, that retreat in which I promise myself to realize, without alloy, the sweet enjoyment of partaking, in the midst of my fellow-citizens, the benign influence of good laws under a free government—the ever favorite object of my heart, and the happy rewards, as I trust, of our mutual cares, labors, and dangers.

Questions and Exercises

1. In which of the states was George Washington born?_____
   What were his childhood interests?_____
   _____

2. What was the extent of his formal education?_____
   _____

3. When was he President of the United States? From_____
   to_____

4. List three of his weaknesses as a speaker. (1)_____
   _____ (2)_____ (3)_____

5. Why was his "Farewell Address" first written in 1792?_____
   _____ When was it given?_____

6. What part of his address is reported to be the most controversial?
   _____

7. What is the basic organizational pattern of the speech?_____
   inductive; _____deductive.

8. Give one example of ethical appeal._____
   _____
   _____

9. Give an example of his use of evidence._____
   _____

10. How does the style of the speech compare to present-day stand-
    ards?_____
    _____

III *REPLY TO HAYNE*

DANIEL WEBSTER
(1782-1852)

The Speaker

Daniel Webster, often called America's greatest orator, was born at Salisbury, New Hampshire, on January 18, 1782. He received his education through private tutoring, at district schools, Exeter Academy, and Dartmouth College. Upon graduation from Dartmouth in 1801, he served an apprenticeship in law, later taught school, and worked briefly as the registrar of deeds in Fryeburg, Maine. He moved to Boston in 1804 where he was admitted to the bar the following year. He moved to Boscawen, New Hampshire, in 1805 and two years later to Portsmouth where he engaged in the private practice of law.

Webster's greatest contributions were in the field of politics. He was first elected Congressman for New Hampshire in 1812 and was re-elected in 1814. In 1816 he moved back to Boston, Massachusetts, where he continued the practice of law. He gained fame in 1818 when he argued the Dartmouth College Case before the United States Supreme Court. In 1822 he was elected Congressman for Massachusetts and was continued in office until 1827, when he became United States Senator. He continued in the Senate until 1841 and again served in the Senate from 1845 to 1850. He became Secretary of State under President Harrison in 1841 and was retained in office under President

Tyler until 1843, when he resigned. He again became Secretary of State under President Fillmore in 1850, which office he held until his death on October 24, 1852, on his farm at Marshfield, Massachusetts. In spite of his long and distinguished career as a lawyer, Congressman, Senator, and Secretary of State, he was keenly disappointed in his continued failures to be nominated for the Presidency.

Between the time of his Fourth of July speech at Hanover, New Hampshire, in 1800 when he was only eighteen, until his final speech on July 25, 1852, at his homecoming at Marshfield, Massachusetts, Webster made hundreds of speeches. Such speeches as his "Reply to Hayne," "Seventh of March Speech 1850," "Bunker Hill Address," and the closing arguments in the Dartmouth College Case and the Knapp-White Murder Case have become firmly entrenched in American literature; others equal in merit are little known. *The Writings and Speeches of Daniel Webster,* National Edition, devotes twelve volumes to the texts and abstracts of his speeches.

Legend has labeled Webster as a sort of "oratorical genius," but history shows that his genius came largely from arduous practice and training. He read widely and could call upon the classics, history, and contemporary literature to support his arguments. As a student he studied written as well as oral communication and had some of his verse and essays published. His communicative skills, in both writing and speaking, made their mark in historic documents as well as in the political debates of the times. All these factors contributed to Webster's reputation as perhaps the most distinguished speaker of his generation.

The Occasion

The famous Webster-Hayne debates extended at intervals throughout most of the Twenty-first Session of Congress, from December 29, 1829, to May 31, 1830. During this period twenty-one Senators delivered a total of sixty-five speeches on a resolution by Senator Foote of Connecticut to limit the selling of Western public lands. The debates were not a two-man affair; rather, Webster and Hayne may be considered the leaders of a bitter controversy which involved a majority of the Senate. The resolution in general concerned the question of Federal versus States' rights and more specifically the question of slavery. Hayne contended that the continued sale of public lands would make the states subservient to the Federal government and that the general government would become independent of the people. Webster countered that the sale of public lands was for the common benefit of all the states and that the states had a community of interests that bound them together. Hayne attempted to consolidate the interests of the West and South against the North largely over the question of slavery. Thus the debates concerned controversial questions on which the Senators bitterly disagreed, especially those Senators representing the Northern and Southern states.

Webster and Hayne were concerned with two audiences—the immediate audience in the Senate and the audience at large consisting of the people of the United States. There is evidence that both speakers were concerned more with the newspaper publicity and its consequent effect on public opinion than they were with convincing their fellow Senators. The likelihood of changing the opinion of the partisan Senators was remote without the pressure of public opinion.

The Speech

The speech that follows is a part of Webster's second reply to Hayne delivered on January 26 and 27, 1830. The speech consisted of some thirty thousand words and required parts of two days to deliver. Webster and Hayne engaged in three debates on the Foote Amendment during the Twenty-first Session of Congress; Webster's second reply is generally considered his most eloquent.

The first part of Webster's second speech dealt with matters of a personal nature apparently designed to increase his ethical appeal. He contrasted Hayne's appeal to fear and his resort to personal bitterness with his own calm and temperance. The main part of his arguments took the form of refutation in which he dealt in turn with the questions of slavery, Federal supremacy, internal improvements, the tariff, and attacks on New England. The unifying force or central idea of the speech hinged on his defense of Federal supremacy. The speech was built to a climax as Webster concluded with "Liberty and Union, now and forever, one and inseparable!"

The speech has much logical appeal since Webster balanced each of his arguments with those of Hayne. It also made effective use of ethical appeal through statements designed to depreciate his opponent's motives and character and to enhance his own. His emotional appeal consisted of references to liberty, freedom, and the preservation of national unity.

The speech that follows was transcribed from a shorthand report and corrected by Webster. The text below was published in Gales and Seaton, *Register of Debates in Congress* (Washington, D.C., 1830), Vol. VI, Part I, pp. 58-80.

MR. PRESIDENT: When the mariner has been tossed for many days in thick weather, and on an unknown sea, he naturally avails himself of the first pause in the storm, the earliest glance of the sun, to take his latitude, and ascertain how far the elements have driven him from his true course. Let us imitate this prudence, and, before we float farther on the waves of this debate, refer to the point from which we departed, that we may at least be able to conjecture where we now are. I ask for the reading of the resolution before the Senate.

[The Secretary read the resolution.]

We have thus heard, Sir, what the resolution is which is actually before us for consideration; and it will readily occur to every one, that it is almost the only subject about which something has not been said in the speech, running through two days, by which the Senate has been entertained by the gentleman from South Carolina. Every topic in the wide range of our public affairs, whether past or present,—every thing, general or local, whether belonging to national politics or party politics, —seems to have attracted more or less of the honorable member's attention, save only the resolution before the Senate. He has spoken of every thing but the public lands; they have escaped his notice. To that subject, in all his excursions, he has not paid even the cold respect of a passing glance.

When this debate, Sir, was to be resumed, on Thursday morning, it so happened that it would have been convenient for me to be elsewhere. The honorable member, however, did not incline to put off the discussion to another day. He had a shot, he said, to return, and he wished to discharge it. That shot, Sir, which he thus kindly informed us was coming, that we might stand out of the way, or prepare ourselves to fall by it and die with decency, has now been received. Under all advantages, and with expectation awakened by the tone which preceded it, it has been discharged, and has spent its force. It may become me to say no more of its effect, than that, if nobody is found, after all, either killed or wounded, it is not the first time, in the history of human affairs, that the vigor and success of the war have not quite come up to the lofty and sounding phrase of the manifesto.

The gentleman, Sir, in declining to postpone the debate, told the Senate, with the emphasis of his hand upon his heart, that there was something rankling *here,* which he wished to relieve. [Mr. Hayne rose, and disclaimed having used the word *rankling.*] It would not, Mr. President, be safe for the honorable member to appeal to those around him, upon the question whether he did in fact make use of that word. But he may have been unconscious of it. At any rate, it is enough that he disclaims it. But still, with or without the use of that particular word, he had yet something *here,* he said, of which he wished to rid himself by an immediate reply. In this respect, Sir, I have a great advantage over the honorable gentleman. There is nothing *here,* Sir, which gives me the slightest uneasiness; neither fear, nor anger, nor that which is sometimes more troublesome than either, the consciousness of having been in the wrong. There is nothing, either originating *here,* or now received *here* by the gentleman's shot. Nothing originating here, for I had not the slightest feeling of unkindness towards the honorable member. Some passages, it is true, had occurred since our acquaintance in this body, which I could have wished might have been otherwise; but I had used philosophy and forgotten them. I paid the honorable member the attention of listening with respect to his first speech; and when he sat down, though surprised, and I must even say astonished, at some of his opinions, nothing was farther from my intention than to commence any personal warfare. Through the whole of the few remarks I made in answer, I avoided, studiously and carefully, every thing which I thought possible to be construed into disrespect. And, Sir, while there is thus nothing originating *here* which I have wished at any time, or now wish, to discharge, I must repeat, also, that nothing has been received *here* which *rankles,* or in any way gives me annoyance. I will not accuse the honorable member of violating the rules of civilized war; I will not say, that he poisoned his arrows. But whether his shafts were, or were not, dipped in that which would have caused rankling if they had reached their destination, there was not, as it happened, quite strength enough in the bow to bring them to their mark. If he wishes now to gather up those shafts, he must look for them elsewhere, they will not be found fixed and quivering in the object at which they were aimed.

The honorable member complained that I had slept on his speech. I must have slept on it, or not slept at all. The moment the honorable member sat down, his friend from Missouri rose, and, with much honeyed commendation of the speech, suggested that the impressions which it had produced were too charming and delightful to be disturbed by other sentiments or other sounds, and proposed that the Senate should adjourn. Would it have been quite amiable in me, Sir, to interrupt this excellent good feeling? Must I not have been absolutely malicious, if I could have thrust myself forward, to destroy sensations thus pleasing? Was it not much better and kinder, both to sleep upon them myself, and to allow others also the pleasure of sleeping upon them? But if it be meant, by sleeping upon his speech, that I took time to prepare a reply to it, it is quite a mistake. Owing to other engagements, I could not employ even the interval between the adjournment of the Senate and its meeting the next morning, in attention to the subject of this debate. Nevertheless, Sir, the mere matter of fact is undoubtedly true. I did sleep on the gentleman's speech, and slept soundly. And I slept equally well on his speech of yesterday, to which I am now replying. It is quite possible that in this respect, also, I possess some advantage over the honorable member, attributable, doubtless, to a cooler temperament on my part; for, in truth, I slept upon his speeches remarkably well.

But the gentleman inquires why *he* was made the object of such a reply. Why was *he* singled out? If an attack has been made on the East, he, he assures us, did not begin it; it was made by the gentleman from Missouri. Sir, I answered the gentleman's speech because I happened to hear it; and because, also, I chose to give an answer to that speech, which, if unanswered, I thought most likely to produce injurious impressions. I did not stop to inquire who was the original drawer of the bill. I found a responsible indorser before me, and it was my purpose to hold him liable, and to bring him to his just responsibility, without delay. But, Sir, this interrogatory of the honorable member was only introductory to another. He proceeded to ask me whether I had turned upon him, in this debate, from the consciousness that I should find an overmatch, if I ventured on a contest with his friend from Missouri. If, Sir, the honorable member, *modestiae gratia,* had chosen thus to defer to his friend, and to pay him a compliment, without intentional disparagement to others, it would have been quite according to the friendly courtesies of debate, and not at all ungrateful to my own feelings. I am not one of those, Sir, who esteem any tribute of regard, whether light and occasional, or more serious and deliberate, which may be bestowed on others, as so much unjustly withholden from themselves. But the tone and manner of the gentleman's question forbid me thus to interpret it. I am not at liberty to consider it as nothing more than a civility to his friend. It had an air of taunt and disparagement, something of the loftiness of asserted superiority, which does not allow me to pass it over without notice. It was put as a question for me to answer, and so put as if it were difficult for me to answer, whether I deemed the member from Missouri an overmatch for myself, in debate here. It seems to me, Sir, that this is extraordinary language, and an extraordinary tone, for the discussions of this body. . . .

I wish now, Sir, to make a remark upon the Virginia resolutions of 1798. I cannot undertake to say how these resolutions were understood by those who passed them. Their language is not a little indefinite. In the case of the exercise by Congress of a dangerous power not granted to them, the resolutions assert the right, on the part of the State, to interfere and arrest the progress of the evil. This is susceptible of more than one interpretation. It may mean no more than that the States may interfere by complaint and remonstrance, or by proposing to the people an alteration of the Federal Constitution. This would all be quite unobjectionable. Or it may be that no more is meant than to assert the general right of revolution, as against all governments, in cases of intolerable oppression. This no one doubts, and this, in my opinion, is all that he who framed the resolution could have meant by it; for I shall not readily believe that he was ever of opinion that a State, under the Constitution and in conformity with it, could, upon the ground of her own opinion of its unconstitutionality, however clear and palpable she might think the case, annul a law of Congress, so far as it should operate on herself, by her own legislative power.

I must now beg to ask, Sir, Whence is this supposed right of the States derived? Where do they find the power to interfere with the laws of the Union? Sir, the opinion which the honorable gentleman maintains is a notion founded in a total misapprehension, in my judgment, of the origin of this government, and of the foundation on which it stands. I hold it to be a popular government, erected by the people; those who administer it, responsible to the people; and itself capable of being amended and modified, just as the people may choose it should be. It is as popular, just as truly emanating from the people, as the State governments. It is created for one purpose; the State governments for another. It has its own powers; they have theirs. There is no more authority with them to arrest the operation of a law of Congress, than with Congress to arrest the operation of their laws. We are here to administer a Constitution emanating immediately from the people, and trusted by them to our administration. It is not the creature of the State governments. It is of no moment to the argument, that certain acts of the State legislatures are necessary to fill our seats in this body. That is not one of their original State powers, a part of the sovereignty of the State. It is a duty which the people, by the Constitution itself, have imposed on the States' legislatures; and which they might have left to be performed elsewhere, if they had seen fit. So they have left the choice of President with electors; but all this does not affect the proposition that this whole government, President, Senate, and House of Representatives, is a popular government. It leaves it still all its popular character. The governor of a State (in some of the

States) is chosen, not directly by the people, but by those who are chosen by the people, for the purpose of performing, among other duties, that of electing a governor. Is the government of the State, on that account, not a popular government? This government, Sir, is the independent offspring of the popular will. It is not the creature of the State legislatures; nay, more, if the whole truth must be told, the people brought it into existence, established it, and have hitherto supported it, for the very purpose, amongst others, of imposing certain salutary restraints on State sovereignties. The States cannot now make war; they cannot contract alliances; they cannot make, each for itself, separate regulations of commerce; they cannot lay imposts; they cannot coin money. If this Constitution, Sir, be the creature of State legislatures, it must be admitted that it has obtained a strange control over the volition of its creators.

The people, then, Sir, erected this government. They gave it a Constitution, and in that Constitution they have enumerated the powers which they bestow on it. They have made it a limited government. They have defined its authority. They have restrained it to the exercise of such powers as are granted; and all others, they declare, are reserved to the States or the people. But, Sir, they have not stopped here. If they had, they would have accomplished but half their work. No definition can be so clear, as to avoid possibility of doubt; no limitation so precise, as to exclude all uncertainty. Who, then, shall construe this grant of the people? Who shall interpret their will, where it may be supposed they have left it doubtful? With whom do they repose this ultimate right of deciding on the powers of the government? Sir, they have settled all this in the fullest manner. They have left it with the government itself, in its appropriate branches. Sir, the very chief end, the main design, for which the whole Constitution was framed and adopted, was to establish a government that should not be obliged to act through State agency, or depend on State opinion and State discretion. The people had had quite enough of that kind of government under the Confederation. Under that system, the legal action, the application of law to individuals, belonged exclusively to the States. Congress could only recommend; their acts were not of binding force, till the States had adopted and sanctioned them. Are we in that condition still? Are we yet at the mercy of State discretion and State construction? Sir, if we are, then vain will be our attempt to maintain the Constitution under which we sit.

But, Sir, the people have wisely provided, in the Constitution itself, a proper suitable mode and tribunal for settling questions of constitutional law. There are in the Constitution grants of powers to Congress, and restrictions on these powers. There are, also, prohibitions on the States. Some authority must, therefore, necessarily exist, having the ultimate jurisdiction to fix and ascertain the interpretation of these grants, restrictions, and prohibitions. The Constitution has itself pointed out, ordained, and established that authority. How has it accomplished this great and essential end? By declaring, Sir, that *"the Constitution, and the laws of the United States made in pursuance thereof, shall be the supreme law of the land, any thing in the constitution or laws of any State to the contrary notwithstanding."*

This, Sir, was the first great step. By this the supremacy of the Constitution and laws of the United States is declared. The people so will it. No State law is to be valid which comes in conflict with the Constitution, or any law of the United States passed in pursuance of it. But who shall decide this question of interference? To whom lies the last appeal? This, Sir, the Constitution itself decides also, by declaring, *"that the judicial power shall extend to all cases arising under the Constitution and laws of the United States."* These two provisions cover the whole ground. They are, in truth, the keystone of the arch! With these it is a government; without them it is a confederation. In pursuance of these clear and express provisions, Congress established, at its very first session, in the judicial act, a mode for carrying them into full effect, and for bringing all questions of constitutional power to the final decision of the Supreme Court. It then, Sir, became a government. It then had the means of self-protection; and but for this, it would, in all probability, have been now among things which are past. Having constituted the government, and declared its powers, the people have further said, that, since somebody must decide on the extent of these powers, the government shall itself decide; subject, always, like other popular governments, to its responsibility to the people. And now, Sir, I repeat, how is it that a State legislature acquires any power to interfere? Who, or what, gives them the right to say to the people, "We, who are your agents and servants for one purpose, will undertake to decide, that your other agents and servants, appointed by you for another purpose, have transcended the authority you gave them!" The reply would be, I think, not impertinent,—"Who made you a judge over another's servants? To their own masters they stand or fall."

Sir, I deny this power of State legislatures altogether. It cannot stand the test of examination. Gentlemen may say, that, in an extreme case, a State government might protect the people from intolerable oppression. Sir, in such a case, the people might protect themselves, without the aid of the State governments. Such a case warrants revolution. It must make, when it comes, a law for itself. A nullifying act of a State legislature cannot alter the case, nor make resistance any more lawful. In maintaining these sentiments, Sir, I am but asserting the rights of the people. I state what they have declared, and insist on their right to declare it. They have chosen to repose this power in the general government, and I think it my duty to support it, like other constitutional powers.

For myself, Sir, I do not admit the competency of South Carolina, or any other State, to prescribe my constitutional duty; or to settle, between me and the people, the validity of laws of Congress, for which I voted. I decline her umpirage. I have not sworn to support the Constitution according to her construction of its clauses. I have not stipulated, by my oath of office or otherwise, to come under any responsibility, except to the people, and those whom they have appointed to pass upon the question, whether laws, supported by my votes, conform to the Constitution of the country. And, Sir, if we look to the general nature of the case, could any thing have been more preposterous, than to make a government for the whole Union, and yet leave its powers subject, not to one interpretation, but to thirteen or twenty-four interpretations? Instead of one tribunal, established by all, responsible to all, with power to decide for all, shall constitutional questions be left to four-and-twenty popular bodies, each at liberty to decide for itself, and none bound to respect the decisions of others; and each at liberty, too, to give a new construction on every new election of its own members? Would any thing, with such a principle in it, or rather with such a destitution of all principle, be fit to be called a government? No, Sir. It should not be denominated a Constitution. It should be called, rather, a collection of topics for everlasting controversy; heads of debate for a disputatious people. It would not be a government. It would not be adequate to any practical good, or fit for any country to live under.

To avoid all possibility of being misunderstood, allow me to repeat again, in the fullest manner, that I claim no powers for the government by forced or unfair construction. I admit that it is a government of strictly limited powers; of enumerated, specified, and particularized powers; and that whatsoever is not granted, is withheld. But notwithstanding all this, and however the grant of powers may be expressed, its limit and extent may yet, in some cases, admit of doubt; and the general government would be good for nothing, it would be incapable of long existing, if some mode had not been provided in which those doubts, as they should arise, might be peaceably, but authoritatively, solved.

And now, Mr. President, let me run the honorable gentleman's doctrine a little into its practical application. Let us look at his probable *modus operandi*. If a thing can be done, an ingenious man can tell *how* it is to be done, and I wish to be informed *how* this State interference is to be put in practice, without violence, bloodshed, and rebellion. We will take the existing case of the tariff law. South Carolina is said to have made up her opinion upon it. If we do not repeal it (as we probably shall not), she will then apply to the case the remedy of her doctrine. She will, we must suppose, pass a law of her legislature, declaring the several acts of Congress, usually called the tariff laws, null and void, so far as they respect South Carolina, or the citizens thereof. So far, all is a paper transaction, and easy enough. But the collector at Charleston is collecting the duties imposed by these tariff laws. He, therefore, must be stopped. The collector will seize the goods if the tariff duties are not paid. The State authorities will undertake their rescue, the marshal, with his posse, will come to the collector's aid, and here the contest begins. The militia of the State will be called out to sustain the nullifying act. They will march, Sir, under a very gallant leader; for I believe the honorable member himself commands the militia of that part of the State. He will raise the *nullifying act* on his standard, and spread it out as his banner! It will have a preamble, setting forth, that the tariff laws are palpable, deliberate, and dangerous violations of the Constitution! He will proceed, with this banner flying, to the custom-house in Charleston,

> All the while,
> Sonorous metal blowing martial sounds.

Arrived at the custom-house, he will tell the collector that he must collect no more duties under any of the tariff laws. This he will be somewhat puzzled to say, by the way, with a grave countenance, considering what hand South Carolina herself had in that of 1816. But, Sir, the collector would not, probably, desist, at his bidding. He would show him the law of Congress, the treasury instruction, and his own oath of office. He would say, he should perform his duty, come what might.

Here would ensue a pause; for they say that a certain stillness precedes the tempest. The trumpeter would hold his breath awhile, and before all this military array should fall on the custom-house, collector, clerks, and all, it is very probable some of those composing it would request of their gallant commander-in-chief to be informed a little upon the point of law; for they have, doubtless, a just respect for his opinions as a lawyer, as well as for his bravery as a soldier. They know he has read Blackstone and the Constitution, as well as Turenne and Vauban. They would ask him, therefore, something concerning their rights in this matter. They would inquire, whether it was not somewhat dangerous to resist a law of the United States. What would be the nature of their offence, they would wish to learn, if they, by military force and array, resisted the execution in Carolina of a law of the United States, and it should turn out, after all, that the law *was constitutional?* He would answer, of course, Treason. No lawyer could give any other answer. John Fries, he would tell them, had learned that, some years ago. How, then, they would ask, do you propose to defend us? We are not afraid of bullets, but treason has a way of taking people off that we do not much relish. How do you propose to defend us? "Look at my floating banner," he would reply; "see there the *nullify-*

ing law!" Is it your opinion, gallant commander, they would then say, that, if we should be indicted for treason, that same floating banner of yours would make a good plea in bar? "South Carolina is a sovereign State," he would reply. That is true; but would the judge admit our plea? "These tariff laws," he would repeat, "are unconstitutional, palpably, deliberately, dangerously." That may all be so; but if the tribunal should not happen to be of that opinion, shall we swing for it? We are ready to die for our country, but it is rather an awkward business, this dying without touching the ground! After all, that is a sort of hemp tax worse than part of the tariff.

Mr. President, the honorable gentleman would be in dilemma, like that of another great general. He would have a knot before him which he could not untie. He must cut it with his sword. He must say to his followers, "Defend yourselves with your bayonets"; and this is war,— civil war.

Direct collision, therefore, between force and force, is the unavoidable result of that remedy for the revision of unconstitutional laws which the gentleman contends for. It must happen in the very first case to which it is applied. Is not this the plain result? To resist by force the execution of a law, generally, is treason. Can the courts of the United States take notice of the indulgence of a State to commit treason? The common saying, that a State cannot commit treason herself, is nothing to the purpose. Can she authorize others to do it? If John Fries had produced an act of Pennsylvania, annulling the law of Congress, would it have helped his case? Talk about it as we will, these doctrines go the length of revolution. They are incompatible with any peaceable administration of the government. They lead directly to disunion and civil commotion; and therefore it is, that at their commencement, when they are first found to be maintained by respectable men, and in a tangible form, I enter my public protest against them all.

The honorable gentleman argues, that if this government be the sole judge of the extent of its own powers, whether that right of judging be in Congress or the Supreme Court, it equally subverts State sovereignty. This the gentleman sees, or thinks he sees, although he cannot perceive how the right of judging, in this matter, if left to the exercise of State legislatures, has any tendency to subvert the government of the

Union. The gentleman's opinion may be, that the right *ought* not to have been lodged with the general government; he may like better such a constitution as we should have under the right of State interference; but I ask him to meet me on the plain matter of fact. I ask him to meet me on the Constitution itself. I ask him if the power is not found there, clearly and visibly found there?

But, Sir, what is this danger, and what are the grounds of it? Let it be remembered, that the Constitution of the United States is not unalterable. It is to continue in its present form no longer than the people who established it shall choose to continue it. If they shall become convinced that they have made an injudicious or inexpedient partition and distribution of power between the State governments and the general government, they can alter that distribution at will.

If any thing be found in the national Constitution, either by original provision or subsequent interpretation, which ought not to be in it, the people know how to get rid of it. If any construction, unacceptable to them, be established, so as to become practically a part of the Constitution, they will amend it, at their own sovereign pleasure. But while the people choose to maintain it as it is, while they are satisfied with it, and refuse to change it, who has given, or who can give, to the State legislatures a right to alter it, either by interference, construction, or otherwise? Gentlemen do not seem to recollect that the people have any power to do any thing for themselves. They imagine there is no safety for them, any longer than they are under the close guardianship of the State legislatures. Sir, the people have not trusted their safety, in regard to the general Constitution, to these hands. They have required other security, and taken other bonds. They have chosen to trust themselves, first, to the plain words of the instrument, and to such construction as the government themselves, in doubtful cases, should put on their own powers, under their oaths of office, and subject to their responsibility to them; just as the people of a State trust their own State governments with a similar power. Secondly, they have reposed their trust in the efficacy of frequent elections, and in their own power to remove their own servants and agents whenever they see cause. Thirdly, they have reposed trust in the judicial power, which, in order that it might be trustworthy, they have made as respectable, as disinterested, and as independent as was practicable. Fourthly, they have seen fit to rely, in case of necessity, or high expediency, on their known and admitted power to alter or amend the Constitution, peaceably and quietly, whenever experience shall point out defects or imperfections. And, finally, the people of the United States have at no time, in no way, directly or indirectly, authorized any State legislature to construe or interpret *their* high instrument of government; much less, to interfere, by their own power, to arrest its course and operation.

If, Sir, the people in these respects had done otherwise than they have done, their constitution could neither have been preserved, nor would it have been worth preserving. And if its plain provisions shall now be disregarded, and these new doctrines interpolated in it, it will become as feeble and helpless a being as its enemies, whether early or more recent, could possibly desire. It will exist in every State but as a poor dependent on State permission. It must borrow leave to be; and will be, no longer than State pleasure, or State discretion, sees fit to grant the indulgence, and to prolong its poor existence.

But, Sir, although there are fears, there are hopes also. The people have preserved this, their own chosen Constitution, for forty years, and have seen their happiness, prosperity, and renown grow with its growth, and strengthen with its strength. They are now, generally, strongly attached to it. Overthrown by direct assault, it cannot be; evaded, undermined, *nullified,* it will not be, if we, and those who shall succeed us here, as agents and representatives of the people, shall conscientiously and vigilantly discharge the two great branches of our public trust, faithfully to preserve, and wisely to administer it.

Mr. President, I have thus stated the reasons of my dissent to the doctrines which have been advanced and maintained. I am conscious of having detained you and the Senate much too long. I was drawn into the debate with no previous deliberation, such as is suited to the discussion of so grave and important a subject. But it is a subject of which my heart is full, and I have not been willing to suppress the utterance of its spontaneous sentiments. I cannot, even now, persuade myself to relinquish it, without expressing once more my deep conviction, that, since it respects nothing less than the Union of the States, it is of most vital and essential importance to the public happiness. I profess, Sir, in my career hitherto, to have kept steadily in view the prosperity and honor of the whole country, and the preservation of our Federal Union. It is to that Union we owe our safety at home, and our consideration and dignity abroad. It is to that Union that we are chiefly indebted for whatever makes us most proud of our country. That Union we reached only by the discipline of our virtues in the severe school of adversity. It had its origin in the necessities of disordered finance, prostrate commerce, and ruined credit. Under its benign influences, these great interests immediately awoke, as from the dead, and sprang forth with newness of life. Every year of its duration has teemed with fresh proofs of its utility and its blessings; and although our territory has stretched out wider and wider, and our population spread farther and farther, they have not outrun its protection or its benefits. It has been to us all a copious fountain of national, social, and personal happiness.

I have not allowed myself, Sir, to look beyond the Union, to see what might lie hidden in the dark recess behind. I have not coolly weighed the chances of preserving liberty when the bonds that unite us together shall be broken asunder. I have not accustomed myself to hang over the precipice of disunion, to see whether, with my short sight, I can fathom the depth of the abyss below; nor could I regard him as a safe counsellor in the affairs of this government, whose thoughts should be mainly bent on considering, not how the Union may be best preserved, but how tolerable might be the condition of the people when it should be broken up and destroyed. While the Union lasts, we have high, exciting, gratifying prospects spread out before us, for us and our children. Beyond that I seek not to penetrate the veil. God grant that in my day, at least, that curtain may not rise! God grant that on my vision never may be opened what lies behind! When my eyes shall be turned to behold for the last time the sun in heaven, may I not see him shining on the broken and dishonored fragments of a once glorious Union; on States dissevered, discordant, belligerent; on a land rent with civil feuds, or drenched, it may be, in fraternal blood! Let their last feeble and lingering glance rather behold the gorgeous ensign of the republic, now known and honored throughout the earth, still full high advanced, its arms and trophies streaming in their original lustre, not a stripe erased or polluted, not a single star obscured, bearing for its motto, no such miserable interrogatory as "What is all this worth?" nor those other words of delusion and folly, "Liberty first and Union afterwards"; but everywhere, spread all over in characters of living light, blazing on all its ample folds, as they float over the sea and over the land, and in every wind under the whole heavens, that other sentiment, dear to every true American heart,—Liberty *and* Union, now and for ever, one and inseparable!

Questions and Exercises

1. When was Daniel Webster born?_____
   Where?_____

2. From what college was he graduated?_____
   _____ When?_____

3. From what two states was he elected to Congress?_____
   _____and_____

4. Besides Congressman, list two other important governmental positions which he held:_____and_____

5. List three factors that led to his eminence as a speaker. (1)_____
   _____ (2)_____
   _____ (3)_____

6. With what principal issue did his "Reply to Hayne" deal?_____
   _____
   What was Webster's position?_____

7. Senators Webster and Hayne were concerned with two audiences.
   What were they?_____
   and_____

8. What was Webster's basic appeal? _____ethical; _____emotional; _____logical.

9. How was his speech prepared for publication?_____

10. Describe the organizational pattern._____
    _____
    _____

IV THE AMERICAN SCHOLAR

RALPH WALDO EMERSON
(1803-1882)

The Speaker

Ralph Waldo Emerson was among the first to popularize the lecture as a means of general education in this country. He was a thinker, an academician, and a man of ideas. Had he lived today, he would likely have been primarily a writer, because he was awkward in social contacts and possessed few aptitudes for speaking. The society of the mid-nineteenth century offered few opportunities for writing as a career, however, because it depended more on oral than on written form for the dissemination of ideas. Emerson satisfied his communicative urges by writing out his addresses and reading them to his audiences.

Born in Boston on May 25, 1803, in humble circumstances, Emerson came from a line of eight generations of ministers. His father, the Reverend William Emerson of the First Unitarian Church in Boston, died when Ralph was eight. In spite of his poverty, Emerson entered Harvard and was graduated in 1821. Here he studied Greek under Edward Everett and rhetoric under Edward Channing, and was greatly influenced by their teachings. He won no honors for scholarship but was class poet and winner of several prizes in speaking and writing. After teaching at his brother's school in Boston, he entered Harvard

Divinity School, graduating in 1826. After his ordination in 1829, he began preaching at Second Unitarian Church in Boston. While his sermons appeared sincere and lucid, they were often dull and uninspiring. His was a positive religion; instead of haranguing his congregation about sin or doctrine, he dealt with the virtues and attitudes of the individual. In preparation, he would jot down five or six ideas on Friday; on Saturday he would correlate them in a written manuscript. He made few revisions, and these usually in the introduction or conclusion.

In 1832 Emerson resigned from his church in Boston because of a disagreement over administering communion. Although continuing to preach occasionally, he devoted most of his time to lecturing on the lyceum circuit and to publishing essays. Emerson spoke mainly on informative subjects and had little taste for debate; he said that he had so much to say that he saw little justification in wrangling over a disputed point with an opponent. Emerson usually spoke from a manuscript; he was not noted for his fluency. His treatment of ethical and literary subjects soon established for him a reputation as one of the foremost American thinkers of his day. He continued to lecture and write until his death on April 27, 1882.

The Occasion

The Phi Beta Kappa address on "The American Scholar" was delivered in the First Parish Church, Cambridge, Massachusetts, on August 31, 1837. It was considered by scholars of his day as perhaps Emerson's most significant work. The audience included students and faculty of Harvard University, members of the Phi Beta Kappa Society, and other distinguished educators—many of the leading scholars and literary men of the time. The lecture stirred considerable controversy. Some interpreted the address as an indictment of much of the traditional Harvard curriculum, but Oliver Wendell Holmes described it as "our intellectual Declaration of Independence." Here, as elsewhere, Emerson was motivated by an enthusiastic desire to communicate mature ideas to his audience. His manner was dignified; his voice, melodious; his preparation, thorough.

The Speech

In his opening remarks Emerson sets the tone of the speech—the American scholar often fails to perform his highest function, namely, "Man Thinking." When in a degenerate state, the scholar "tends to become a mere thinker or, still worse, the parrot of other men's thinking." Emerson proceeds to delineate the three major educational forces which influence the scholar: nature, books, and action. Then he discusses the duties of the scholar. He concludes with a plea—the scholar should rely on his individual instinct. Because of his prominence Emerson was not compelled to use a large quantity of supporting evidence, although he does make frequent use of comparisons and examples. The language is eloquent and dignified. Generally Emerson utilizes the deductive method. He states his points, explains them, and supports them with a variety of forms. His transitional statements between ideas are particularly effective. The text that follows was written and read to the audience and later prepared by Emerson for publication in Ralph Waldo Emerson, *Nature, Addresses, and Lectures* (Boston: Houghton Mifflin Co., 1876), pp. 83-115.

MR. PRESIDENT AND GENTLEMEN: I greet you on the recommencement of our literary year. Our anniversary is one of hope, and, perhaps, not enough of labor. We do not meet for games of strength or skill, for the recitation of histories, tragedies, and odes, like the ancient Greeks; for parliaments of love and poesy, like the Troubadours; nor for the advancement of science, like our contemporaries in the British and European capitals. Thus far, our holiday has been simply a friendly sign of the survival of the love of letters amongst a people too busy to give to letters any more. As such it is precious as the sign of an indestructible instinct. Perhaps the time is already come when it ought to be, and will be, something else; when the sluggard intellect of this continent will look from under its iron lids and fill the postponed expectation of the world with something better than the exertions of mechanical skill. Our day of dependence, our long apprenticeship to the learning of other lands, draws to a close. The millions that around us are rushing into life, cannot always be fed on the sere remains of foreign harvests. Events, actions arise, that must be sung, that will sing themselves. Who can doubt that poetry will revive and lead in a new age, as the star in the constellation Harp, which now flames in our zenith, astronomers announce, shall one day be the pole-star for a thousand years?

In this hope I accept the topic which not only usage but the nature of our association seem to prescribe to this day,—the American Scholar. Year by year we come up hither to read one more chapter of his biography. Let us inquire what light new days and events have thrown on his character and his hopes.

It is one of those fables which out of an unknown antiquity convey an unlooked-for wisdom, that the gods, in the beginning, divided Man into men, that he might be more helpful to himself; just as the hand was divided into fingers, the better to answer its end.

The old fable covers a doctrine ever new and sublime; that there is One Man,—present to all particular men only partially, or through one faculty; and that you must take the whole society to find the whole man. Man is not a farmer, or a professor, or an engineer, but he is all. Man is priest, and scholar, and statesman, and producer, and soldier. In the *divided* or social state these functions are parcelled out to individuals, each of whom aims to do his stint of the joint work, whilst each other performs his. The fable implies that the individual, to possess himself, must sometimes return from his own labor to embrace all the other laborers. But, unfortunately, this original unit, this fountain of power, has been so distributed to multitudes, has been so minutely subdivided and peddled out, that it is spilled into drops, and cannot be gathered. The state of society is one in which the members have suffered amputation from the trunk, and strut about so many walking monsters,—a good finger, a neck, a stomach, an elbow, but never a man.

Man is thus metamorphosed into a thing, into many things. The planter, who is Man sent out into the field to gather food, is seldom cheered by any idea of the true dignity of his ministry. He sees his bushel and his cart, and nothing beyond, and sinks into the farmer, instead of Man on the farm. The tradesman scarcely ever gives an ideal worth to his work, but is ridden by the routine of his craft, and the soul is subject to dollars. The priest becomes a form; the attorney a statute-book; the mechanic a machine; the sailor a rope of the ship.

In this distribution of functions the scholar is the delegated intellect. In the right state he is *Man Thinking*. In the degenerate state, when the victim of society, he tends to become a mere thinker, or still worse, the parrot of other men's thinking.

In this view of him, as Man Thinking, the theory of his office is contained. Him Nature solicits with all her placid, all her monitory pictures; him the past instructs; him the future invites. Is not indeed every man a student, and do not all things exist for the student's behoof? And, finally, is not the true scholar the only true master? But the old oracle said, "All things have two handles: beware of the wrong one." In life, too often, the scholar errs with mankind and forfeits his privilege. Let us see him in his school, and consider him in reference to the main influences he receives.

I. The first in time and the first in importance of the influences upon the mind is that of nature. Every day, the sun; and, after sunset, Night and her stars. Ever the winds blow; ever the grass grows. Every day, men and women, conversing—beholding and beholden. The scholar is he of all men whom this spectacle most engages. He must settle its value in his mind. What is nature to him? There is never a beginning, there is never an end, to the inexplicable continuity of this web of God, but always circular power returning into itself. Therein it resembles his own spirit, whose beginning, whose ending, he never can find,—so entire, so boundless. Far too as her splendors shine, system on system shooting like rays, upward, downward, without centre, without circumference,—in the mass and in the particle, Nature hastens to render account of herself to the mind. Classification begins. To the young mind every thing is individual, stands by itself. By and by, it finds how to join two things and see in them one nature; then three, then three thousand; and so, tyrannized over by its own unifying instinct, it goes on tying things together, diminishing anomalies, discovering roots running under ground whereby contrary and remote things cohere and flower out from one stem. It presently learns that since the dawn of history there has been a constant accumulation and classifying of facts. But what is classification but the perceiving that these objects are not chaotic, and are not foreign, but have a law which is also a law of the human mind? The astronomer discovers that geometry, a pure abstraction of the human mind, is the measure of planetary motion. The chemist finds proportions and intelligible method throughout matter; and science is nothing but the finding of analogy, identity, in the most remote parts. The ambitious soul sits down before each refractory fact; one after another reduces all strange constitutions, all new powers, to their class and their law, and goes on forever to animate the last fibre of organization, the outskirts of nature, by insight.

Thus to him, to his schoolboy under the bending dome of day, is suggested that he and it proceed from one root; one is leaf and one is flower; relation, sympathy, stirring in every vein. And what is that root? Is not that the soul of his soul? A thought too bold; a dream too wild. Yet when this spiritual light shall have revealed the law of more earthly natures,—when he has learned to worship the soul, and to see that the natural philosophy that now is, is only the first gropings of its gigantic hand, he shall look forward to an ever expanding knowledge as to a becoming creator. He shall see that nature is the opposite of the soul, answering to it part for part. One is seal and one is print. Its beauty is the beauty of his own mind. Its laws are the laws of his own mind. Nature then becomes to him the measure of his attainments. So much of nature as he is ignorant of, so much of his own mind does he not yet possess. And, in fine, the ancient precept, "Know thyself," and the modern precept, "Study nature," become at last one maxim.

II. The next great influence into the spirit of the scholar is the mind of the Past,—in whatever form, whether of literature, of art, of institutions, that mind is inscribed. Books are the best type of the influence of the past, and perhaps we shall get at the truth,—learn the amount of this influence more conveniently,—by considering their value alone.

The theory of books is noble. The scholar of the first age received into him the world around; brooded thereon; gave it the new arrangement of his own mind, and uttered it again. It came into him life; it went out from him truth. It came to him short-lived actions; it went out from him immortal thoughts. It came to him business; it went from him poetry. It was dead fact; now, it is quick thought. It can stand, and it can go. It now endures, it now flies, it now inspires. Precisely in proportion to the depth of mind from which it issued, so high does it soar, so long does it sing.

Or, I might say, it depends on how far the process had gone, of transmuting life into truth. In proportion to the completeness of the distillation, so will the purity and imperishableness of the product be. But none is quite perfect. As no air-pump can by any means make a perfect vacuum, so neither can any artist entirely exclude the conventional, the local, the perishable from his book, or write a book of pure thought, that shall be as efficient, in all respects, to a remote posterity, as to contemporaries, or rather to the second age. Each age, it is found, must write its own books; or rather, each generation for the next succeeding. The books of an older period will not fit this.

Yet hence arises a grave mischief. The sacredness which attaches to the act of creation, the act of thought, is transferred to the record. The poet chanting was felt to be a divine man: henceforth the chant is divine also. The writer was a just and wise spirit; henceforward it is settled the book is perfect; as love of the hero corrupts into worship of his statue. Instantly the book becomes noxious: the guide is a tyrant. The sluggish and perverted mind of the multitude, slow to open to the incursions of Reason, having once so opened, having once received this book, stands upon it, and makes an outcry if it is disparaged. Colleges are built on it. Books are written on it by thinkers, not by Man Thinking; by men of talent, that is, who start wrong, who set out from accepted dogmas, not from their own sight of principles. Meek young men grow up in libraries, believing it their duty to accept the views which Cicero, which Locke, which Bacon, have given; forgetful that Cicero, Locke, and Bacon were only young men in libraries when they wrote these books.

Hence, instead of Man Thinking, we have the bookworm. Hence the book-learned class, who value books, as such; not as related to nature and the human constitution, but as making a sort of Third Estate with the world and the soul. Hence the restorers of readings, the emendators, the bibliomaniacs of all degrees.

Books are the best of things, well used; abused, among the worst. What is the right use? What is the one end which all means go to effect? They are for nothing but to inspire. I had better never see a book than to be warped by its attraction clean out of my own orbit, and made a satellite instead of a system. The one thing in the world, of value, is the active soul. This every man is entitled to; this every man contains within him, although in almost all men obstructed and as yet unborn. The soul active sees absolute truth and utters truth, or creates. In this action it is genius; not the privilege of here and there a favorite, but the sound estate of every man. In its essence it is progressive. The book, the college, the school of art, the institution of any kind, stop with some past utterance of genius. This is good, say they,—let us hold by this. They pin me down. They look backward and not forward. But genius looks forward: the eyes of man are set in his forehead, not in his hindhead: man hopes: genius creates. Whatever talents may be, if the man create not, the pure efflux of the Deity is not his;—cinders and smoke there may be, but not yet flame. There are creative manners, there are creative actions, and creative words; manners, actions, words, that is, indicative of no custom or authority, but springing spontaneous from the mind's own sense of good and fair.

On the other part, instead of being its own seer, let it receive from another mind its truth, though it were in torrents of light, without periods of solitude, inquest, and self-recovery, and a fatal disservice is done. Genius is always sufficiently the enemy of genius by over-influence. The literature of every nation bears me witness. The English dramatic poets have Shakespearized now for two hundred years.

Undoubtedly there is a right way of reading, so it be sternly subordinated. Man Thinking must not be subdued by his instruments. Books are for the scholar's idle times. When he can read God directly, the hour is too precious to be wasted in other men's transcripts of their readings. But when the intervals of darkness come, as come they must, —when the sun is hid and the stars withdraw their shining,—we repair to the lamps which were kindled by their ray, to guide our steps to the East again, where the dawn is. We hear, that we may speak. The Arabian proverb says, "A fig tree, looking on a fig tree, becometh fruitful."

It is remarkable, the character of the pleasure we derive from the best books. They impress us with the conviction that one nature wrote and the same reads. We read the verses of one of the great English

poets, of Chaucer, of Marvell, of Dryden, with the most modern joy,
—with a pleasure, I mean, which is in great part caused by the abstraction of all *time* from their verses. There is some awe mixed with the
joy of our surprise, when this poet, who lived in some past world, two
or three hundred years ago, says that which lies close to my own soul,
that which I also had well-nigh thought and said. But for the evidence
thence afforded to the philosophical doctrine of the identity of all
minds, we should suppose some preestablished harmony, some foresight of souls that were to be, and some preparation of stores for their
future wants, like the fact observed in insects, who lay up food before
death for the young grub they shall never see.

I would not be hurried by any love of system, by any exaggeration
of instincts, to underrate the Book. We all know, that as the human
body can be nourished on any food, though it were boiled grass and the
broth of shoes, so the human mind can be fed by any knowledge. And
great and heroic men have existed who had almost no other information than by the printed page. I only would say that it needs a strong
head to bear that diet. One must be an inventor to read well. As the
proverb says, "He that would bring home the wealth of the Indies,
must carry out the wealth of the Indies." There is then creative reading as well as creative writing. When the mind is braced by labor and
invention, the page of whatever book we read becomes luminous with
manifold allusion. Every sentence is doubly significant, and the sense
of our author is as broad as the world. We then see, what is always
true, that as the seer's hour of vision is short and rare among heavy
days and months, so is its record, perchance, the least part of his volume. The discerning will read, in his Plato or Shakespeare, only that
least part,—only the authentic utterances of the oracle;—all the rest
he rejects, were it never so many times Plato's and Shakespeare's.

Of course there is a portion of reading quite indispensable to a wise
man. History and exact science he must learn by laborious reading.
Colleges, in like manner, have their indispensable office,—to teach elements. But they can only highly serve us when they aim not to drill,
but to create; when they gather from far every ray of various genius
to their hospitable halls, and by the concentrated fires, set the hearts
of their youth on flame. Thought and knowledge are natures in which

apparatus and pretension avail nothing. Gowns and pecuniary foundations, though of towns of gold, can never countervail the least sentence
or syllable of wit. Forget this, and our American colleges will recede
in their public importance, whilst they grow richer every year.

III. There goes in the world a notion that the scholar should be a
recluse, a valetudinarian,—as unfit for any handiwork or public labor
as a penknife for an axe. The so-called "practical men" sneer at specu-
lative men, as if, because they speculate or *see*, they could do nothing.
I have heard it said that the clergy,—who are always, more universally than any other class, the scholars of their day,—are addressed as
women; that the rough, spontaneous conversation of men they do not
hear, but only a mincing and diluted speech. They are often virtually
disfranchised; and indeed there are advocates for their celibacy. As far
as this is true of the studious classes, it is not just and wise. Action is
with the scholar subordinate, but it is essential. Without it he is not
yet man. Without it thought can never ripen into truth. Whilst the
world hangs before the eye as a cloud of beauty, we cannot even see
its beauty. Inaction is cowardice, but there can be no scholar without the heroic mind. The preamble of thought, the transition through
which it passes from the unconscious to the conscious, is action. Only
so much do I know, as I have lived. Instantly we know whose words
are loaded with life, and whose not.

The world,—this shadow of the soul, or *other me*,—lies wide
around. Its attractions are the keys which unlock my thoughts and
make me acquainted with myself. I run eagerly into this resounding
tumult. I grasp the hands of those next me, and take my place in the
ring to suffer and to work, taught by an instinct that so shall the dumb
abyss be vocal with speech. I pierce its order; I dissipate its fear; I
dispose of it within the circuit of my expanding life. So much only of
life as I know by experience, so much of the wilderness have I van-
quished and planted, or so far have I extended my being, my dominion.
I do not see how any man can afford, for the sake of his nerves and his
nap, to spare any action in which he can partake. It is pearls and rubies
to his discourse. Drudgery, calamity, exasperation, want, are instructors
in eloquence and wisdom. The true scholar grudges every opportunity
of action past by, as a loss of power. It is the raw material out of which

the intellect moulds her splendid products. A strange process, too, this by which experience is converted into thought, as a mulberry leaf is converted into satin. The manufacture goes forward at all hours.

The actions and events of our childhood and youth are now matters of calmest observation. They lie like fair pictures in the air. Not so with our recent actions,—with the business which we now have in hand. On this we are quite unable to speculate. Our affections as yet circulate through it. We no more feel or know it than we feel the feet, or the hand, or the brain of our body. The new deed is yet a part of life,—remains for a time immersed in our unconscious life. In some contemplative hour it detaches itself from the life like a ripe fruit, to become a thought of the mind. Instantly it is raised, transfigured; the corruptible has put on incorruption. Henceforth it is an object of beauty, however base its origin and neighborhood. Observe too the impossibility of antedating this act. In its grub state, it cannot fly, it cannot shine, it is a dull grub. But suddenly, without observation, the selfsame thing unfurls beautiful wings, and is an angel of wisdom. So is there no fact, no event, in our private history, which shall not, sooner or later, lose its adhesive, inert form, and astonish us by soaring from our body into the empyrean. Cradle and infancy, school and playground, the fear of boys, and dogs, and ferules, the love of little maids and berries, and many another fact that once filled the whole sky, are gone already; friend and relative, profession and party, town and country, nation and world, must also soar and sing.

Of course, he who has put forth his total strength in fit actions has the richest return of his wisdom. I will not shut myself out of this globe of action, and transplant an oak into a flowerpot, there to hunger and pine; nor trust the revenue of some single faculty, and exhaust one vein of thought, much like those Savoyards, who, getting their livelihood by carving shepherds, shepherdesses, and smoking Dutchmen, for all Europe, went out one day to the mountain to find stock, and discovered that they had whittled up the last of their pine trees. Authors we have, in numbers, who have written out their vein, and who, moved by a commendable prudence, sail for Greece or Palestine, follow the trapper into the prairie, or ramble round Algiers, to replenish their merchantable stock.

If it were only for a vocabulary, the scholar would be covetous of action. Life is our dictionary. Years are well spent in country labors; in town; in the insight into trades and manufactures; in frank intercourse with many men and women; in science; in art; to the one end of mastering in all their facts a language by which to illustrate and embody our perceptions. I learn immediately from any speaker how much he has already lived, through the poverty or the splendor of his speech. Life lies behind us as the quarry from whence we get tiles and copestones for the masonry of to-day. This is the way to learn grammar. Colleges and books only copy the language which the field and the work-yard made.

But the final value of action, like that of books, and better than books, is that it is a resource. That great principle of Undulation in nature, that shows itself in the inspiring and expiring of the breath; in desire and satiety; in the ebb and flow of the sea; in day and night; in heat and cold; and, as yet more deeply ingrained in every atom and every fluid, is known to us under the name of Polarity,—these "fits of easy transmission and reflection," as Newton called them, are the law of nature because they are the law of spirit.

The mind now thinks, now acts, and each fit reproduces the other. When the artist has exhausted his materials, when the fancy no longer paints, when thoughts are no longer apprehended and books are a weariness,—he has always the resource *to live*. Character is higher than intellect. Thinking is the function. Living is the functionary. The stream retreats to its source. A great soul will be strong to live, as well as strong to drink. Does he lack organ or medium to impart his truths? He can still fall back on this elemental force of living them. This is a total act. Thinking is a partial act. Let the grandeur of justice shine in his affairs. Let the beauty of affection cheer his lowly roof. Those "far from fame," who dwell and act with him, will feel the force of his constitution in the doings and passages of the day better than it can be measured by any public and designed display. Time shall teach him that the scholar loses no hour which the man lives. Herein he unfolds the sacred germ of his instinct, screened from influence. What is lost in seemliness is gained in strength. Not out of those on whom systems of education have exhausted their culture, comes the helpful giant to destroy the old or to build the new, but out of un-handselled savage nature; out of terrible Druids and Berserkers come at last Alfred and Shakespeare.

I hear therefore with joy whatever is beginning to be said of the dignity and necessity of labor to every citizen. There is virtue yet in the hoe and the spade, for learned as well as for unlearned hands. And labor is everywhere welcome; always we are invited to work; only be this limitation observed, that a man shall not for the sake of wider activity sacrifice any opinion to the popular judgments and modes of action.

I have now spoken of the education of the scholar by nature, by books, and by action. It remains to say somewhat of his duties.

They are such as become Man Thinking. They may all be comprised in self-trust. The office of the scholar is to cheer, to raise, and to guide men by showing them facts amidst appearances. He plies the slow, unhonored, and unpaid task of observation. Flamsteed and Herschel, in their glazed observatories, may catalogue the stars with the praise of all men, and the results being splendid and useful, honor is sure. But he, in his private observatory, cataloguing obscure and nebulous stars of the human mind, which as yet no man has thought of as such,—watching days and months sometimes for a few facts; correcting still his old records;—must relinquish display and immediate fame. In the long period of his preparation he must betray often an ignorance and shiftlessness in popular arts, incurring the disdain of the able who shoulder him aside. Long he must stammer in his speech; often forego the living for the dead. Worse yet, he must accept—how often!—poverty and solitude. For the ease and pleasure of treading the old road, accepting the fashions, the education, the religion of society, he takes the cross of making his own, and, of course, the self-accusation, the faint heart, the frequent uncertainty and loss of time, which are the nettles and tangling vines in the way of the self-relying and self-directed; and the state of virtual hostility in which he seems to stand to society, and especially to educated society. For all this loss and scorn, what offset? He is to find consolation in exercising the highest functions of human nature. He is one who raises himself from private considerations and breathes and lives on public and illustrious thoughts. He is the world's eye. He is the world's heart. He is to resist the vulgar prosperity that retrogrades ever to barbarism, by preserving and communicating heroic sentiments, noble biographies, melodious verse, and the conclusions of history. Whatsoever oracles the human heart, in all emergencies, in all solemn hours, has uttered as its commentary on the world of actions,—these he shall receive and impart. And whatsoever new verdict Reason from her inviolable seat pronounces on the passing men and events of to-day,—this he shall hear and promulgate.

These being his functions, it becomes him to feel all confidence in himself, and to defer never to the popular cry. He and he only knows the world. The world of any moment is the merest appearance. Some great decorum, some fetish of a government, some ephemeral trade, or war, or man, is cried up by half mankind and cried down by the other half, as if all depended on this particular up or down. The odds are that the whole question is not worth the poorest thought which the scholar has lost in listening to the controversy. Let him not quit his belief that a popgun is a popgun, though the ancient and honorable of the earth affirm it to be the crack of doom. In silence, in steadiness, in severe abstraction, let him hold by himself; add observation to observation, patient of neglect, patient of reproach, and bide his own time—happy enough if he can satisfy himself alone that this day he has seen something truly. Success treads on every right step. For the instinct is sure, that prompts him to tell his brother what he thinks. He then learns that in going down into the secrets of his own mind he has descended into the secrets of all minds. He learns that he who has mastered any law in his private thoughts, is master to that extent of all men whose language he speaks, and of all into whose language his own can be translated. The poet, in utter solitude remembering his spontaneous thoughts and recording them, is found to have recorded that which men in crowded cities find true for them also. The orator distrusts at first the fitness of his frank confessions, his want of knowledge of the persons he addresses, until he finds that he is the complement of his hearers;—that they drink his words because he fulfills for them their own nature; the deeper he dives into his privatest, secretest presentiment, to his wonder he finds this is the most acceptable, most public, and universally true. The people delight in it; the better part of every man feels, This is my music; this is myself.

In self-trust all the virtues are comprehended. Free should the scholar be,—free and brave. Free even to the definition of freedom, "without any hindrance that does not arise out of his own constitution." Brave; for fear is a thing which a scholar by his very function puts behind him. Fear always springs from ignorance. It is a shame to him if his tranquility, amid dangerous times, arise from the presumption that like children and women his is a protected class; or if he seeks a temporary peace by the diversion of his thoughts from politics or vexed questions, hiding his head like an ostrich in the flowering bushes, peeping into microscopes, and turning rhymes, as a boy whistles to keep his courage up. So is the danger a danger still; so is the fear worse. Manlike let him turn and face it. Let him look into its eye and search its nature, inspect its origin,—see the whelping of this lion— which lies no great way back; he will then find in himself a perfect comprehension of its nature and extent; he will have made his hands meet on the other side, and can henceforth defy it and pass on superior. The world is his who can see through its pretension. What deafness, what stone-blind custom, what overgrown error you behold is there only by sufferance,—by your sufferance. See it to be a lie, and you have already dealt it its mortal blow.

Yes, we are the cowed,—we the trustless. It is a mischievous notion that we are come late into nature; that the world was finished a long time ago. As the world was plastic and fluid in the hands of God, so it is ever to so much of his attributes as we bring to it. To ignorance and sin, it is flint. They adapt themselves to it as they may; but in proportion as a man has any thing in him divine, the firmament flows before him and takes his signet and form. Not he is great who can alter matter, but he who can alter my state of mind. They are the kings of the world who give the color of their present thought to all nature and all art, and persuade men by the cheerful serenity of their carrying the matter, that this thing which they do is the apple which the ages have desired to pluck, now at last ripe, and inviting nations to the harvest. The great man makes the great thing. Wherever Macdonald sits, there is the head of the table. Linnaeus makes botany the most alluring of studies, and wins it from the farmer and the herb-woman; Davy, chemistry; and Cuvier, fossils. The day is always his who works in it with serenity and great aims. The unstable estimates of men crowd to him whose mind is filled with a truth, as the heaped waves of the Atlantic follow the moon.

For this self-trust, the reason is deeper than can be fathomed,—darker than can be enlightened. I might not carry with me the feeling of my audience in stating my own belief. But I have already shown the ground of my hope, in adverting to the doctrine that man is one. I believe man has been wronged; he has wronged himself. He has almost lost the light that can lead him back to his prerogatives. Men are become of no account. Men in history, men in the world of to-day, are bugs, are spawn, and are called "the mass" and "the herd." In a century, in a millennium, one or two men; that is to say, one or two approximations to the right state of every man. All the rest behold in the hero or the poet their own green and crude being,—ripened; yes, and are content to be less, so *that* may attain to its full stature. What a testimony, full of grandeur, full of pity, is borne to the demands of his own nature, by the poor clansman, the poor partisan, who rejoices in the glory of his chief. The poor and the low find some amends to their immense moral capacity, for their acquiescence in a political and social inferiority. They are content to be brushed like flies from the path of a great person, so that justice shall be done by him to that common nature which it is dearest desire of all to see enlarged and glorified. They sun themselves in the great man's light, and feel it to be their own element. They cast the dignity of man from their downtrod selves upon the shoulders of a hero, and will perish to add one drop of blood to make that great heart beat, those giant sinews combat and conquer. He lives for us, and we live in him.

Men, such as they are, very naturally seek money or power; and power because it is as good as money,—the "spoils," so called, "of office." And why not? for they aspire to the highest, and this, in their sleep-walking, they dream is highest. Wake them and they shall quit the false good and leap to the true, and leave governments to clerks and desks. This revolution is to be wrought by the gradual domestication of the idea of Culture. The main enterprise of the world for splendor, for extent, is the upbuilding of a man. Here are the materials strewn along the ground. The private life of one man shall be a more illustrious monarchy, more formidable to its enemy, more sweet and serene in its influence to its friend, than any kingdom in history. For a man, rightly viewed, comprehendeth the particular natures of all men. Each philosopher, each bard, each actor has only done for me, as by a delegate, what one day I can do for myself. The books which once we valued more than the apple of the eye, we have quite exhausted. What is that but saying that we have come up with the point of view which the universal mind took through the eyes of one scribe; we have been that man, and have passed on. First, one, then another, we drain all cisterns, and waxing greater by all these supplies, we crave a better and more abundant food. The man has never lived that can feed us ever. The human mind cannot be enshrined in a person who shall set a barrier on any one side to this unbounded, unboundable empire. It is one central fire, which, flaming now out of the lips of Etna, lightens the capes of Sicily, and now out of the throat of Vesuvius, illuminates the towers and vineyards of Naples. It is one light which beams out of a thousand stars. It is one soul which animates all men.

But I have dwelt perhaps tediously upon this abstraction of the Scholar. I ought not to delay longer to add what I have to say of nearer reference to the time and to this country.

Historically, there is thought to be a difference in the ideas which predominate over successive epochs, and there are data for marking the genius of the Classic, of the Romantic, and now of the Reflective or Philosophical age. With the views I have intimated of the oneness or the identity of the mind through all individuals, I do not much dwell on these differences. In fact, I believe each individual passes through all three. The boy is a Greek; the youth, romantic; the adult, reflective. I deny not, however, that a revolution in the leading idea may be distinctly enough traced.

Our age is bewailed as the age of Introversion. Must that needs be evil? We, it seems, are critical; we are embarrassed with second thoughts; we cannot enjoy any thing for hankering to know whereof the pleasure consists; we are lined with eyes; we see with our feet; the time is infected with Hamlet's unhappiness,—

Sicklied o'er with the pale cast of thought

It is so bad then? Sight is the last thing to be pitied. Would we be blind? Do we fear lest we should outsee nature and God, and drink truth dry? I look upon the discontent of the literary class as a mere announcement of the fact that they find themselves not in the state of mind of their fathers, and regret the coming state as untried; as a boy dreads the water before he has learned that he can swim. If there is any period one would desire to be born in, is it not the age of Revolution; when the old and the new stand side by side and admit of being compared; when the energies of all men are searched by fear and by hope; when the historic glories of the old can be compensated by the rich possibilities of the new era? This time, like all times, is a very good one, if we but know what to do with it.

I read with some joy of the auspicious signs of the coming days, as they glimmer already through poetry and art, through philosophy and science, through church and state.

One of these signs is the fact that the same movement which effected the elevation of what was called the lowest class in the state, assumed in literature a very marked and as benign an aspect. Instead of the sublime and beautiful, the near, the low, the common, was explored and poetized. That which had been negligently trodden under foot by those who were harnessing and provisioning themselves for long journeys into far countries, is suddenly found to be richer than all foreign parts. The literature of the poor, the feelings of the child, the philosophy of the street, the meaning of household life, are the topics of the time. It is a great stride. It is a sign—is it not?—of new vigor when the extremities are made active, when currents of warm life run into the hands and the feet. I ask not for the great, the remote, the romantic; what is doing in Italy or Arabia; what is Greek art, or Provençal minstrelsy; I embrace the common, I explore and sit at the feet of the familiar, the low. Give me insight into to-day, and you may have the antique and future worlds. What would we really know the meaning of? The meal in the firkin; the milk in the pan; the ballad in the street; the news of the boat; the glance of the eye; the form and the gait of the body;—show me the ultimate reason of these matters; show me the sublime presence of the highest spiritual cause lurking, as always it does lurk, in these suburbs and extremities of nature; let me see every trifle bristling with the polarity that ranges it instantly on an eternal law; and the shop, the plough, and the ledger referred to the like cause by which light undulates and poets sing;—and the world lies no longer a dull miscellany and lumber-room, but has form and order; there is no trifle, there is no puzzle, but one design unites and animates the farthest pinnacle and the lowest trench.

This idea has inspired the genius of Goldsmith, Burns, Cowper, and, in a newer time, of Goethe, Wordsworth, and Carlyle. This idea they have differently followed and with various success. In contrast with their writing, the style of Pope, of Johnson, of Gibbon, looks cold and pedantic. This writing is blood-warm. Man is surprised to find that things near are not less beautiful and wondrous than things remote. The near explains the far. The drop is a small ocean. A man is related to all nature. This perception of the worth of the vulgar is fruitful in discoveries. Goethe, in this very thing the most modern of the moderns, has shown us, as none ever did, the genius of the ancients.

There is one man of genius who has done much for this philosophy of life, whose literary value has never yet been rightly estimated;—I mean Emanuel Swedenborg. The most imaginative of men, yet writing with the precision of a mathematician, he endeavored to engraft a purely philosophical Ethics on the popular Christianity of his time. Such an attempt of course must have difficulty which no genius could surmount. But he saw and showed the connection between nature and the affections of the soul. He pierced the emblematic or spiritual character of the visible, audible, tangible world. Especially did his shade-loving muse hover over and interpret the lower parts of nature; he showed the mysterious bond that allies moral evil to the foul material forms, and has given in epical parables a theory of insanity, of beasts, of unclean and fearful things.

Another sign of our times, also marked by an analogous political movement, is the new importance given to the single person. Every thing that tends to insulate the individual,—to surround him with barriers of natural respect, so that each man shall feel the world is his, and man shall treat with man as a sovereign state with a sovereign state, —tends to true union as well as greatness. "I learned," said the melancholy Pestalozzi, "that no man in God's wide earth is either willing or able to help any other man." Help must come from the bosom alone. The scholar is that man who must take up into himself all the ability of the time, all the contributions of the past, all the hopes of the future. He must be an university of knowledges. If there be one lesson more than another which should pierce his ear, it is, The world is nothing, the man is all; in yourself is the law of all nature, and you know not yet how a globule of sap ascends; in yourself slumbers the whole of Reason; it is for you to know all; it is for you to dare all. Mr. President and Gentlemen, this confidence in the unsearched might of man belongs, by all motives, by all prophecy, by all preparation, to the American Scholar. We have listened too long to the courtly muses of Europe. The spirit of the American freeman is already suspected to be timid, imitative, tame. Public and private avarice make the air we breathe thick and fat. The scholar is decent, indolent, complaisant. See already the tragic consequence. The mind of this country, taught to aim at low objects, eats upon itself. There is no work for any but the decorous and the complaisant. Young men of the fairest promise, who begin life upon our shores, inflated by the mountain winds, shined upon by all the stars of God, find the earth below not in unison with these, but are hindered from action by the disgust which the principles on which business is managed inspire, and turn drudges, or die of disgust, some of them suicides. What is the remedy? They did not yet see, and thousands of young men as hopeful now crowding to the barriers for the career do not yet see, that if the single man plant himself indomitably on his instincts, and there abide, the huge world will come round to him. Patience,—patience; with the shades of all the good and great for company; and for solace the perspective of your own infinite life; and for work the study and the communication of principles, the making those instincts prevalent, the conversion of the world. Is it not the chief disgrace in the world, not to be an unit;—not to be reckoned one character;—not to yield that peculiar fruit which each man was created to bear, but to be reckoned in the gross, in the hundred, or the thousand, of the party, the section, to which we belong; and our opinion predicted geographically, as the north, or the south? Not so, brother and friends—please God, ours shall not be so. We will walk on our own feet; we will work with our hands; we will speak our own minds. The study of letters shall be no longer a name for pity, for doubt, and for sensual indulgence. The dread of man and the love of man shall be a wall of defence and a wreath of joy around all. A nation of men will for the first time exist, because each believes himself inspired by the Divine Soul which also inspires all men.

Questions and Exercises

1. List three professions which Ralph Waldo Emerson followed:
   (1)_____ (2)_____ (3)_____
2. Where was he born?_____ When?_____
   Into what type of economic status?_____
3. Where did he attend undergraduate school?_____
   Divinity school?_____
4. What was the occasion for his speech "The American Scholar"?
   _____
5. Of whom did his audience consist?_____
   _____
6. What was the central idea of the speech?_____
   _____
7. How did he prepare his speech for delivery?_____
   _____
8. List the main divisions of his speech._____
   _____
   _____
9. What two forms of support did he use most?_____
   _____and_____
10. Of what did the conclusion consist?_____
    _____
    _____

V GETTYSBURG ADDRESS

ABRAHAM LINCOLN
(1809-1865)

The Speaker

Abraham Lincoln's use of oral communication presents a study in paradoxes. His "Gettysburg Address" received the highest vote on the ballot conducted for this study, yet his awkward bearing, high-pitched voice, and nonfluent speech constitute the antithesis of desired presentation skills. He received but one year of formal education, yet his inquiring mind, background of information, and knowledge of human nature characterize the educated man. Perhaps his life presents a good example of one whose able-man characteristics—intelligence, character, and good will—compensated for his deficiencies in communicative skills. His self-education shows the heights a man can attain on his own initiative. He exemplifies the able man in action.

Lincoln was born in a log cabin near Hodgenville, Kentucky, on February 12, 1809. His early years, spent in Kentucky until 1816, in Indiana until 1830, and then in Illinois, afforded little opportunity for formal education; however, he read everything available, sought every opportunity to listen to speakers, and engaged others in lively discussion and conversation.

His experiences were largely in the field of law and politics. He was elected in 1834 to the Illinois Legislature, where he remained until 1842. During this period he served an apprenticeship in law and was admitted to the Illinois bar in 1837. He made two unsuccessful attempts to secure nomination for Congress: in 1842 and again in 1844. He was elected to the House of Representatives and served one term, from 1847 to 1849. After returning to his law practice, he ran for the United States Senate in 1854 and again in 1858 but was defeated both times. During the 1858 campaign a series of debates which he held with his Democratic opponent, Stephen A. Douglas, did much to give him national prominence. An address at Cooper Institute, New York, on February 27, 1860, helped to secure his nomination by the Republican party the following May for the Presidency of the United States. He won the election in 1860 and was re-elected in 1864. He was shot by John Wilkes Booth while attending a play at Ford's Theatre, Washington, and died on April 15, 1865.

The Occasion

Lincoln's "Gettysburg Address" was given at the dedication of the cemetery at Gettysburg, Pennsylvania, on November 19, 1863. The Battle of Gettysburg, considered by many as the turning point of the Civil War, was fought on July 1-3, 1863. The states that lost soldiers at the Battle of Gettysburg obtained grounds on a part of the battlefield and had the dead removed there for burial. The cemetery was established as a private corporation with commissioners representing seventeen states. The purpose of the dedication ceremony was to consecrate the grounds of the cemetery and pay homage to those who had lost their lives in the battle.

Edward Everett of Boston, one of the most popular speakers of that era, was chosen to give the principal address. He had served in turn as minister, professor of Greek at Harvard, president of Harvard, United States Senator, and Secretary of State. President Lincoln was invited to give a "few appropriate remarks" in keeping with the occasion. The audience of more than fifteen thousand people included many important governmental and military officials, bereaved families, and citizens of the area.

The Speech

Edward Everett's eloquent and carefully prepared address required two hours for delivery; Lincoln's speech took no more than three minutes. Who could have anticipated that, almost one hundred years later, few people could even remember the name of the principal orator, while almost all school children could quote at least parts of Lincoln's "remarks" from memory?

Although a brief speech, Lincoln's "Gettysburg Address" restated much of his political philosophy—that a government embodying the ideal of equality of men should be preserved; that the doctrine of the rights of man should be protected; that the concept of government of, by, and for the people should prevail. The chronological order, past-present-future, formed the organizational pattern. Lincoln started with a statement of our original concepts of liberty and equality. Then he discussed the present danger to those concepts caused by the Civil War. Finally, he emphasized the task remaining, to protect our freedom and concept of government based on the individual.

The text that follows is known as "the Bliss copy." It was written some three months after the delivery of the speech itself. Although historians disagree on exactly when and how the speech was prepared, it is believed that Lincoln's first draft was written in Washington several days before the ceremony. A revised draft, the one Lincoln held as he spoke, was written on the evening before and on the morning of the dedication. Other revisions and copies were provided for Secretary John Hay for deposit in the Library of Congress, for Judge Wills for preservation with other documents of the occasion, and for use at a sanitary fair in New York City. A revised copy was written at the request of George Bancroft for use at the Baltimore Soldier's and Sailor's Fair, but finding this copy unsuited for lithographing purposes, Lincoln made another copy which has become the accepted standard text. This text of the speech follows from John G. Nicolay and John Hay,

Complete Works of Abraham Lincoln (New York: Appleton-Century-Crofts, 1894-1905), Vol. 9, pp. 209-210.

Four score and seven years ago our fathers brought forth on this continent, a new nation, conceived in Liberty, and dedicated to the proposition that all men are created equal.

Now we are engaged in a great civil war, testing whether that nation or any nation so conceived and so dedicated, can long endure. We are met on a great battle-field of that war. We have come to dedicate a portion of that field, as a final resting place for those who here gave their lives that that nation might live. It is altogether fitting and proper that we should do this.

But, in a larger sense, we can not dedicate—we can not consecrate—we can not hallow—this ground. The brave men, living and dead, who struggled here, have consecrated it, far above our poor power to add or detract. The world will little note, nor long remember what we say here, but it can never forget what they did here. It is for us the living, rather, to be dedicated here to the unfinished work which they who fought here have thus far so nobly advanced. It is rather for us to be here dedicated to the great task remaining before us—that from these honored dead we take increased devotion to that cause for which they gave the last full measure of devotion—that we here highly resolve that these dead shall not have died in vain—that this nation, under God, shall have a new birth of freedom—and that government of the people, by the people, for the people, shall not perish from the earth.

Questions and Exercises

1. Where was Abraham Lincoln born?_____
   In what state did he live when elected President?_____

2. What were the economic circumstances of his early life?_____
   _____

3. Describe his manner of delivery._____
   _____

4. What event in his Senatorial campaign of 1858 led to his national prominence?_____

5. What was the occasion of his "Gettysburg Address"?_____
   _____

6. Who was the principal speaker for the occasion?_____

7. What was the central idea of the speech?_____
   _____
   _____

8. How was the speech organized?_____
   _____

9. Describe the style of the speech._____
   _____
   _____

10. Why, in your opinion, did his speech become so well known?
    _____
    _____

VI SECOND INAUGURAL ADDRESS

ABRAHAM LINCOLN
(1809-1865)

The Occasion

Lincoln was re-elected president in 1864 by an overwhelming majority of five hundred thousand votes and carried all states but three—Kentucky, Delaware, and New Jersey. By the time of his second inauguration on March 4, 1865, it was apparent that the war would soon be over. Lee surrendered at Appomattox on April 9, a little more than a month after the inauguration. The spirit of the country was one of relief.

The inauguration ceremonies were held at the east portico of the Capitol. In spite of the cold and dreary weather, an audience estimated at fifty thousand attended. Although the usual governmental dignitaries were present, the bulk of the audience consisted of average citizens favorable to Lincoln's war policies and philosophy of government. Lincoln had his critics, however. Less than a year before the inauguration, one faction of the Republican party had written a platform condemning him for his conduct of the war and declaring him a political and military failure. By the time of the inauguration, the spirit of a majority of his listeners was one of optimism and appreciation.

The Speech

Although the speech was short, requiring less than six minutes to deliver, it was considered by Lincoln and many historians as perhaps his greatest speech. It reflected the growth of Lincoln both as a man and as a speaker. Early in his career Lincoln appeared to speak largely for himself, next for his party, and then for the Union; but in his "Second Inaugural Address," he spoke for mankind. His development went from the personal to the partisan, and then to the universal. Lincoln appeared to speak from the depths of his heart with almost sublime and prophetic authority.

The organizational pattern, like that of the "Gettysburg Address," follows a chronological order of past-present-future. He began by contrasting the conditions that prevailed at the time of his first inauguration with those existing at the second inauguration. He next discussed slavery as the underlying cause of existing conditions, but avoided placing the blame on either side. He concluded with an expression of hope for universal peace and understanding.

The basic appeal is largely ethical. The highly ethical character of the man comes through in such statements as "Both [sides] read the same Bible, and pray to the same God." ". . . but let us judge not that we be not judged." "With malice toward none; with charity for all; . . . let us strive . . . to do all which may achieve and cherish a just and lasting peace. . . ." The text that follows was reprinted from *Inaugural Addresses of the Presidents of the United States* (Washington, D.C.: United States Government Printing Office, 1961), 87th Congress, 1st Session, House Document No. 218, pp. 127-128.

FELLOW-COUNTRYMEN: At this second appearing to take the oath of the presidential office there is less occasion for an extended address than there was at the first. Then a statement somewhat in detail of a course to be pursued seemed fitting and proper. Now, at the expiration of four years, during which public declarations have been constantly called forth on every point and phase of the great contest which still absorbs the attention and engrosses the energies of the nation, little that is new could be presented. The progress of our arms, upon which all else chiefly depends, is as well known to the public as to myself, and it is, I trust, reasonably satisfactory and encouraging to all. With high hope for the future, no prediction in regard to it is ventured.

On the occasion corresponding to this four years ago all thoughts were anxiously directed to an impending civil war. All dreaded it, all sought to avert it. While the inaugural address was being delivered from this place, devoted altogether to *saving* the Union without war, insurgent agents were in the city seeking to *destroy* it without war— seeking to dissolve the Union and divide effects by negotiation. Both parties deprecated war, but one of them would *make* war rather than let the nation survive, and the other would *accept* war rather than let it perish, and the war came.

One-eighth of the whole population was colored slaves, not distributed generally over the Union, but localized in the southern part of it. These slaves constituted a peculiar and powerful interest. All knew that this interest was somehow the cause of the war. To strengthen, perpetuate, and extend this interest was the object for which the insurgents would rend the Union even by war, while the Government claimed no right to do more than to restrict the territorial enlargement of it. Neither party expected for the war the magnitude or the duration which it has already attained. Neither anticipated that the *cause* of the conflict might cease with or even before the conflict itself should cease. Each looked for an easier triumph, and a result less fundamental and astounding. Both read the same Bible and pray to the same God, and each invokes His aid against the other. It may seem strange that any men should dare to ask a just God's assistance in wringing their bread from the sweat of other men's faces, but let us judge not, that we be not judged. The prayers of both could not be answered. That of neither has been answered fully. The Almighty has His own purposes. "Woe unto the world because of offenses; for it must needs be that offenses come, but woe to that man by whom the offense cometh." If we shall suppose that American slavery is one of those offenses which, in the providence of God, must needs come, but which, having continued through His appointed time, He now wills to remove, and that He gives to both North and South this terrible war as the woe due to those by whom the offense came, shall we discern therein any departure from those divine attributes which the believers in a living God always ascribe to Him? Fondly do we hope, fervently do we pray, that this mighty scourge of war may speedily pass away. Yet, if God wills that it continue until all the wealth piled by the bondsman's two hundred and fifty years of unrequited toil shall be sunk, and until every drop of blood drawn with the lash shall be paid by another drawn with the sword, as was said three thousand years ago, so still it must be said, "The judgments of the Lord are true and righteous altogether."

With malice toward none, with charity for all, with firmness in the right as God gives us to see the right, let us strive on to finish the work we are in, to bind up the nation's wounds, to care for him who shall have borne the battle and for his widow and his orphan, to do all which may achieve and cherish a just and lasting peace among ourselves and with all nations.

Questions and Exercises

1. For how many years did Abraham Lincoln serve as President? _____ When?_____

2. When did he die?_____ Under what circumstances? _____

3. What do you consider his principal source of greatness?_____ _____

4. What political party did he represent?_____

5. How many states did he lose in the presidential campaign of 1864?_____ List them._____

6. What was the setting for his "Second Inaugural Address"?_____ _____ _____

7. Describe the organizational pattern._____ _____ _____

8. Give one example of ethical appeal._____ _____ _____

9. Give one example of logical appeal._____ _____ _____

10. What method was used in the introduction?_____ _____ _____

VII *THE NEW SOUTH*

HENRY W. GRADY
(1850-1889)

The Speaker

On December 22, 1886, Henry W. Grady, at age thirty-six, made a speech in New York City entitled "The New South" that established him as the South's outstanding spokesman for reconciliation with the North. Until his death three years and one day later, he made numerous speeches and wrote many articles as editor of the Atlanta *Constitution* that solidified his position as the South's champion of reconciliation. He established a national reputation as a Southern spokesman at a time when a voice for the New South was sorely needed. The forces that led to war had called forth orators of renown; the forces for peace following the war had failed to attract orators of comparable ability and reputation. The Southerner was looked upon as the troublemaker, the one who suppressed the Negro's vote, encouraged lynchings, harbored resentment, and desired revenge. The South needed a spokesman to enunciate its message of a changed attitude, a desire for harmony, a preference for national over sectional interests. Grady became that spokesman.

Henry W. Grady was born in Athens, Georgia, on May 24, 1850. He attended public schools only two years, from 1859 to 1861. In 1866, he entered the sophomore class at the University of Georgia and was graduated two years later. He studied law at the University of Virginia, but left after his first year to enter the profession of journalism. After serving as editor of the Rome *Daily-Commercial*, he became publisher of the Atlanta *Herald* and later the Atlanta *Courier*, but both papers declared bankruptcy. He became part owner and managing editor of the Atlanta *Constitution* in 1880, in which position he continued until his death on December 23, 1889. He died of pneumonia contracted during his trip to Boston, where he delivered his speech "The Race Problem."

Grady gave early indications of his proficiency in communication, both written and oral. In college he became interested in the activities of the literary societies, excelled in debating and other types of speaking, and showed great interest in the study of literature and rhetoric. He was a prodigious reader, and continued to be one until his death. His extraordinary memory enabled him to quote his speeches verbatim immediately after writing them. His unusual command of language served him well both as an editor and as a spokesman for the new South.

The Occasion

Grady's speech, "The New South" was given before the New England Society of New York City, an organization of prominent business and professional men with strong conservative leanings. The well-known organization, founded in 1805, was noted for its distinguished membership, which included such men as J. Pierpont Morgan, Russell Sage, Elihu Root, and Seth Thomas. It prided itself on securing the most distinguished speakers of the period to address its meetings. Speakers appearing on the same program as Grady included Reverend Thomas D. Talmage, William W. Phelps, General W. T. Sherman, General J. M. Schofield, and Reverend Henry Van Dyke, Jr. Grady was the first Southerner ever to be invited to address the organization. He was reputed to be a member of the progressive forces at work in the South toward reconciliation, and the membership of the Society wanted a firsthand report from him.

The prevailing circumstances presented a difficult speaking situation for Grady. The natural animosities of the Northern Republican leaders toward the South occasioned by the Civil War had been intensified by the election of Grover Cleveland, the first Democratic President, in 1884. Many members of the society had large sums invested in the South and were fearful of the effect of the election on their investments.

Reverend Talmage and General Sherman preceded Grady on the program. Their speeches were highly prejudicial against the South. Talmage praised the return of the victorious Northern armies and Sherman related an incident which depreciated the position of the Southerner. When General Sherman concluded, the audience stood and enthusiastically sang "Marching through Georgia." One can imagine the mixed emotions which the young Georgia editor felt as he arose to defend the New South.

The Speech

The introduction comprises almost one-half of the speech. Grady realized that the hostility of the audience toward his subject required that he create a favorable attitude for himself to ensure a receptive attitude for his message. The methods he used showed a keen perception of audience reactions. He began by quoting Benjamin H. Hill, a man highly acceptable to his audience. Then he in turn expressed appreciation for being the first Southerner asked to address the Society, commented on the American concept of fairness in considering opposing ideas, injected well-chosen humor designed to ensure an open-minded attitude, and used indirect suggestion to show a common bond of tradition between the North and the South. These methods apparently put his listeners into the proper frame of mind for his speech.

The central theme of the speech was to show the changed attitude reflected in the spirit of the New South. Grady developed three points, using the deductive arrangement, to bring out the central idea: (1) what the South has accomplished, (2) the Southerners' treatment of the Negro, and (3) the loyalty of the South. The points were developed more by explaining general concepts than by using specific details, but toward the end he added the weight of his own convictions that a new spirit existed in the South. He concluded the speech with a stirring challenge—that the North lay aside its prejudices and accept the friendship extended by the New South.

Newspaper accounts termed the speech impromptu. Historians have revealed that Grady had a carefully prepared, extemporaneous speech which he adapted well to the remarks of the preceding speakers. The text that follows was taken from the *Proceedings* of the Society, reprinted by Joel Chandler Harris, *Henry W. Grady: His Life, Writings, and Speeches* (New York: Cassell Publishing Co., 1890), pp. 15-16.

"There was a South of slavery and secession—that South is dead. There is a South of union and freedom—that South, thank God, is living, breathing, growing every hour." These words, delivered from the immortal lips of Benjamin H. Hill, at Tammany Hall in 1866, true then, and truer now, I shall make my text to-night.

Mr. President and Gentlemen: Let me express to you my appreciation of the kindness by which I am permitted to address you. I make this abrupt acknowledgment advisedly, for I feel that if, when I raise my provincial voice in this ancient and august presence, I could find courage for no more than the opening sentence, it would be well if, in that sentence, I had met in a rough sense my obligation as a guest, and had perished, so to speak, with courtesy on my lips and grace in my heart. [*Laughter.*] Permitted through your kindness to catch my second wind, let me say that I appreciate the significance of being the first Southerner to speak at this board, which bears the substance, if it surpasses the semblance, of original New England hospitality [*Applause*], and honors a sentiment that in turn honors you, but in which my personality is lost, and the compliment to my people made plain. [*Laughter.*]

I bespeak the utmost stretch of your courtesy to-night. I am not troubled about those from whom I come. You remember the man whose wife sent him to a neighbor with a pitcher of milk, and who, tripping on the top step, fell, with such casual interruptions as the landing afforded, into the basement; and while picking himself up had the pleasure of hearing his wife call out: "John, did you break the pitcher?"

"No, I didn't," said John, "but I be dinged if I don't!" [*Laughter.*]

So, while those who call to me from behind may inspire me with energy if not with courage, I ask an indulgent hearing from you. I beg that you will bring your full faith in American fairness and frankness to judgment upon what I shall say. There was an old preacher once who told some boys of the Bible lesson he was going to read in the morning. The boys finding the place, glued together the connecting pages. [*Laughter.*] The next morning he read on the bottom of one page: "When Noah was one hundred and twenty years old he took unto himself a wife, who was"—then turning the page—"one hundred and forty cubits long [*Laughter*], forty cubits wide, built of gopher-wood [*Laughter*], and covered with pitch inside and out." [*Loud and continued laughter.*] He was naturally puzzled at this. He read it again, verified it, and then said: "My friends, this is the first time I ever met this in the Bible, but I accept it as an evidence of the assertion that we are fearfully and wonderfully made." [*Immense laughter.*] If I could get you to hold such faith to-night I could proceed cheerfully to the task I otherwise approach with a sense of consecration.

Pardon me one word, Mr. President, spoken for the sole purpose of getting into the volumes that go out annually freighted with the rich eloquence of your speakers—the fact that the Cavalier as well as the Puritan was on the continent in its early days, and that he was "up and able to be about." [*Laughter.*] I have read your books carefully and I find no mention of that fact, which seems to me an important one for preserving a sort of historical equilibrium if for nothing else.

Let me remind you that the Virginia Cavalier first challenged France on this continent—that Cavalier John Smith gave New England its very name, and was so pleased with the job that he has been handing his own name around ever since—and that while Miles Standish was cutting off men's ears for courting a girl without her parents' consent, and forbade men to kiss their wives on Sunday, the Cavalier was courting everything in sight, and that the Almighty had vouchsafed great increase to the Cavalier colonies, the huts in the wilderness being full as the nests in the woods.

But having incorporated the Cavalier as a fact in your charming little books I shall let him work out his own salvation, as he has always done with engaging gallantry, and we will hold no controversy as to his merits. Why should we? Neither Puritan nor Cavalier long survived as such. The virtues and traditions of both happily still live for the inspiration of their sons and the saving of the old fashion. [*Applause.*] But both Puritan and Cavalier were lost in the storm of the first Revolution; and the American citizen, supplanting both and stronger than either, took possession of the Republic bought by their common blood and fashioned to wisdom, and charged himself with teaching men government and establishing the voice of the people as the voice of God. [*Applause.*]

My friend Dr. Talmage has told you that the typical American has yet to come. Let me tell you that he has already come. [*Applause.*] Great types like valuable plants are slow to flower and fruit. But from the union of these colonist Puritans and Cavaliers, from the straightening of their purposes and the crossing of their blood, slow perfecting through a century, came he who stands as the first typical American, the first who comprehended within himself all the strength and gentleness, all the majesty and grace of this Republic—Abraham Lincoln. [*Loud and continued applause.*] He was the sum of Puritan and Cavalier, for in his ardent nature were fused the virtues of both, and in the depths of his great soul the faults of both were lost. [*Renewed applause.*] He was greater than Puritan, greater than Cavalier, in that he was American [*Renewed applause.*] and that in his homely form were first gathered the vast and thrilling forces of his ideal government—charging it with such tremendous meaning and so elevating it above human suffering that martyrdom, though infamously aimed, came as a fitting crown to a life consecrated from the cradle to human liberty. [*Loud and prolonged cheering.*] Let us, each cherishing the traditions and honoring his fathers, build with reverent hands to the type of this simple but sublime life, in which all types are honored; and in our common glory as Americans there will be plenty and to spare for your forefathers and for mine. [*Renewed cheering.*]

In speaking to the toast with which you have honored me, I accept the term, "The New South," as in no sense disparaging to the Old. Dear to me, sir, is the home of my childhood and the traditions of my people. I would not, if I could, dim the glory they won in peace and war, or by word or deed take aught from the splendor and grace of their civilization—never equaled and, perhaps, never to be equaled in its chivalric strength and grace. There is a New South, not through protest against the Old, but because of new conditions, new adjustments and, if you please, new ideas and aspirations. It is to this that I address myself, and to the consideration of which I hasten lest it become the Old South before I get to it. Age does not endow all things with strength and virtue, nor are all new things to be despised. The shoemaker who put over his door "John Smith's shop. Founded in 1760," was more than matched by his young rival across the street who hung out this sign: "Bill Jones. Established 1886. No old stock kept in this shop."

Dr. Talmage has drawn for you, with a master's hand, the picture of your returning armies. He has told you how, in the pomp and circumstance of war, they came back to you, marching with proud and victorious tread, reading their glory in a nation's eyes! Will you bear with me while I tell you of another army that sought its home at the close of the late war—an army that marched home in defeat and not in victory—in pathos and not in splendor, but in glory that equaled yours, and to hearts as loving as ever welcomed heroes home. Let me picture to you the footsore Confederate soldier, as, buttoning up in his faded gray jacket the parole which was to bear testimony to his children of his fidelity and faith, he turned his face southward from Appomattox in April, 1865. Think of him as ragged, half-starved, heavy-hearted, enfeebled by want and wounds; having fought to exhaustion, he surrenders his gun, wrings the hands of his comrades in silence, and lifting his tear-stained and pallid face for the last time to the graves that dot the old Virginia hills, pulls his gray cap over his brow and begins the slow and painful journey. What does he find— let me ask you, who went to your homes eager to find in the welcome you had justly earned, full payment for four years' sacrifice—what does he find when, having followed the battle-stained cross against overwhelming odds, dreading death not half so much as surrender, he reaches the home he left so prosperous and beautiful? He finds his house in ruins, his farm devastated, his slaves free, his stock killed, his barns empty, his trade destroyed, his money worthless; his social system, feudal in its magnificence, swept away; his people without law or legal status, his comrades slain, and the burdens of others heavy on his shoulders. Crushed by defeat, his very traditions are gone; without money, credit, employment, material or training; and, besides all this, confronted with the gravest problem that ever met human intelligence —the establishing of a status for the vast body of his liberated slaves.

What does he do—this hero in gray with a heart of gold? Does he sit down in sullenness and despair? Not for a day. Surely God, who had stripped him of his prosperity, inspired him in his adversity. As ruin was never before so overwhelming, never was restoration swifter. The soldier stepped from the trenches into the furrow; horses that had charged Federal guns march before the plow, and fields that ran red with human blood in April were green with the harvest in June; women reared in luxury cut up their dresses and made breeches for their husbands, and, with a patience and heroism that fit women always as a garment, gave their hands to work. There was little bitterness in all this. Cheerfulness and frankness prevailed. "Bill Arp" struck the key-note when he said: "Well, I killed as many of them as they did of me, and now I am going to work." [*Laughter and applause.*] Or the soldier returning home after defeat and roasting some corn on the roadside, who made the remark to his comrades: "You may leave the South if you want to, but I am going to Sandersville, kiss my wife and raise a crop, and if the Yankees fool with me any more I will whip 'em again." [*Renewed applause.*] I want to say to General Sherman—who is considered an able man in our hearts, though some people think he is a kind of careless man about fire—that from the ashes he left us in 1864 we have raised a brave and beautiful city; that somehow or other we have caught the sunshine in the bricks and mortar of our homes, and have builded therein not one ignoble prejudice or memory. [*Applause.*]

But in all this what have we accomplished? What is the sum of our work? We have found out that in the general summary the free Negro counts more than he did as a slave. We have planted the schoolhouse on the hilltop and made it free to white and black. We have sowed towns and cities in the place of theories and put business above politics. [*Applause.*] We have challenged your spinners in Massachusetts and your iron-makers in Pennsylvania. We have learned that the $400,000,-

000 annually received from our cotton crop will make us rich, when the supplies that make it are home-raised. We have reduced the commercial rate of interest from twenty-four to six per cent, and are floating four per cent bonds. We have learned that one Northern immigrant is worth fifty foreigners, and have smoothed the path to southward, wiped out the place where Mason and Dixon's line used to be, and hung our latch-string out to you and yours. [*Prolonged cheers.*] We have reached the point that marks perfect harmony in every household, when the husband confesses that the pies which his wife cooks are as good as those his mother used to bake; and we admit that the sun shines as brightly and the moon as softly as it did "before the war." [*Laughter.*] We have established thrift in city and country. We have fallen in love with work. We have restored comfort to homes from which culture and elegance never departed. We have let economy take root and spread among us as rank as the crabgrass which sprang from Sherman's cavalry camps, until we are ready to lay odds on the Georgia Yankee, as he manufactures relics of the battlefield in a one-story shanty and squeezes pure olive oil out of his cotton-seed, against any down-easter that ever swapped wooden nutmegs for flannel sausages in the valleys of Vermont. [*Loud and continuous laughter.*] Above all, we know that we have achieved in these "piping times of peace" a fuller independence for the South than that which our fathers sought to win in the forum by their eloquence or compel on the field by their swords. [*Loud applause.*]

It is a rare privilege, sir, to have had part, however humble, in this work. Never was nobler duty confided to human hands than the uplifting and upbuilding of the prostrate and bleeding South, misguided perhaps, but beautiful in her suffering, and honest, brave and generous always. [*Applause.*] In the record of her social, industrial, and political illustrations we await with confidence the verdict of the world.

But what of the Negro? Have we solved the problem he presents or progressed in honor and equity towards the solution? Let the record speak to the point. No section shows a more prosperous laboring population than the Negroes of the South; none in fuller sympathy with the employing and land-owning class. He shares our school fund, has the fullest protection of our laws and the friendship of our people. Self-interest, as well as honor, demand that he should have this. Our future, our very existence depend upon our working out this problem in full and exact justice. We understand that when Lincoln signed the Emancipation Proclamation, your victory was assured; for he then committed you to the cause of human liberty, against which the arms of man cannot prevail [*Applause*]; while those of our statesmen who trusted to make slavery the cornerstone of the Confederacy doomed us to defeat as far as they could, committing us to a cause that reason could not defend or the sword maintain in the sight of advancing civilization. [*Renewed applause.*] Had Mr. Toombs said, which he did not say, that he would call the roll of his slaves at the foot of Bunker Hill, he would have been foolish, for he might have known that whenever slavery became entangled in war it must perish, and that the chattel in human flesh ended forever in New England when your fathers—not to be blamed for parting with what didn't pay—sold their slaves to our fathers—not to be praised for knowing a paying thing when they saw it. [*Laughter.*] The relations of the Southern people with the Negro are close and cordial. We remember with what fidelity for four years he guarded our defenceless women and children, whose husbands and fathers were fighting against his freedom. To his eternal credit be it said that whenever he struck a blow for his own liberty he fought in open battle, and when at last he raised his black and humble hands that the shackles might be struck off, those hands were innocent of wrong against his helpless charges, and worthy to be taken in loving grasp by every man who honors loyalty and devotion. [*Applause.*] Ruffians have maltreated him, rascals have misled him, philanthropists established a bank for him, but the South, with the North, protects against injustice to this simple and sincere people. To liberty and enfranchisement is as far as law can carry the Negro. The rest must be left to conscience and common sense. It should be left to those among whom his lot is cast, with whom he is indissolubly connected and whose prosperity depends upon their possessing his intelligent sympathy and confidence. Faith has been kept with him in spite of calumnious assertions to the contrary by those who assume to speak for us or by frank opponents. Faith will be kept with him in the future, if the South holds her reason and integrity. [*Applause.*]

But have we kept faith with you? In the fullest sense, yes. When Lee surrendered—I don't say when Johnston surrendered, because I understand he still alludes to the time when he met General Sherman last as the time when he "determined to abandon any further prosecution of the struggle"—when Lee surrendered, I say, and Johnston quit, the South became, and has since been, loyal to this Union. We fought hard enough to know that we were whipped, and in perfect frankness accepted as final the arbitrament of the sword to which we had appealed. The South found her jewel in the toad's head of defeat. The shackles that had held her in narrow limitations fell forever when the shackles of the Negro slave were broken. [*Applause*.] Under the old regime the Negroes were slaves to the South, the South was a slave to the system. The old plantation, with its simple police regulation and its feudal habit, was the only type possible under slavery. Thus we gathered in the hands of a splendid and chivalric oligarchy the substance that should have been diffused among the people, as the rich blood, under certain artificial conditions, is gathered at the heart, filling that with affluent rapture, but leaving the body chill and colorless. [*Applause*.]

The Old South rested everything on slavery and agriculture, unconscious that these could neither give nor maintain healthy growth. The New South presents a perfect democracy, the oligarchs leading in the popular movement—a social system compact and closely knitted, less splendid on the surface but stronger at the core—a hundred farms for every plantation, fifty homes for every palace, and a diversified industry that meets the complex needs of this complex age.

The New South is enamored of her new work. Her soul is stirred with the breath of a new life. The light of a grander day is falling fair on her face. She is thrilling with the consciousness of growing power and prosperity. As she stands upright, full-statured and equal among the people of the earth, breathing the keen air and looking out upon the expanding horizon, she understands that her emancipation came because in the inscrutable wisdom of God her honest purpose was crossed and her brave armies were beaten. [*Applause*.]

This is said in no spirit of time-serving or apology. The South has nothing for which to apologize. She believes that the late struggle between the States was war and not rebellion, revolution and not conspiracy, and that her convictions were as honest as yours. I should be unjust to the dauntless spirit of the South and to my own convictions if I did not make this plain in this presence. The South has nothing to take back. In my native town of Athens is a monument that crowns its central hills—a plain, white shaft. Deep cut into its shining side is a name dear to me above the names of men, that of a brave and simple man who died in brave and simple faith. Not for all the glories of New England—from Plymouth Rock all the way—would I exchange the heritage he left me in his soldier's death. To the foot of that shaft I shall send my children's children to reverence him who ennobled their name with his heroic blood. But, sir, speaking from the shadow of that memory, which I honor as I do nothing else on earth, I say that the cause in which he suffered and for which he gave his life was adjudged by higher and fuller wisdom than his or mine, and I am glad that the omniscient God held the balance of battle in His Almighty hand, and that human slavery was swept forever from American soil—the American Union saved from the wreck of war. [*Loud applause.*]

This message, Mr. President, comes to you from consecrated ground. Every foot of the soil about the city in which I live is sacred as a battleground of the Republic. Every hill that invests it is hallowed to you by the blood of your brothers, who died for your victory, and doubly hallowed to us by the blood of those who died hopeless, but undaunted, in defeat—sacred soil to all of us, rich with memories that make us purer and stronger and better, silent but stanch witnesses in its red desolation of the matchless valor of American hearts and the deathless glory of American arms—speaking an eloquent witness in its white peace and prosperity to the indissoluble union of American States and the imperishable brotherhood of the American people. [*Immense cheering.*]

Now, what answer has New England to this message? Will she permit the prejudices of war to remain in the hearts of the conquerors, when it has died in the hearts of the conquered? [*Cries of "No! No!"*] Will she transmit this prejudice to the next generation, that in their hearts, which never felt the generous ardor of conflict, it may perpetuate itself? [*"No! No!"*] Will she withhold, save in strained courtesy, the hand which straight from his soldier's heart Grant offered to Lee at Appomattox? Will she make the vision of a restored and happy people, which gathered above the couch of your dying captain, filling his heart with grace, touching his lips with praise and glorifying his path to the grave; will she make this vision on which the last sight of his expiring soul breathed a benediction, a cheat and a delusion? [*Tumultuous cheering and shouts of "No! No!"*] If she does, the South, never abject in asking for comradeship, must accept with dignity its refusal; but if she does not; if she accepts in frankness and sincerity this message of goodwill and friendship, then will the prophecy of Webster, delivered in this very Society forty years ago amid tremendous applause, be verified in its fullest and final sense, when he said: "Standing hand to hand and clasping hands, we should remain united as we have been for sixty years, citizens of the same country, members of the same government, united, all united now and united forever. There have been difficulties, contentions, and controversies, but I tell you that in my judgment

> Those opposed eyes,
> Which like the meteors of a troubled heaven,
> All of one nature, of one substance bred,
> Did lately meet in th' intestine shock,
> Shall now, in mutual well-beseeming ranks,
> March all one way.

[*Prolonged applause.*]

Questions and Exercises

1. Why was Henry W. Grady called "a spokesman for the South"?
   _____

2. Where was he born?_____ When?_____
   When did he die?_____

3. From what university was he graduated?_____
   Where did he study law?_____

4. What activities in his college life led to his development as a
   speaker?_____
   _____

5. What was his profession?_____

6. Where did he give his speech "The New South"?_____
   Who composed his audience?_____
   _____

7. What is the central idea of the speech?_____
   _____
   _____

8. In your opinion, why is the introduction so long?_____
   _____

9. What are the main divisions of the speech?_____
   _____
   _____

10. Of what does the conclusion consist?_____
    _____
    _____

VIII *ATLANTA EXPOSITION ADDRESS*

BOOKER T. WASHINGTON
(*about* 1856-1915)

The Speaker

No other speaker in this anthology accomplished so much from humble beginnings as did Booker T. Washington. Throughout his rise from slave to world-renowned citizen, Washington linked his life with a cause and held tenaciously to it in spite of adversities. That cause was to improve the lot of his race—the Negro. Some historians estimate that Washington made up to four thousand speeches in his lifetime—speeches before Northern whites for funds to carry on his educational program; speeches before Southern whites for social acceptance of his race; speeches before his own race to challenge them and show them how to improve their own station in life. No other Negro leader did more for his race at a time when help was so greatly needed.

The exact date of Washington's birth is not known but his biographers believe it was in 1856, in Franklin County, Virginia. Following emancipation he moved to Malden, West Virginia, where he received a minimum of elementary education largely at night school while he worked by day in a salt furnace and coal mine. His intense desire for education resulted in his entrance in Hampton Institute in 1872; he was graduated in three years. After graduating, he taught school in Malden, West Virginia, for two years, then attended Wayland Seminary in Washington, D.C., in 1878 and 1879, and taught in Hampton Institute from 1879 to 1881. In 1881 he became principal of Tuskegee Institute in Tuskegee, Alabama, where he remained until his death on November 14, 1915. He was buried on the campus of Tuskegee Institute.

Washington became the leading spokesman for the Negro both in the North and in the South. His was a program of conservative action which called for an opportunity for his race to improve its own position in life. He advocated vocational training for the majority of his race and contended that the Negro should make himself indispensable to his community. He believed that the Negro could help promote understanding and tolerance if he could demonstrate his worth to the community in which he lived.

The Occasion

Washington's "Atlanta Exposition Address" was delivered at the opening of the Atlanta Cotton States and International Exposition on September 18, 1895, in Atlanta, Georgia. The Atlanta Exposition was an important occasion, one of the landmarks in the history of the state. Prior to the opening of the exposition, Washington had been selected to accompany a distinguished delegation to the national Capitol in Washington, D.C., for the purpose of appearing before a Senate committee in quest of funds for the exposition. The success of this mission made the exposition possible and Washington was lauded for his speech before the committee.

In completing plans for the exposition, the directors decided in favor of erecting a separate building devoted entirely to displaying the progress of the Negro since emancipation. The directorship of this project was offered to Washington but he declined because of pressing duties at Tuskegee Institute. Later the directors extended an invitation to Washington to speak at the opening ceremonies of the exposition.

111

He accepted with mixed emotions of pride and apprehension because he was the first Negro to be asked to address an audience of white citizens on so important a national occasion.

Washington, his wife, and three children left Tuskegee for Atlanta the day before the opening of the exposition. They were met by a committee which escorted them to their boardinghouse. Atlanta was packed with people from all parts of the United States as well as from many foreign countries. The novelty of a former slave addressing so important an audience had created unusual interest in the opening ceremonies. Early the next morning a committee escorted Washington to his place in the procession leading to the exposition grounds. The three hours required for the procession to reach the exposition grounds were hours of intense heat, a factor which added to Washington's fears and misgivings.

The ceremonies were begun with short addresses by the governor of Georgia and other dignitaries responsible for the exposition. Washington was introduced by the governor amid enthusiastic cheering, especially from the Negro section. For the next fifteen minutes, Washington held the rapt attention of the audience. When he concluded, his listeners broke into spontaneous applause as the governor rushed across the platform to shake Washington's hand. The next morning newspapers throughout the country printed the address in full and for months afterward carried favorable editorial comments about it. Washington's position as a national leader in education was thus firmly established.

The Speech

The most difficult feat in Washington's "Atlanta Exposition Address" was his adaptation to an audience of varying attitudes and emotional feelings toward his subject. Four distinct groups were present: a large number of Negroes favorable to him as their spokesman; a smaller group of Northern whites in sympathy with the plight of his people; a larger group of Southern whites skeptical of both his motives and his ability; and a small group of foreign dignitaries curious about the history-making proceedings. To secure a favorable hearing from such a heterogenous group required skill and tact. The speech was least favorably received by his own race, some of whom thought he had been too favorable in his remarks about the Southern whites and had not spoken out strongly enough for the rights of the Negro.

The introduction, body, and conclusion are clearly distinguishable in the arrangement of the speech. The introduction required no more than two minutes. After an opening statement about the numbers and importance of the Negro population in the South, Washington paid tribute to the directors of the exposition for their generous recognition of his race and expressed confidence that the Negro would contribute to the progress of the South.

He moved from the introduction to the body by means of a detailed narrative illustration which pointed up the central idea and served as a unifying force for the speech. Instead of stating his thesis as a proposition, he led into it through an illustration. The theme unfolds by such statements as ". . . we [the Negro] shall prosper in proportion as we learn to dignify and glorify common labour and put brains and skill into the common occupations of life. . . ." "No race can prosper till it learns that there is as much dignity in tilling a field as in writing a poem."

The conclusion, like the introduction, is about two minutes long. Washington again expressed appreciation for the opportunity offered the Negro by the exposition and pledged the best efforts of his race toward building the prosperity of the South. The text that follows was taken from *Up From Slavery* by Booker T. Washington (Garden City, N.Y.: Doubleday & Company, Inc., 1948), pp. 218-225. Copyright 1901, 1929, by Booker T. Washington. Reprinted by permission of Doubleday & Company, Inc.

MR. PRESIDENT AND GENTLEMEN OF THE BOARD OF DIRECTORS AND CITIZENS: One-third of the population of the South is of the Negro race. No enterprise seeking the material, civil, or moral welfare of this section can disregard this element of our population and reach the highest success. I but convey to you, Mr. President and Directors, the sentiment of the masses of my race when I say that in no way have the value and manhood of the American Negro been more fittingly and generously recognized than by the managers of this magnificent Exposition at every stage of its progress. It is a recognition that will do more to cement the friendship of the two races than any occurrence since the dawn of our freedom.

Not only this, but the opportunity here afforded will awaken among us a new era of industrial progress. Ignorant and inexperienced, it is not strange that in the first years of our new life we began at the top instead of at the bottom; that a seat in Congress or the state legislature was more sought than real estate or industrial skill; that the political convention or stump speaking had more attractions than starting a dairy farm or truck garden.

A ship lost at sea for many days suddenly sighted a friendly vessel. From the mast of the unfortunate vessel was seen a signal, "Water, water; we die of thirst!" The answer from the friendly vessel at once came back, "Cast down your bucket where you are." And a third and fourth signal for water was answered, "Cast down your bucket where you are." The captain of the distressed vessel, at last heeding the injunction, cast down his bucket, and it came up full of fresh, sparkling water from the mouth of the Amazon River. To those of my race who depend on bettering their condition in a foreign land or who underestimate the importance of cultivating friendly relations with the Southern white man, who is their next-door neighbour, I would say: "Cast down your bucket where you are"—cast it down in making friends in every manly way of the people of all races by whom we are surrounded.

Cast it down in agriculture, mechanics, in commerce, in domestic service, and in the professions. And in this connection it is well to bear in mind that whatever other sins the South may be called to bear when it comes to business, pure and simple, it is in the South that the Negro is given a man's chance in the commercial world, and in nothing is this Exposition more eloquent than in emphasizing this chance. Our greatest danger is that in the great leap from slavery to freedom we may overlook the fact that the masses of us are to live by the productions of our hands, and fail to keep in mind that we shall prosper in proportion as we learn to dignify and glorify common labour and put brains and skill into the common occupations of life; shall prosper in proportion as we learn to draw the line between the superficial and the substantial, the ornamental gew-gaws of life and the useful. No race can prosper till it learns that there is as much dignity in tilling a field as in writing a poem. It is at the bottom of life we must begin, and not at the top. Nor should we permit our grievances to overshadow our opportunities.

To those of the white race who look to the incoming of those of foreign birth and strange tongue and habits for the prosperity of the South, were I permitted I would repeat what I say to my own race, "Cast down your bucket where you are." Cast it down among the eight millions of Negroes whose habits you know, whose fidelity and love you have tested in days when to have proved treacherous meant the ruin of your firesides. Cast down your bucket among these people who have, without strikes and labour wars, tilled your fields, cleared your forests, builded your railroads and cities, and brought forth treasures from the bowels of the earth, and helped make possible this magnificent representation of the progress of the South. Casting down your bucket among my people, helping and encouraging them as you are doing on these grounds, and to education of head, hand, and heart, you will find that they will buy your surplus land, make blossom the waste places in your fields, and run your factories. While doing this, you can be sure in the future, as in the past, that you and your families will be surrounded by the most patient, faithful, law-abiding, and unresentful people that the world has seen. As we have proved our loyalty to you in the past, in nursing your children, watching by the sick-bed of your mothers and fathers, and often following them with tear-dimmed eyes to their graves, so in the future, in our humble way, we shall stand by you with a devotion that no foreigner can approach, ready to lay down our lives, if need be, in defence of yours, interlacing our industrial, commercial, civil, and religious life with yours in a way that shall make the interests of both races one. In all things that are purely social we can be as separate as the fingers, yet one as the hand in all things essential to mutual progress.

There is no defence or security for any of us except in the highest intelligence and development of all. If anywhere there are efforts tending to curtail the fullest growth of the Negro, let these efforts be turned into stimulating, encouraging, and making him the most useful and intelligent citizen. Effort or means so invested will pay a thousand per cent interest. These efforts will be twice blessed—"blessing him that gives and him that takes."

There is no escape through law of man or God from the inevitable:—

> The laws of changeless justice bind
> Oppressor with oppressed;
> And close as sin and suffering joined
> We march to fate abreast.

Nearly sixteen millions of hands will aid you in pulling the load upward; or they will pull against you the load downward. We shall constitute one-third and more of the ignorance and crime of the South, or one-third its intelligence and progress; we shall contribute one-third to the business and industrial prosperity of the South, or we shall prove a veritable body of death, stagnating, depressing, retarding every effort to advance the body politic.

Gentlemen of the Exposition, as we present to you our humble effort at an exhibition of our progress, you must not expect overmuch. Starting thirty years ago with ownership here and there in a few quilts and pumpkins and chickens (gathered from miscellaneous sources), remember the path that has led from these to the inventions and production of agricultural implements, buggies, steam-engines, newspapers, books, statuary, carving, paintings, the management of drug-stores and banks, has not been trodden without contact with thorns and thistles. While we take pride in what we exhibit as a result of our independent efforts, we do not for a moment forget that our part in this exhibition would fall far short of your expectations but for the constant help that has come to our educational life, not only from the Southern states, but especially from Northern philanthropists, who have made their gifts a constant stream of blessing and encouragement.

The wisest among my race understand that the agitation of questions of social equality is the extremest folly, and that progress in the enjoyment of all the privileges that will come to us must be the result of severe and constant struggle rather than of artificial forcing. No race that has anything to contribute to the markets of the world is long in any degree ostracised. It is important and right that all privileges of the law be ours, but it is vastly more important that we be prepared for the exercises of these privileges. The opportunity to earn a dollar in a factory just now is worth infinitely more than the opportunity to spend a dollar in an opera-house.

In conclusion, may I repeat that nothing in thirty years has given us more hope and encouragement, and drawn us so near to you of the white race, as this opportunity offered by the Exposition; and here bending, as it were, over the altar that represents the results of the struggles of your race and mine, both starting practically empty-handed three decades ago, I pledge that in your effort to work out the great and intricate problem which God has laid at the doors of the South, you shall have at all times the patient, sympathetic help of my race; only let this be constantly in mind, that, while from representations in these buildings of the product of field, of forest, of mine, of factory, letters, and art, much good will come, yet far above and beyond material benefits will be that higher good, that, let us pray God, will come, in a blotting out of sectional differences and racial animosities and suspicions, in a determination to administer absolute justice, in a willing obedience among all classes to the mandates of law. This, this, coupled with our material prosperity, will bring into our beloved South a new heaven and a new earth.

Questions and Exercises

1. Why is there uncertainty about the date of Booker T. Washington's birth?_____
   Where was he born?_____
2. Where did he attend college?_____
   _____
3. With what educational institution was he associated for thirty-three years?_____ What was his position?_____
   _____
4. To what cause did he devote much of his life?_____
   _____
5. What was the setting for his "Atlanta Exposition Address"?_____
   _____
6. What was unusual about his audience?_____
   _____
   _____
7. State the central idea of the speech._____
   _____
   _____
8. What purpose did the narrative illustration used early in the speech serve?_____
   _____
9. What method was used in the introduction?_____
   _____
10. What were the reactions to the speech?_____
    _____
    _____

IX *CROSS OF GOLD*

WILLIAM JENNINGS BRYAN
(1860-1925)

The Speaker

William Jennings Bryan lived at a time when the downtrodden common man greatly needed a spokesman; Bryan rose to the occasion and established a hold on the populace unparalleled in the history of the country. During the latter part of the nineteenth century when Bryan was at his peak, big business held a stranglehold on the nation's economy which made the workingman's and farmer's lives almost intolerable. It was a period when the large trusts held monopolistic control over almost all phases of the economy; "the rich got richer and the poor grew poorer"; the farmer bitterly complained of "ten-cent corn and ten per cent interest." These conditions caused Mary E. Lease, a Populist speaker, to introduce a phrase which became a battle cry for the farmer: "Raise less corn and more hell." Bryan, by popular choice, became the spokesman of these depressed groups; he became known as "The Great Commoner."

William Jennings Bryan was born in Salem, Illinois, on March 19, 1860, the son of a lawyer and judge; he was born in an environment that respected the power of oral communication. After graduating from high school, he attended Whipple Academy in 1876-1877, then enrolled in Illinois College where he was graduated in 1881 as valedictorian of his class. Upon graduation he enrolled in Union College of Law in Chicago. Bryan took his law degree in 1883 and was admitted to the Illinois bar the same year. One intense interest pervaded his training—speaking activities. Records at Illinois College show that he took almost all the courses offered in elocution and oratory, was an enthusiastic member of the literary societies, and engaged in speaking contests at every opportunity. In his early years at the college he may not have been the most successful speech participant, but all agreed that he was the most persistent and enthusiastic. Facility in speaking was his consuming passion, a trait which brought him fame in later years.

Bryan's lifework consisted of practicing law, engaging in politics, editing newspapers, and lecturing before all types of audiences. Upon graduation from law school, he practiced in Jacksonville, Illinois, from 1883 to 1887 and then at Lincoln, Nebraska. He was elected to Congress in 1890, re-elected in 1892, and defeated for United States Senator in 1894. He became editor of the Omaha *World Herald* in 1894 and served until 1896 when he was selected as the Democratic nominee for the Presidency, largely through the influence of his "Cross of Gold Speech" delivered before the Democratic Convention. Although Bryan waged a vigorous campaign, he was defeated by McKinley by a narrow margin of 500,000 votes. The campaign was an uneven fight. The Republicans enlisted thousands of workers in house-to-house canvass, blanketed the country with hundreds of speakers, and raised more than $7,000,000 for campaign expenses. Bryan did almost all his own campaigning, traveled over 18,000 miles, and made some six hundred speeches, but his party raised only $300,000 for the campaign.

Bryan reached the height of his popularity during the campaign of 1896, but he remained a political power for another twenty years. He was nominated by the Democrats again in 1900 but was defeated by McKinley. In 1908 he again was nominated, but lost the race to Taft. In the 1912 Democratic Convention, he played an important part in securing the nomination for Wilson, who appointed Bryan his Secretary of State. Between his campaigns for the Presidency he served, in turn, as colonel in the Spanish-American War, editor of *The Com-*

moner, lecturer on a world tour, and lawyer in many important court trials. During his declining years he spoke frequently in favor of prohibition and for a return to fundamentalist religion. He died on July 26, 1925, at the end of the famous Scopes trial in which he acted as prosecutor against Clarence Darrow, who was defense attorney in the Tennessee schoolteacher evolution case.

The Occasion

Bryan's "Cross of Gold" speech was given at the Democratic National Convention in Chicago, on July 8, 1896. Between the time of his defeat for the United States Senate in 1894 and the time of the convention, Bryan had toured the country speaking in favor of bimetallism. He came to the convention fully prepared to continue the fight. Since the platform committee could not reach a compromise between the advocates of bimetallism and those of the gold standard, two reports were submitted to the convention. Bryan led the group favoring bimetallism and it was decided that he should conclude the debate on the convention floor. Prior to Bryan's speech, the delegates had become worn out from listening to endless discussion under adverse conditions. The acoustics were poor in the convention hall and many of the delegates could hardly hear the speakers who preceded Bryan.

When Bryan started to speak in a deliberate, confident manner, his penetrating voice carrying easily throughout the hall, the weary delegates became aroused. The more Bryan talked, the more aroused the delegates became. Soon the entire assembly of twenty thousand started rising with tumultuous applause at the end of each sentence. At the end of the speech, the delegates broke into an emotional frenzy unparalleled in any previous convention. Bryan captured the audience and in so doing ensured his nomination for the Presidency.

The Speech

Bryan's "Cross of Gold" speech bulked large in emotional appeal. Critics maintain that the speech contained little argument and no new ideas. Perhaps Bryan intended it so, for the prevailing conditions did not call for an argument. The audience was in a suggestible mood. The majority of the delegates already thought as Bryan did; they desired a spokesman to voice those thoughts in a strong and emotional manner, to articulate their resentment of the injustices to the common man. Bryan rose to the occasion and gave the audience what it wanted.

In the introduction, Bryan began by referring to his opponents as distinguished gentlemen, depreciated his own importance when compared to the principle that he upheld, and stated his intention to uphold the cause of liberty—the cause of humanity. He then gave a brief history of the bimetallic controversy which led into the body of his speech.

The body of the speech consists largely of answers to points raised by preceding speakers. In each argument he upheld the interests of the common man against those of big business and contended that the free coinage of silver would benefit the workingman. Although he made use of ethical and logical appeal, his chief appeal was emotional. Through the liberal use of illustrative material and figurative language, he succeeded in arousing the people to an emotional pitch. He seemed more concerned with attacking the advocates of the gold standard than with showing the advantages of the bimetallic standard. Critics state that the speech was an appeal to the heart rather than the head.

The conclusion sounds a note of confidence and an appeal to fight. It ends with the now famous analogy, "You shall not press down upon the brow of labor this crown of thorns, you shall not crucify mankind upon a cross of gold." The text that follows is from *Speeches of William Jennings Bryan* (New York: Funk and Wagnalls, 1909), Vol. I, pp. 238-249.

I WOULD BE presumptuous, indeed, to present myself against the distinguished gentlemen to whom you have listened if this were a mere measuring of abilities; but this is not a contest between persons. The humblest citizen in all the land, when clad in the armor of a righteous cause, is stronger than all the hosts of error. I come to speak to you in defense of a cause as holy as the cause of liberty—the cause of humanity.

When this debate is concluded, a motion will be made to lay upon the table the resolution offered in commendation of the administration, and also the resolution offered in condemnation of the administration. We object to bringing this question down to the level of persons. The individual is but an atom; he is born, he acts, he dies; but principles are eternal; and this has been a contest over a principle.

Never before in the history of this country has there been witnessed such a contest as that through which we have just passed. Never before in the history of American politics has a great issue been fought out as this issue has been, by the voters of a great party. On the fourth of March, 1895, a few Democrats, most of them members of Congress, issued an address to the Democrats of the nation, asserting that the money question was the paramount issue of the hour; declaring that a majority of the Democratic party had the right to control the action of the party on this paramount issue; and concluding with the request that the believers in the free coinage of silver in the Democratic party should organize, take charge of, and control the policy of the Democratic party. Three months later, at Memphis, an organization was perfected, and the silver Democrats went forth openly and courageously proclaiming their belief, and declaring that, if successful, they would crystallize into a platform the declaration which they had made. Then began the conflict. With a zeal approaching the zeal which inspired the Crusaders who followed Peter the Hermit, our silver Democrats went forth from victory unto victory until they are now assembled, not to discuss, not to debate, but to enter up the judgment already rendered by the plain people of this country. In this contest brother has been arrayed against brother, father against son. The warmest ties of love, acquaintance and association have been disregarded; old leaders have been cast aside when they have refused to give expression to the sentiments of those whom they would lead, and new leaders have sprung up to give direction to this cause of truth. Thus has the contest been waged, and we have assembled here under as binding and solemn instructions as were ever imposed upon representatives of the people.

We do not come as individuals. As individuals we might have been glad to compliment the gentleman from New York [Senator Hill], but we know that the people for whom we speak would never be willing to put him in a position where he could thwart the will of the Democratic party. I say it was not a question of persons, it was a question of principle, and it is not with gladness, my friends, that we find ourselves brought into conflict with those who are now arrayed on the other side.

The gentleman who preceded me [ex-Governor Russell] spoke of the State of Massachusetts; let me assure him that not one present in all this convention entertains the least hostility to the people of the State of Massachusetts, but we stand here representing the people who are the equals, before the law, of the greatest citizens in the State of Massachusetts. When you [*turning to the gold delegates*] come before us and tell us that we are about to disturb your business interests, we reply that you have disturbed our business interests by your course.

We say to you that you have made the definition of a business man too limited in its application. The man who is employed for wages is as much a business man as his employer, the attorney in a country town is as much a business man as the corporation counsel in a great metropolis; the merchant at the cross-roads store is as much a business man as the merchant of New York; the farmer who goes forth in the morning and toils all day—who begins in the spring and toils all summer—and who by the application of brain and muscle to the natural resources of the country creates wealth, is as much a business man as the man who goes upon the board of trade and bets upon the price of grain; the miners who go down a thousand feet into the earth, or climb two thousand feet upon the cliffs, and bring forth from their hiding places the precious metals to be poured into the channels of trade are as much business men as the few financial magnates who, in a back room, corner the money of the world. We come to speak for this broader class of business men.

Ah, my friends, we say not one word against those who live upon the Atlantic coast, but the hardy pioneers who have braved all the dangers of the wilderness, who have made the desert to blossom as the rose—the pioneers away out there [*pointing to the West*], who rear their children near to Nature's heart, where they can mingle their voices with the voices of the birds—out there where they have erected school houses for the education of their young, churches where they praise their Creator, and cemeteries where rest the ashes of their dead —these people, we say, are as deserving of the consideration of our party as any people in this country. It is for these that we speak. We do not come as aggressors. Our war is not a war of conquest; we are fighting in the defense of our homes, our families, and posterity. We have petitioned, and our petitions have been scorned; we have entreated, and our entreaties have been disregarded; we have begged, and they have mocked when our calamity came. We beg no longer; we petition no more. We defy them.

The gentleman from Wisconsin has said that he fears a Robespierre. My friends, in this land of the free you need not fear that a tyrant will spring up from among the people. What we need is an Andrew Jackson to stand, as Jackson stood, against the encroachments of organized wealth.

They tell us that this platform was made to catch votes. We reply to them that changing conditions make new issues, that the principles on which Democracy rests are as everlasting as the hills, but that they must be applied to new conditions as they arise. Conditions have arisen, and we are here to meet those conditions. They tell us that the income tax ought not be brought in here; that it is a new idea. They criticize us for our criticism of the Supreme Court of the United States. My friends, we have not criticized; we have simply called attention to what you already know. If you want criticisms, read the dissenting opinions of the court. There you will find criticisms. They say that we passed an unconstitutional law; we deny it. The income tax law was not unconstitutional when it was passed; it was not unconstitutional when it went before the Supreme Court for the first time; it did not become unconstitutional until one of the judges changed his mind, and we cannot be expected to know when a judge will change his mind. The income tax is just. It simply intends to put the burdens of government upon the backs of the people. I am in favor of an income tax. When I find a man who is not willing to bear his share of the burdens of the government which protects him, I find a man who is unworthy to enjoy the blessings of a government like ours.

They say that we are opposing national bank currency; it is true. If you will read what Thomas Benton said, you will find he said that, in searching history, he could find but one parallel to Andrew Jackson; that was Cicero, who destroyed the conspiracy of Cataline and saved Rome. Benton said that Cicero only did for Rome what Jackson did for us when he destroyed the bank conspiracy and saved America. We say in our platform that we believe that the right to coin and issue money is a function of government. We believe it. We believe that it is a part of sovereignty, and can no more with safety be delegated to private individuals than we could afford to delegate to private individuals the power to make penal statutes or levy taxes. Mr. Jefferson, who was once regarded as good Democratic authority, seems to have differed in opinion from the gentleman who has addrest us on the part of the minority. Those who are opposed to this proposition tell us that the issue of paper money is a function of the bank, and that the Government ought to go out of the banking business. I stand with Jefferson rather than with them, and tell them, as he did, that the issue of money is a function of government, and that banks ought to go out of the governing business.

They complain about the plank which declares against life tenure in office. They have tried to strain it to mean that which it does not mean. What we oppose by that plank is the life tenure which is being built up in Washington, and which excludes from participation in official benefits the humbler members of society.

Let me call your attention to two or three important things. The gentleman from New York says that he will propose an amendment to the platform providing that the proposed change in our monetary system shall not affect contracts already made. Let me remind you that there is no intention of affecting those contracts which according to present laws are made payable in gold; but if he means to say that we cannot change our monetary system without protecting those who have loaned money before the change was made, I desire to ask him where, in law or in morals, he can find justification for not protecting the debtors when the act of 1873 was passed, if he now insists that we must protect the creditors.

He says he will also propose an amendment which will provide for the suspension of free coinage if we fail to maintain the parity within a year. We reply that when we advocate a policy which we believe will be successful, we are not compelled to raise a doubt as to our own sincerity by suggesting what we shall do if we fail. I ask him, if he would apply his logic to us, why he does not apply it to himself. He says he wants this country to try to secure an international agreement. Why does he not tell us what he is going to do if he fails to secure an international agreement? There is more reason for him to do that than there is for us to provide against the failure to maintain the parity. Our opponents have tried for twenty years to secure an international agreement, and those are waiting for it most patiently who do not want it at all.

And now, my friends, let me come to the paramount issue. If they ask us why it is that we say more on the money question than we say upon the tariff question, I reply that, if protection has slain its thousands, the gold standard has slain its tens of thousands. If they ask us why we do not embody in our platform all the things that we believe in, we reply that when we have restored the money of the Constitution all other necessary reforms will be possible; but that until this is done there is no other reform that can be accomplished.

Why is it that within three months such a change has come over the country? Three months ago, when it was confidently asserted that those who believe in the gold standard would frame our platform and nominate our candidate, even the advocates of the gold standard did not think that we could elect a President. And they had good reason for their doubt, because there is scarcely a State here today asking for the gold standard which is not in the absolute control of the Republican party. But note the change. Mr. McKinley was nominated at St. Louis upon a platform which declared for the maintenance of the gold standard until it can be changed into bimetallism by international agreement. Mr. McKinley was the most popular man among the Republicans, and three months ago everybody in the Republican party prophesied his election. How is it to-day? Why, the man who was once pleased to think that he looked like Napoleon—that man shudders to-day when he remembers that he was nominated on the anniversary of the battle of Waterloo. Not only that, but as he listens he can hear with ever-increasing distinctness the sounds of the waves as they beat upon the lonely shores of St. Helena.

Why this change? Ah, my friends, is not the reason for the change evident to any one who will look at the matter? No private character, however pure, no personal popularity, however great, can protect from the avenging wrath of an indignant people a man who will declare that he is in favor of fastening the gold standard upon this country, or who is willing to surrender the right of self-government and place the legislative control of our affairs in the hands of foreign potentates and powers.

We go forth confident that we shall win. Why? Because upon the paramount issue of this campaign there is not a spot of ground upon which the enemy will dare to challenge battle. If they tell us that the gold standard is a good thing, we shall point to their platform and tell them that their platform pledges the party to get rid of the gold standard and substitute bimetallism. If the gold standard is a good thing, why try to get rid of it? I call your attention to the fact that some of the very people who are in this convention to-day and who tell us that we ought to declare in favor of international bimetallism—thereby declaring that the gold standard is wrong and that the principle of bimetallism is better—these very people four months ago were open and avowed advocates of the gold standard, and were then telling us that we could not legislate two metals together, even with the aid of all the world. If the gold standard is a good thing, we ought to declare in favor of its retention and not in favor of abandoning it; and if the gold standard is a bad thing, why should we wait until other nations are willing to help us to let go? Here is the line of battle, and we care not upon which issue they force the fight; we are prepared to meet them on either issue or on both. If they tell us that the gold standard is the standard of civilization, we reply to them that this, the most enlightened of all the nations of the earth, has never declared for a gold standard and that both the great parties this year are declaring against it. If the gold standard is the standard of civilization, why, my friends, should we not have it? If they come to meet us on that issue we can present the history of our nation. More than that; we can tell them that they will search the pages of history in vain to find a single instance where the common people have ever declared themselves in favor of the gold standard. They can find where the holders of fixt investments have declared for a gold standard, but not where the masses have.

Mr. Carlisle said in 1878 that this was a struggle between "the idle holders of idle capital" and "the struggling masses, who produce the wealth and pay the taxes of the country"; and, my friends, the question we are to decide is: Upon which side will the Democratic party fight; upon the side of "the idle holders of idle capital" or upon the side of "the struggling masses"? That is the question which the party must answer first, and then it must be answered by each individual hereafter. The sympathies of the Democratic party, as shown by the platform, are on the side of the struggling masses who have ever been the foundation of the Democratic party. There are two ideas of government. There are those who believe that, if you will only legislate to make the well-to-do prosperous, their prosperity will leak through on those below. The Democratic idea, however, has been that if you legislate to make the masses prosperous, their prosperity will find its way up through every class which rests upon them.

You come to us and tell us that the great cities are in favor of the gold standard; we reply that the great cities rest upon our broad and fertile prairies. Burn down your cities and leave our farms, and your cities will spring up again as if by magic; but destroy our farms and the grass will grow in the streets of every city in the country.

My friends, we declare that this nation is able to legislate for its own people on every question, without waiting for the aid or consent of any other nation on earth; and upon that issue we expect to carry every State in the Union. I shall not slander the inhabitants of the fair State of Massachusetts nor the inhabitants of the State of New York by saying that, when they are confronted with the proposition, they will declare that this nation is not able to attend to its own business. It is the issue of 1776 over again. Our ancestors, when but three millions in number, had the courage to declare their political independence of every other nation; shall we, their descendants, when we have grown to seventy millions, declare that we are less independent than our fore-fathers? No, my friends, that will never be the verdict of our people. Therefore we care not upon what lines the battle is fought. If they say bimetallism is good, but that we cannot have it until the other nations help us, we reply that, instead of having a gold standard because England has, we will restore bimetallism, and then let England have bimetallism because the United States has it. If they dare to come out in the open field and defend the gold standard as a good thing, we will fight them to the uttermost. Having behind us the producing masses of this nation and the world, supported by the commercial interests, the laboring interests, and the toilers everywhere, we will answer their demand for a gold standard by saying to them: You shall not press down upon the brow of labor this crown of thorns, you shall not crucify mankind upon a cross of gold.

Questions and Exercises

1. Give the place and date of William Jennings Bryan's birth._____

_____

2. What evidence is there of his high academic attainment at Illinois College?_____
   From what school did he obtain his law degree?_____

3. What activities in his training had bearing on his development as a speaker?_____

_____

4. Why did he become known as "The Great Commoner"?_____

_____

5. In what professions did he engage?_____

_____

6. What was the audience situation for his "Cross of Gold" speech?

_____

7. What was the reaction to the speech?_____

_____

_____

8. Give a sentence that illustrates the style of the speech._____

_____

_____

9. What form of proof predominated? _____ethical; _____emotional; _____logical.

10. Describe the organizational pattern._____

_____

_____

PART II
CONTEMPORARY
SPEECHES
after 1900

X THE MAN WITH THE MUCK RAKE

THEODORE ROOSEVELT
(1858-1919)

The Speaker

Theodore Roosevelt exemplifies the self-made speaker. Although his formal education was superior, he neglected training in oral communication because he did not plan to go into public life and, therefore, felt little need for such training. A program of self-training was thrust upon him when he became a candidate for the New York Assembly in 1882. During his remaining thirty-seven years, he made thousands of speeches on four continents to many types of audiences. It was Roosevelt, the man, who drew large audiences. The force of his personality overshadowed his lack of skills in oral communication.

During his day, Roosevelt's reputation as a speaker suffered because he lacked the flamboyant, oratorical style characteristic of the prevailing period of elocution. Today, his speaking is more highly regarded because the oratorical flourish no longer prevails. His thorough background of information and ideas, his high ethical principles, and his maturity of judgment cause him to be regarded today among the most effective speakers in history.

Theodore Roosevelt, the twenty-sixth President of the United States, was born in New York City, October 27, 1858. He came from famous ancestors who settled originally in Manhattan in 1650. His father was a prosperous merchant; his mother came from a prominent family of Georgia. Roosevelt married Alice Hathaway Lee of Boston in 1880; she died in 1884. Two years later he married Edith Kermit Carow of New York City. One child was born to his first marriage and five to his second.

Roosevelt, frail as a youth, received private tutoring until he entered Harvard in 1876. His high scholastic attainment is shown by his election to Phi Beta Kappa and his final standing of twenty-first in a class of 158. He excelled in written communication but his training and practice in speaking were meager and inconspicuous. After graduation from Harvard in 1880, he studied law at New York University and later at Columbia.

His distinguished political career began with his election to the New York State Assembly, where he served from 1882 to 1884. After engaging in ranching in South Dakota, he returned to New York City in 1886 and was defeated in his race for mayor. He served on the United States Service Commission from 1889 to 1895 and as president of the Police Commission of New York City from 1895 to 1897. He became Assistant Secretary of the Navy in 1897 but resigned in May, 1898, to become a Rough Rider, a lieutenant colonel of the First United States Volunteer Cavalary in the Spanish-American War. His exploits as a Rough Rider enhanced his popularity. He was elected Governor of New York in November, 1898. In March, 1900, he was elected Vice-President under Republican William McKinley; and six months later, after the assassination of McKinley, he succeeded to the Presidency. He was elected President in 1904 but declined to run again in 1908.

After retiring from the Presidency, Roosevelt gained further fame for his big-game hunting in Africa and from his lecture tour of England and Europe. He returned to politics in 1912 when he bolted the Republican party and became the nominee for President on the Bull Moose or Progressive party ticket. Following his defeat by Woodrow Wilson, he explored the Brazilian wilderness for the next two years. The remainder of his life was spent in public service, making speeches and writing. He served in turn as contributing editor of *The Outlook* and editorial writer for the *Metropolitan* and the Kansas City *Star*. His speaking skills decreased during his declining years, but few men in history used speech so effectively to shape social and political reforms.

Roosevelt died in his sleep from a blood clot in his heart on January 6, 1919.

The Occasion

Roosevelt's famous speech, "The Man with the Muck Rake," was given during his second term as President, on April 14, 1906, on the occasion of the laying of the cornerstone for the Congressional Office Building in Washington, D.C. During the late nineteenth and early twentieth centuries, big business held a stranglehold on the nation's economy. Roosevelt earlier initiated a movement to break up the big trusts with their monopolistic controls. Numerous writers took up the cry and wrote bitter denunciations of big business and indeed of the capitalistic system. Such writers as Ida M. Tarbell, Lincoln Steffens, Burton J. Henrick, and Thomas W. Lawson wrote exposés of the practices in the oil industry, municipal governments, life insurance companies, and business financing. Magazines like *McClure's, Everybody's, Cosmopolitan,* and *The American* clamored for articles on the malfeasances of business and allied evils such as child labor, false advertising, and political corruption.

Apparently Roosevelt thought that such exposés had gone too far and were undermining the public trust in American enterprises. He attempted to mollify the feelings of distrust caused by so many articles and speeches against big business. In short, he sought to reaffirm his confidence in big business and to allay the feelings of distrust of the general public. Roosevelt first presented the idea of his speech in an informal address to the Gridiron Club in March, 1906, and a month later addressed it to a Washington audience.

His audience consisted of a distinguished assemblage including members of both houses of Congress, the Supreme Court, the Diplomatic Corps, and the general public. Present were many businessmen who strongly favored the thesis of his speech.

The Speech

Roosevelt began by referring to the occasion in noting the growth of the national capital since the laying of the cornerstone of the Capitol Building. He explained that this growth paralleled that of the nation as a whole, that the increase in wealth had outstripped that of the population. He compared the attitude of many who criticized the evils attendant to such growth to the Man with the Muck Rake in Bunyan's *Pilgrim's Progress*—the man who could look no way but down and who always raked the filth toward him. He labeled these extreme critics "mud-slingers" or "muck rakers."

The central theme called for restraint in criticizing the questionable practices of big businessmen. Roosevelt exercised the skillful device of advocating both sides at the same time. He recognized the value of destructive criticism yet condemned those who carried such criticism too far. He warned against attributing the evil practices of some men to all men and contended that the majority of industrialists were honest men of high principles who had contributed much to the nation's growth.

The arrangement is didactic in form. He stated his points, then expanded them through explanation and reasoning. Yet it is difficult to outline his speech in one-two-three order, for each new point is an extension of the previous point. Toward the end, he raised the question of how to contend with the problems of amassing enormous fortunes. He made several suggestions but did not develop them in detail. His programs for progressive taxation and federal supervision of interstate commerce were presented as matters to ponder rather than as definite proposals.

The forms of support consist mainly of explanation and reasoning. He used several specific instances, some comparison, and two quotations, but no detailed illustrations or statistics. The moralistic theme, quotation from the Bible, and references to honesty and high ideals created ethical appeal. There are few direct emotional appeals but the speech bulks large in logical appeal. The style is formal, the sentences are studied and balanced, and the structure shows a tight forensic form. The speech reveals careful preparation in minute detail.

The text that follows is from *The Works of Theodore Roosevelt,* Memorial Edition (New York: Charles Scribner's Sons, 1923-1925), Vol. 18, pp. 571-585.

Over a century ago Washington laid the corner-stone of the Capitol in what was then little more than a tract of wooded wilderness here beside the Potomac. We now find it necessary to provide by great additional buildings for the business of the government. This growth in the need for the housing of the government is but a proof and example of the way in which the nation has grown and the sphere of action of the national government has grown. We now administer the affairs of a nation in which the extraordinary growth of population has been outstripped by the growth of wealth and the growth in complex interests. The material problems that face us to-day are not such as they were in Washington's time, but the underlying facts of human nature are the same now as they were then. Under altered external form we war with the same tendencies toward evil that were evident in Washington's time, and are helped by the same tendencies for good. It is about some of these that I wish to say a word to-day.

In Bunyan's "Pilgrim's Progress" you may recall the description of the Man with the Muck Rake, the man who could look no way but downward, with the muck rake in his hand; who was offered a celestial crown for his muck rake, but who would neither look up nor regard the crown he was offered, but continued to rake to himself the filth of the floor.

In "Pilgrim's Progress" the Man with the Muck Rake is set forth as the example of him whose vision is fixed on carnal instead of on spiritual things. Yet he also typifies the man who in this life consistently refuses to see aught that is lofty, and fixes his eyes with solemn intentness only on that which is vile and debasing. Now it is very necessary that we should not flinch from seeing what is vile and debasing. There is filth on the floor, and it must be scraped up with the muck rake; and there are times and places where this service is the most needed of all the services that can be performed. But the man who never does anything else, who never thinks or speaks or writes save of his feats with the muck rake, speedily becomes, not a help to society, not an incitement to good, but one of the most potent forces for evil.

There are, in the body politic, economic and social, many and grave evils, and there is urgent necessity for the sternest war upon them. There should be relentless exposure of and attack upon every evil man, whether politician or business man, every evil practice, whether in politics, in business, or in social life. I hail as a benefactor every writer or speaker, every man who, on the platform, or in book, magazine, or newspaper, with merciless severity makes such attack, provided always that he in his turn remembers that the attack is of use only if it is absolutely truthful. The liar is no whit better than the thief, and if his mendacity takes the form of slander, he may be worse than most thieves. It puts a premium upon knavery untruthfully to attack an honest man, or even with hysterical exaggeration to assail a bad man with untruth. An epidemic of indiscriminate assault upon character does no good, but very great harm. The soul of every scoundrel is gladdened whenever an honest man is assailed, or even a scoundrel is untruthfully assailed.

Now, it is easy to twist out of shape what I have just said, easy to affect to misunderstand it, and, if it is slurred over in repetition, not difficult really to misunderstand it. Some persons are sincerely incapable of understanding that to denounce mud-slinging does not mean the indorsement of whitewashing; and both the interested individuals who need whitewashing, and those others who practise mud-slinging, like to encourage such confusion of ideas. One of the chief counts against those who make indiscriminate assault upon men in business or men in public life is that they invite a reaction which is sure to tell powerfully in favor of the unscrupulous scoundrel who really ought to be attacked, who ought to be exposed, who ought, if possible, to be put in the penitentiary. If Aristides is praised overmuch as just, people get tired of hearing it; and overcensure of the unjust finally and from similar reasons results in their favor.

Any excess is almost sure to invite a reaction; and, unfortunately, the reaction, instead of taking the form of punishment of those guilty of the excess, is very apt to take the form either of punishment of the unoffending or of giving immunity, and even strength, to offenders. The effort to make financial or political profit out of the destruction of character can only result in public calamity. Gross and reckless assaults on character, whether on the stump or in newspaper, magazine, or book, create a morbid and vicious public sentiment, and at the same time act as a profound deterrent to able men of normal sensitiveness and tend to prevent them from entering the public service at any price. As an instance in point, I may mention that one serious difficulty encountered in getting the right type of men to dig the Panama Canal is the certainty that they will be exposed, both without, and, I am sorry to say, sometimes within, Congress, to utterly reckless assaults on their character and capacity.

At the risk of repetition, let me say again that my plea is not for immunity to, but for the most unsparing exposure of, the politician who betrays his trust, of the big business man who makes or spends his fortune in illegitimate or corrupt ways. There should be a resolute effort to hunt every such man out of the position he has disgraced. Expose the crime, and hunt down the criminal; but remember that even in the case of crime, if it is attacked in sensational, lurid, and untruthful fashion, the attack may do more damage to the public mind than the crime itself. It is because I feel that there should be no rest in the endless war against the forces of evil that I ask that the war be conducted with sanity as well as resolution. The men with the muck rakes are often indispensable to the well-being of society; but only if they know when to stop raking the muck, and to look upward to the celestial crown above them, to the crown of worthy endeavor. There are beautiful things above and round about them; and if they gradually grow to feel that the whole world is nothing but muck, their power of usefulness is gone. If the whole picture is painted black, there remains no hue whereby to single out the rascals for distinction from their fellows. Such painting finally induces a kind of moral color-blindness; and people affected by it come to the conclusion that no man is really black and no man really white, but that all are gray. In other words, they believe neither in the truth of the attack nor in the honesty of the man who is attacked; they grow as suspicious of the accusation as of the offense; it becomes well-nigh hopeless to stir them either to wrath against wrongdoing or to enthusiasm for what is right; and such a mental attitude in the public gives hope to every knave, and is the despair of honest men.

To assail the great and admitted evils of our political and industrial life with such crude and sweeping generalizations as to include decent men in the general condemnation means the searing of the public conscience. There results a general attitude either of cynical belief in and indifference to public corruption or else of a distrustful inability to discriminate between the good and the bad. Either attitude is fraught with untold damage to the country as a whole. The fool who has not sense to discriminate between what is good and what is bad is well-nigh as dangerous as the man who does discriminate and yet chooses the bad. There is nothing more distressing to every good patriot, to every good American, than the hard, scoffing spirit which treats the allegation of dishonesty in a public man as a cause for laughter. Such laughter is worse than the crackling of thorns under a pot, for it denotes not merely the vacant mind, but the heart in which high emotions have been choked before they could grow to fruition.

There is any amount of good in the world, and there never was a time when loftier and more disinterested work for the betterment of mankind was being done than now. The forces that tend for evil are great and terrible, but the forces of truth and love and courage and honesty and generosity and sympathy are also stronger than ever before. It is a foolish and timid, no less than a wicked, thing to blink the fact that the forces of evil are strong, but it is even worse to fail to take into account the strength of the forces that tell for good. Hysterical sensationalism is the very poorest weapon wherewith to fight for lasting righteousness. The men who, with stern sobriety and truth, assail the many evils of our time, whether in the public press, or in magazines, or in books, are the leaders and allies of all engaged in the work for social and political betterment. But if they give good reasons for distrust of what they say, if they chill the ardor of those who demand truth as a primary virtue, they thereby betray the good cause, and play into the hands of the very men against whom they are nominally at war.

In his "Ecclesiastical Polity" that fine old Elizabethan divine, Bishop Hooker, wrote:

> He that goeth about to persuade a multitude that they are not so well governed as they ought to be shall never want attentive and favorable hearers, because they know the manifold defects whereunto every kind of regimen is subject; but the secret lets and difficulties which in public proceeding are innumerable and inevitable, they have not ordinarily the judgment to consider."

This truth should be kept constantly in mind by every free people desiring to preserve the sanity and poise indispensable to the permanent success of self-government. Yet, on the other hand, it is vital not to permit this spirit of sanity and self-command to degenerate into mere mental stagnation. Bad though a state of hysterical excitement is, and evil though the results are which come from the violent oscillations such excitement invariably produces, yet a sodden acquiescence in evil is even worse. At this moment we are passing through a period of great unrest—social, political, and industrial unrest. It is of the utmost importance for our future that this should prove to be not the unrest of mere rebelliousness against life, of mere dissatisfaction with the inevitable inequality of conditions, but the unrest of a resolute and eager ambition to secure the betterment of the individual and the nation. So far as this movement of agitation throughout the country takes the form of a fierce discontent with evil, of a determination to punish the authors of evil, whether in industry or politics, the feeling is to be heartily welcomed as a sign of healthy life.

If, on the other hand, it turns into a mere crusade of appetite against appetite, a contest between the brutal greed of the "have-nots" and the brutal greed of the "haves," then it has no significance for good, but only for evil. If it seeks to establish a line of cleavage, not along the line which divides good men from bad, but along that other line, running at right angles thereto, which divides those who are well off from those who are less well off, then it will be fraught with immeasurable harm to the body politic.

We can no more and no less afford to condone evil in the man of capital than evil in the man of no capital. The wealthy man who exults because there is a failure of justice in the effort to bring some trust magnate to an account for his misdeeds is as bad as, and no worse than, the so-called labor leader who clamorously strives to excite a foul class feeling on behalf of some other labor leader who is implicated in murder. One attitude is as bad as the other and no worse; in each case the accused is entitled to exact justice; and in neither case is there need of action by others which can be construed into an expression of sympathy for crime. There is nothing more antisocial in a democratic republic like ours than such vicious class-consciousness. The multi-millionaires who band together to prevent the enactment of proper laws for the supervision of the use of wealth, or to assail those who resolutely enforce such laws, or to exercise a hidden influence upon the political destinies of parties or individuals in their own personal interest, are a menace to the whole community; and a menace at least as great is offered by those laboring men who band together to defy the law, and by their openly used influence to coerce law-upholding public officials. The apologists for either class of offenders are themselves enemies of good citizenship; and incidentally they are also, to a peculiar degree, the enemies of every honest-dealing corporation and every law-abiding labor-union.

It is a prime necessity that if the present unrest is to result in permanent good, the emotion shall be translated into action, and that the action shall be marked by honesty, sanity, and self-restraint. There is mighty little good in a mere spasm of reform. The reform that counts is that which comes through steady, continuous growth; violent emotionalism leads to exhaustion.

It is important to this people to grapple with the problems connected with the amassing of enormous fortunes and the use of those fortunes, both corporate and individual, in business. We should discriminate in the sharpest way between fortunes well won and fortunes ill won; between those gained as an incident to performing great services to the community as a whole, and those gained in evil fashion by keeping just within the limits of mere law-honesty. Of course no amount of charity in spending such fortunes in any way compensates for misconduct in making them. As a matter of personal conviction, and without pretending to discuss the details or formulate the system, I feel that we shall ultimately have to consider the adoption of some such scheme as that of a progressive tax on all fortunes, beyond a certain amount, either given in life or devised or bequeathed upon death to any individual— a tax so framed as to put it out of the power of the owner of one of these enormous fortunes to hand on more than a certain amount to any one individual; the tax, of course, to be imposed by the national and not the State government. Such taxation should, of course, be aimed merely at the inheritance or transmission in their entirety of those fortunes swollen beyond all healthy limits.

Again, the national government must in some form exercise supervision over corporations engaged in interstate business—and all large corporations are engaged in interstate business,—whether by license or otherwise, so as to permit us to deal with the far-reaching evils of over-capitalization. This year we are making a beginning in the direction of serious effort to settle some of these economic problems by the railway rate legislation. Such legislation, if so framed, as I am sure it will be, as to secure definite and tangible results, will amount to something of itself; and it will amount to a great deal more in so far as it is taken as a first step in the direction of a policy of superintendence and control over corporate wealth engaged in interstate commerce, this superintendence and control not to be exercised in a spirit of malevolence toward the men who have created the wealth, but with the firm purpose both to do justice to them and to see that they in their turn do justice to the public at large.

The first requisite in the public servants who are to deal in this shape with corporations, whether as legislators or as executives, is honesty. This honesty can be no respecter of persons. There can be no such thing as unilateral honesty. The danger is not really from corrupt corporations; it springs from the corruption itself, whether exercised for or against corporations.

The eighth commandment reads, "Thou shalt not steal." It does not read, "Thou shalt not steal from the rich man." It does not read, "Thou shalt not steal from the poor man." It reads simply and plainly, "Thou shalt not steal." No good whatever will come from that warped and mock morality which denounces the misdeeds of men of wealth and forgets the misdeeds practised at their expense; which denounces bribery, but blinds itself to blackmail; which foams with rage if a corporation secures favors by improper methods, and merely leers with hideous mirth if the corporation is itself wronged. The only public servant who can be trusted honestly to protect the rights of the public against the misdeeds of a corporation is that public man who will just as surely protect the corporation itself from wrongful aggression. If a public man is willing to yield to popular clamor and do wrong to the men of wealth or to rich corporations, it may be set down as certain that if the opportunity comes he will secretly and furtively do wrong to the public in the interest of a corporation.

But, in addition to honesty, we need sanity. No honesty will make a public man useful if that man is timid or foolish, if he is a hot-headed zealot or an impracticable visionary. As we strive for reform, we find that it is not at all merely the case of a long up-hill pull. On the contrary, there is almost as much of breeching work as of collar work; to depend only on traces means that there will soon be a runaway and an upset. The men of wealth who to-day are trying to prevent the regulation and control of their business in the interest of the public by the proper government authorities will not succeed, in my judgment, in checking the progress of the movement. But if they did succeed, they would find that they had sown the wind and would surely reap the whirlwind, for they would ultimately provoke the violent excesses which accompany a reform coming by convulsion instead of by steady and natural growth.

On the other hand, the wild preachers of unrest and discontent, the wild agitators against the entire existing order, the men who act crookedly, whether because of sinister design or from mere puzzle-headedness, the men who preach destruction without proposing any substitute for what they intend to destroy, or who propose a substitute which would be far worse than the existing evils,—all these men are the most dangerous opponents of real reform. If they get their way, they will lead the people into a deeper pit than any into which they would fall under the present system. If they fail to get their way, they will still do incalculable harm by provoking the kind of reaction which, in its revolt against the senseless evil of their teaching, would enthrone more securely than ever the very evils which their misguided followers believe they are attacking.

More important than aught else is the development of the broadest sympathy of man for man. The welfare of the wage-worker, the welfare of the tiller of the soil—upon this depends the welfare of the entire country; their good is not to be sought in pulling down others; but their good must be the prime object of all our statesmanship.

Materially we must strive to secure a broader economic opportunity for all men, so that each shall have a better chance to show the stuff of which he is made. Spiritually and ethically we must strive to bring about clean living and right thinking. We appreciate that the things of the body are important; but we appreciate also that the things of the soul are immeasurably more important. The foundation-stone of national life is, and ever must be, the high individual character of the average citizen.

145

Questions and Exercises

1. Why is Theodore Roosevelt termed "a self-made speaker"?_____
   _____
   _____

2. What was his chief weakness as a speaker?_____
   _____

3. From what college was he graduated?_____
   Give evidence of his scholastic attainment._____
   _____

4. When did he become President of the United States?_____
   Under what circumstances?_____
   _____

5. To what political party did he belong as President?_____
   What party did he represent in his presidential campaign of 1912?
   _____

6. What was the occasion for his speech "The Man with the Muck
   Rake"?_____
   _____

7. What is the central idea of the speech?_____
   _____

8. What is the significance of the title?_____
   _____
   _____

9. Give one example of ethical appeal._____
   _____
   _____

10. Describe the organizational pattern._____
    _____
    _____

XI *DECLARATION OF WAR*

WOODROW WILSON
(1856-1924)

The Speaker

Woodrow Wilson exemplifies the well-trained speaker. From boyhood, he aspired to become a leader and he seemed to sense that effective speaking would help him attain his aspirations. As a youth, he practiced speaking under rigid standards set up by his father, listened to the outstanding speakers of his day, and studied the significant speeches and speakers of history. At college he delivered orations, participated in the speaking activities of the literary societies, and engaged in college debates. As a teacher, he encouraged his students to participate in debates on current issues and served briefly as debate coach. He was annually voted the outstanding lecturer at Princeton.

Upon entering the political arena, Wilson was well prepared to put his communicative skills and his wide background of knowledge to constructive use. That his early training served him well is borne out by history. The professors who selected the speeches for this anthology by a poll chose three of Wilson's addresses, the most of any speaker's.

Thomas Woodrow Wilson was born on December 28, 1856, at Staunton, Virginia. He later dropped the "Thomas" to give his name a more euphonious sound. His family moved to Augusta, Georgia, in 1858, where he lived until age fourteen when he moved to Columbia,

South Carolina. His precollege training consisted of private tutoring, largely by his father. In 1873, he entered Davidson College but withdrew because of illness. In 1875, he entered Princeton; he was graduated in 1879. He entered law school at the University of Virginia the same year but withdrew the next year because of ill health. After studying law at home, he was admitted to the Georgia bar in 1882. He gave up the practice of law after one year to enter the graduate school of Johns Hopkins, where he received his Doctor of Philosophy degree in 1886.

As a student, Wilson excelled in English, rhetoric, composition, and declamation; he made only average marks in Latin, Greek, and mathematics. The literary societies commanded his greatest interest. He was especially active in the politics of the societies and in the forensic activities which they sponsored. He also gained valuable experience in written communication as editor of the university paper. Wilson engaged in the type of extracurricular activities that added to a well-rounded education and that, at the same time, gave him pleasure.

Woodrow Wilson made significant contributions to education and politics. He taught at Bryn Mawr from 1885 to 1888, at Wesleyan from 1888 to 1890, and at Princeton from 1890 to 1892, when he was elected to the presidency of Princeton. He remained as president of Princeton until 1910, when he resigned to run for governor of New Jersey. He was elected governor and two years later became the Democratic nominee for President against William Howard Taft, the Republican candidate, and Theodore Roosevelt, the Progressive candidate. Wilson won in 1912 and was re-elected President in 1916, when he defeated Charles Evans Hughes. He suffered a paralytic stroke on September 25, 1919, while on a cross-country speaking tour in behalf of the League of Nations. He never completely recovered and died almost five years later in Washington, D.C., on February 3, 1924.

Wilson took himself and his principles seriously. He had a powerful and analytical mind, an unusual store of knowledge, and the communicative skills which enabled him to present his views forcibly and lucidly. His high moral principles, his strong religious convictions, and his intolerance of mediocrity made him impatient with opposition and often bitter in defeat. His ambition caused him to drive himself eventually beyond the endurance of his frail body. He never forgave the American people for rejecting the League of Nations and he died a bitter and disappointed man. Yet these characteristics caused him to contribute much to his age and perhaps to future ages.

The Occasion

Wilson's message, calling for a declaration of war against Germany, was delivered before a joint session of Congress on April 2, 1917. From the time of the neutrality proclamation on August 4, 1914, Wilson had worked incessantly to keep the United States out of war. He was reelected President on the slogan, "He kept us out of war," and apparently his most fervent wish was to make good his promise. Yet he was torn between his desires to maintain the neutrality of the United States and to aid Great Britain, whose political institutions he had championed since his college days.

The forces for declaring war gradually wore down Wilson's resistance. The pressures came from all sides—the war hawks in his Cabinet, our ambassador to Great Britain, the big-business interests, the British and French propaganda machines, and finally the German declaration of unrestricted submarine warfare. Wilson had hoped for a "peace without victory" which would enable the United States, as the principal neutral, to exert its influence for establishing the League of Nations. Even after this procedure became impossible, Wilson attempted to bind the Allies to a statement of purpose embodying an international organization. With the continued sinking of American vessels by German submarines, Wilson realized the futility of maintaining neutrality. Therefore, on April 2, 1917, he called the Congress into special session and gave the most momentous speech of his life.

Wilson's war message was so intensely personal that he alone composed it. He consulted only his trusted assistant, Edward M. House, and then only after the speech had been completed. House made but one minor change, which Wilson accepted. During the delivery of the speech, Wilson seemed perturbed by the frequent applause. After the speech, he immediately went back to the White House. He remarked to his faithful secretary, Joseph P. Tumulty, about how strange it seemed to hear his speech of death applauded. According to Tumulty, he put his head on the table and wept.

Wilson's immediate audience consisted of the members of both Houses of Congress, the Supreme Court, the Cabinet, the diplomatic corps, and a packed gallery. His secondary audience consisted of the citizens throughout the nation, indeed of the world. He appeared to be speaking more to mankind in general than to his immediate audience.

The Speech

Wilson's war message required thirty-two minutes to deliver. As he entered the packed House chambers at 8:40 in the evening, he received a great ovation. He read the speech from his manuscript in his pleasant, well-modulated, tenor voice.

The basic organizational pattern is chronological—past-present-future. After referring to the occasion, the solemn events that made necessary the extraordinary session, he reviewed the recent events of German submarine warfare that had killed thousands of American citizens on neutral vessels. He then returned to the present—the German actions had resulted in a war against mankind. As a result, he said, "We will not choose the path of submission." He then explained his recommendations asking for a declaration of war. He looked toward the future in outlining the steps necessary for prosecuting the war and toward a League of Nations for maintaining the peace after the war.

The speech is largely of the expository-argumentative type. Its basic appeal is to reason. Although the occasion was charged with emotion, Wilson appeared deliberately to play down any appeals to the emotions. He said, "The choice we make . . . must be made with moderation of counsel and a temperament of judgment befitting our character. . . . We must put excited feelings away." Wilson's high ethical principles and moral standards permeate the speech; for example, "We have no quarrel with the German people. We have no feelings towards them but one of sympathy and friendship."

The style is somewhat academic but clear and forceful. He used the telling phrase effectively; for example, "The present German submarine warfare against commerce is a warfare against mankind." "The world must be made safe for democracy." "We are but one of the champions of the rights of mankind." Most important, the speech reflects the agony of a man who must perform a distasteful but necessary duty. The following text was taken from the *Congressional Record*, 65th Congress, Vol. 55, April 12, 1917, pp. 102-103.

GENTLEMEN OF THE CONGRESS: I have called the Congress into extraordinary session because there are serious, very serious choices of policy to be made, and made immediately, which it was neither right nor constitutionally permissible that I should assume the responsibility of making.

On the third of February last I officially laid before you the extraordinary announcement of the Imperial German Government that on and after the first day of February it was its purpose to put aside all restraints of law or of humanity and use its submarines to sink every vessel that sought to approach either the ports of Great Britain and Ireland or the western coasts of Europe or any of the ports controlled by the enemies of Germany within the Mediterranean. That had seemed to be the object of the German submarine warfare earlier in the war, but since April of last year the Imperial Government had somewhat restrained the commanders of its undersea craft in conformity with its promise then given to us that passenger boats should not be sunk and that due warning would be given to all other vessels which its submarines might seek to destroy, when no resistance was offered or escape attempted, and care taken that their crews were given at least a fair chance to save their lives in their open boats. The precautions taken were meager and haphazard enough, as was proved in distressing instance after instance in the progress of the cruel and unmanly business, but a certain degree of restraint was observed. The new policy has swept every restriction aside. Vessels of every kind, whatever their flag, their character, their cargo, their destination, their errand, have been ruthlessly sent to the bottom without warning and without thought of help or mercy for those on board, the vessels of friendly neutrals along with those of belligerents. Even hospital ships and ships carrying relief to the sorely bereaved and stricken people of Belgium, though the latter were provided with safe conduct through the proscribed areas by the German Government itself and were distinguished by unmistakable marks of identity, have been sunk with the same reckless lack of compassion or of principle.

I was for a little while unable to believe that such things would in fact be done by any government that had hitherto subscribed to humane practices of civilized nations. International law had its origin in the attempt to set up some law which would be respected and observed upon the seas, where no nation had right of dominion and where lay the free highways of the world. By painful stage after stage has that law been built up, with meager enough results, indeed, after all was accomplished that could be accomplished, but always with a clear view, at least, of what the heart and conscience of mankind demanded. This minimum of right the German Government has swept aside, under the plea of retaliation and necessity and because it had no weapons which it could use at sea except these which it is impossible to employ as it is employing them without throwing to the wind all scruples of humanity or of respect for the understandings that were supposed to underlie the intercourse of the world. I am not now thinking of the loss of property involved, immense and serious as that is, but only of the wanton and wholesale destruction of the lives of noncombatants, men, women, and children, engaged in pursuits which have always, even in the darkest periods of modern history, been deemed innocent and legitimate. Property can be paid for; the lives of peaceful and innocent people cannot be. The present German submarine warfare against commerce is a warfare against mankind.

It is a war against all nations. American ships have been sunk, American lives taken, in ways which it has stirred us very deeply to learn of, but the ships and people of other neutral and friendly nations have been sunk and overwhelmed in the waters in the same way. There has been no discrimination. The challenge is to all mankind. Each nation must decide for itself how it will meet it. The choice we make for ourselves must be made with a moderation of counsel and a temperateness of judgment befitting our character and our motives as a nation. We must put excited feeling away. Our motive will not be revenge or the victorious assertion of the physical might of the nation, but only the vindication of right, of human right, of which we are only a single champion.

When I addressed the Congress on the twenty-sixth of February last I thought that it would suffice to assert our neutral rights with arms, our right to use the seas against unlawful interference, our right to keep our people safe against unlawful violence. But armed neutrality, it now appears, is impracticable. Because submarines are in effect outlaws when used as the German submarines have been used against merchant shipping, it is impossible to defend ships against their attacks as the law of nations has assumed that merchantmen would defend themselves against privateers or cruisers, visible craft giving chase upon the open sea. It is common prudence in such circumstances, grim necessity indeed, to endeavor to destroy them before they have shown their own intention. They must be dealt with upon sight, if dealt with at all. The German Government denies the right of neutrals to use arms at all within the areas of the sea which it has proscribed, even in the defense of rights which no modern publicist has ever before questioned their right to defend. The intimation is conveyed that the armed guards which we have placed on our merchant ships will be treated as beyond the pale of law and subject to be dealt with as pirates would be. Armed neutrality is ineffectual enough at best; in such circumstances and in the face of such pretensions it is worse than ineffectual; it is likely only to produce what it was meant to prevent; it is practically certain to draw us into the war without either the rights or the effectiveness of belligerents. There is one choice we cannot make, we are incapable of making; we will not choose the path of submission and suffer the most sacred rights of our nation and our people to be ignored or violated. The wrongs against which we now array ourselves are no common wrongs; they cut to the very roots of human life.

With a profound sense of the solemn and even tragical character of the step I am taking and of the grave responsibilities which it involves, but in unhesitating obedience to what I deem my constitutional duty, I advise that the Congress declare the recent course of the Imperial German Government to be in fact nothing less than war against the Government and people of the United States; that it formally accept the status of belligerent which has thus been thrust upon it; and that it take immediate steps not only to put the country in a more thorough state of defense, but also to exert all its power and employ all its resources to bring the Government of the German Empire to terms and end the war.

What this will involve is clear. It will involve the utmost practicable cooperation in counsel and action with the governments now at war with Germany, and, as incident to that, the extension to those governments of the most liberal financial credits, in order that our resources may so far as possible be added to theirs. It will involve the organization and mobilization of all the material resources of the country to supply the materials of war and serve the incidental needs of the nation in the most abundant and yet the most economical and efficient way possible. It will involve the immediate full equipment of the navy in all respects but particularly in supplying it with the best means of dealing with the enemy's submarines. It will involve the immediate addition to the armed forces of the United States already provided for by law in case of war of at least five thousand men, who should, in my opinion, be chosen upon the principle of universal liability to service, and also the authorization of subsequent additional increments of equal force so soon as they may be needed and can be handled in training. It will involve also, of course, the granting of adequate credits to the Government, sustained, I hope, so far as they can equitably be sustained by the present generation, by well-conceived taxation.

I say sustained so far as may be equitable by taxation because it seems to me that it would be most unwise to base the credits which will now be necessary entirely on money borrowed. It is our duty, I most respectfully urge, to protect our people so far as we may against the very serious hardships and evils which would be likely to arise out of the inflation which would be produced by vast loans.

In carrying out the measures by which these things are to be accomplished we should keep constantly in mind the wisdom of interfering as little as possible in our own preparation and in the equipment of our own military forces with the duty—for it will be a very practical duty—of supplying the nations already at war with Germany with the materials which they can obtain only from us or by our assistance. They are in the field and we should help them in every way to be effective there.

I shall take the liberty of suggesting, through the several executive departments of the Government, for the consideration of your committees, measures for the accomplishment of the several objects I have mentioned. I hope that it will be your pleasure to deal with them as having been framed after very careful thought by the branch of the Government upon whom the responsibility of conducting the war and safeguarding the nation will most directly fall.

While we do these things, these deeply momentous things, let us be very clear, and make very clear to all the world, what our motives and our objects are. My own thought has not been driven from its habitual and normal course by the unhappy events of the last two months, and I do not believe that the thought of the nation has been altered or clouded by them. I have exactly the same things in mind now that I had in mind when I addressed the Senate on the twenty-second of January last; the same that I had in mind when I addressed the Congress on the third of February and on the twenty-sixth of February. Our object now, as then, is to vindicate the principles of peace and justice in the life of the world as against selfish and autocratic power, and to set up among the really free and self-governed peoples of the world such a concert of purpose and of action as will henceforth ensure the observance of those principles. Neutrality is no longer feasible or desirable where the peace of the world is involved and the freedom of its peoples, and the menace to that peace and freedom lies in the existence of autocratic governments, backed by organized force which is controlled wholly by their will, not by the will of their people. We have seen the last of neutrality in such circumstances. We are at the beginning of an age in which it will be insisted that the same standards of conduct and of responsibility for wrong done shall be observed among nations and their governments that are observed among the individual citizens of civilized States.

We have no quarrel with the German people. We have no feeling towards them but one of sympathy and friendship. It was not upon their impulse that their government acted in entering this war. It was not with their previous knowledge or approval. It was a war determined upon as wars used to be determined upon in the old, unhappy days when peoples were nowhere consulted by their rulers and wars were provoked and waged in the interest of dynasties or of little groups of ambitious men who were accustomed to use their fellowmen as pawns and tools. Self-governed nations do not fill their neighbor states with spies or set the course of intrigue to bring about some critical posture of affairs which will give them an opportunity to strike and make conquest. Such designs can be successfully worked out only under cover and where no one has the right to ask questions. Cunningly contrived plans of deception or aggression, carried, it may be, from generation to generation, can be worked out and kept from the light only within the privacy of courts or behind the carefully guarded confidences of a narrow and privileged class. They are happily impossible where public opinion commands and insists upon full information concerning all the nation's affairs.

A steadfast concert for peace can never be maintained except by a partnership of democratic nations. No autocratic government could be trusted to keep faith within it or observe its covenants. It must be a league of honor, a partnership of opinion. Intrigue would eat its vitals away; the plottings of inner circles who could plan what they would and render account to no one would be a corruption seated at its very heart. Only free peoples can hold their purpose and their honor steady to a common end and prefer the interests of mankind to any narrow interest of their own.

Does not every American feel that assurance has been added to our hope for the future peace of the world by the wonderful and heartening things that have been happening within the last few weeks in Russia? Russia was known by those who knew her best to have been always in fact democratic at heart in all the vital habits of her thought, in all the intimate relationships of her people that spoke their natural instinct, their habitual attitude towards life. The autocracy that crowned the summit of her political structure, long as it had stood and terrible as was the reality of its power, was not in fact Russian in origin, character, or purpose; and now it has been shaken off and the great, generous Russian people have been added, in all their naive majesty and might, to the forces that are fighting for freedom in the world, for justice, and for peace. Here is a fit partner for a League of Honor.

One of the things that has served to convince us that the Prussian autocracy was not and could never be our friend is that from the very outset of the present war it has filled our unsuspecting communities, and even our offices of government, with spies and set criminal intrigues everywhere afoot against our national unity of counsel, our peace within and without, our industries and our commerce. Indeed, it is now evident that its spies were here even before the war began; and it is unhappily not a matter of conjecture but a fact proved in our courts of justice that the intrigues which have more than once come perilously near to disturbing the peace and dislocating the industries of the country have been carried on at the instigation, with the support, and even under the personal direction of official agents of the Imperial Government accredited to the Government of the United States. Even in checking these things and trying to extirpate them we have sought to put the most generous interpretation possible upon them because we knew that their source lay, not in any hostile feeling of the German people toward us (who were, no doubt, as ignorant of them as we ourselves were), but only in the selfish designs of a government that did what it pleased and told its people nothing. But they have played their part in serving to convince us at last that that government entertains no real friendship for us, and means to act against our peace and security at its convenience. That it means to stir up enemies against us at our very doors the intercepted note to the German Minister at Mexico City is eloquent evidence.

We are accepting this challenge of hostile purpose because we know that in such a government, following such methods, we can never have a friend; and that in the presence of its organized power, always lying in wait to accomplish we know not what purpose, there can be no assured security for the democratic governments of the world. We are now about to accept the gauge of battle with this natural foe to liberty and shall, if necessary, spend the whole force of the nation to check and nullify its pretensions and its power. We are glad, now that we see the facts with no veil of false pretense about them, to fight thus for the ultimate peace of the world and for the liberation of its peoples, the German peoples included; for the rights of nations, great and small, and the privilege of men everywhere to choose their way of life and of obedience. The world must be made safe for democracy. Its peace must be planted upon the tested foundations of political liberty. We have no selfish ends to serve. We desire no conquest, no dominion. We seek no indemnities for ourselves, no material compensation for the sacrifices we shall freely make. We are but one of the champions of the rights of mankind. We shall be satisfied when those rights have been made as secure as the faith and the freedom of nations can make them.

Just because we fight without rancor and without selfish object, seeking nothing for ourselves but what we shall wish to share with all free peoples, we shall, I feel confident, conduct our operations as belligerents without passion and ourselves observe with proud punctilio the principles of right and of fair play we profess to be fighting for.

I have said nothing of the government allied with the Imperial Government of Germany because they have not made war upon us or challenged us to defend our right and our honor. The Austro-Hungarian Government has, indeed, avowed its unqualified endorsement and acceptance of the reckless and lawless submarine warfare adopted now without disguise by the Imperial German Government, and it has therefore not been possible for this Government to receive Count Tarnowski, the Ambassador recently accredited to this Government by the Imperial and Royal Government of Austria-Hungary; but that Government has not actually engaged in warfare against citizens of the United States on the seas, and I take the liberty, for the present at least, of postponing a discussion of our relations with the authorities at Vienna. We enter this war only where we are clearly forced into it because there are no other means of defending our rights.

It will be all the easier for us to conduct ourselves as belligerents in a high spirit of right and fairness because we act without animus, not with enmity toward a people or with the desire to bring any injury or disadvantage upon them, but only in armed opposition to an irresponsible government which has thrown aside all considerations of humanity and of right and is running amuck. We are, let me say again, the sincere friends of the German people, and shall desire nothing so much as the early reëstablishment of intimate relations of mutual advantage between us,—however hard it may be for them, for the time being, to believe that this is spoken from our hearts. We have borne with their present government through all these bitter months because of that friendship, exercising a patience and forbearance which would otherwise have been impossible. We shall, happily, still have an opportunity to prove that friendship in our daily attitude and actions toward the millions of men and women of German birth and native sympathy who live among us and share our life, and we shall be proud to prove it towards all who are in fact loyal to their neighbors and to the Government in the hour of test. They are, most of them, as true and loyal Americans as if they had never known any other fealty or allegiance. They will be prompt to stand with us in rebuking and restraining the few who may be of a different mind and purpose. If there should be disloyalty, it will be dealt with with a firm hand of stern repression; but, if it lifts its head at all, it will lift it only here and there and without countenance except from a lawless and malignant few.

It is a distressing and oppressive duty, Gentlemen of the Congress, which I have performed in thus addressing you. There are, it may be, many months of fiery trial and sacrifice ahead of us. It is a fearful thing to lead this great peaceful people into war, into the most terrible and disastrous of all wars, civilization itself seeming to be in the balance. But the right is more precious than peace, and we shall fight for the things which we have always carried nearest our hearts—for democracy, for the right of those who submit to authority to have a voice in their own governments, for the rights and liberties of small nations, for a universal dominion of right by such a concert of free peoples as shall bring peace and safety to all nations and make the world itself at last free. To such a task we can dedicate our lives and our fortunes, everything that we are and everything that we have, with the pride of those who know that the day has come when America is privileged to spend her blood and her might for the principles that gave her birth and happiness and the peace which she has treasured. God helping her, she can do no other.

Questions and Exercises

1. Why is Woodrow Wilson termed "a well-trained speaker"? _____
   _____
   _____

2. Where was he born?_____ When?_____
   When did he die?_____ Where?_____

3. What was the highest college degree that he attained?_____
   _____ Where?_____

4. When was he president of Princeton University?_____
   Why did he resign?_____

5. Who were his opponents in the presidential campaign of 1912?
   _____

6. What was the date of his speech declaring war against Germany?
   _____ Who composed his audience?_____
   _____

7. What is the basic organizational pattern?_____
   _____

8. Give one example of logical proof._____
   _____
   _____

9. Describe the style of the speech._____
   _____
   _____

10. What were his basic forms of support?_____
    _____
    _____

XII *THE FOURTEEN POINTS SPEECH*

WOODROW WILSON
(1856-1924)

The Occasion

Four days after Wilson's "War Message," Congress had passed and the President had signed the War Resolution; the United States was at war on April 6, 1917. Wilson reached the peak of his career as a war leader. Through the force of his personality, his effective communicative skills, his high ethical standards, and his sincere spiritual fervor, he aroused the people from their apathy and created a spirit essential to waging war.

The time between Wilson's "War Message" and his "Fourteen Points" speech was a period of "gasless" Sundays, "meatless" and "heatless" days, and "Liberty Bonds." The volunteer army plan was abandoned in favor of a draft system which eventually included all able-bodied men between the ages of eighteen and forty-five. Taxes were increased, new taxes were devised, large loans were floated, industries and laborers were commandeered, occupations and businesses were regimented, and freedom of speech and freedom of the press were restricted. Wilson's persuasive powers did much to convince the public of the necessity for these deprivations.

Wilson employed his skills at clothing noble sentiments in lofty and telling phrases by framing war aims and presenting them to Congress and to the people. In his early diplomatic notes he emphasized American rights of commerce and travel. His "War Message" went beyond practical considerations to more lofty ideals for making "the world safe for democracy." Later he extended his ideals to include a "war for democracy" and a "war to end war." His most complete message stating his specific objectives came in his famous "Fourteen Points" speech, delivered before Congress on January 8, 1918.

Although his "War Message" was the final act in getting the United States into war, his "Fourteen Points" speech paved the way for an early end to the war. Wilson's proposals were so right and equitable that German morale weakened and thus Germany was brought to early surrender. The German high command sought peace based on Wilson's Fourteen Points.

Wilson's immediate audience for his "Fourteen Points" speech was the same as for his War Message—a joint session of the two Houses of Congress and packed galleries. Through the press and diplomatic channels, however, he reached a much larger audience—the world as a whole. The idealism expressed in the message did much to arouse the American people to new heights of patriotism and to weaken the German people's faith in their own cause.

The Speech

Although the Fourteen Points announced by Wilson were not all original with him, he gave them a new emphasis and expressed for the first time the conditions prerequisite for the cooperation of the United States in ending the war. The chief points of political significance were: open covenants of peace, freedom of navigation, the removal of economic barriers to world trade, reduction of armaments, impartial adjustment of colonial claims, and a general association of nations. The remaining points pertained to territorial matters of specific nations.

Like his "War Message," Wilson's "Fourteen Points" speech is of the expository-argumentative type. He began by explaining the purpose of his speech. His statement of principles, he said, was in response to desires expressed by the Central Empires to discuss "the objects of war and the possible bases of a general peace." He reviewed the previous statements of peace and settlement made by countries of the Central Powers and of Russia and contended that the Central Powers' statement constituted no concessions at all. He then discussed Russia's plight and the reasonableness of her statements. Next, he discussed some criteria for an acceptable statement of principles, stated and briefly explained his fourteen points, and discussed his motives in presenting them—"It is the principle of justice to all peoples . . . to live on equal terms of liberty and safety with one another. . . ."

The speech has a maximum of logical appeal, a minimum of emotional appeal, and bulks large in ethical appeal by the expression of lofty ideals. The forms of support consist primarily of explanation, reasoning, historical examples, and repetition; no statistics or quotations from authority are used. The style is forceful and contains many telling phrases. It contains much alliteration; for example, "processes of peace," "principle and purpose," "confusions of counsel," and "fearless frankness." The speech represents Wilson at his best. It is taken from *Congressional Record,* Vol. 56, January 8, 1918, pp. 680-681.

GENTLEMEN OF THE CONGRESS: Once more, as repeatedly before, the spokesmen of the Central Empires have indicated their desire to discuss the objects of the war and the possible bases of a general peace. Parleys have been in progress at Brest-Litovsk between representatives of the Central Powers, to which the attention of all the belligerents has been invited for the purpose of ascertaining whether it may be possible to extend these parleys into a general conference with regard to terms of peace and settlement. The Russian representatives presented not only a perfectly definite statement of the principles upon which they would be willing to conclude peace but also an equally definite program of the concrete application of those principles. The representatives of the Central Powers, on their part, presented an outline of settlement which, if much less definite, seemed susceptible of liberal interpretation until their specific program of practical terms was added. That program proposed no concessions at all either to the sovereignty of Russia or to the preferences of the populations with whose fortunes it dealt, but meant, in a word, that the Central Empires were to keep every foot of territory their armed forces had occupied,—every province, every city, every point of vantage,—as a permanent addition to their territories and their power. It is reasonable conjecture that the general principles of settlement which they at first suggested originated with the more liberal statesmen of Germany and Austria, the men who have begun to feel the force of their own peoples' thought and purpose, while the concrete terms of actual settlement came from the military leaders who have no thought but to keep what they have got. The negotiations have been broken off. The Russian representatives were sincere and in earnest. They cannot entertain such proposals of conquest and domination.

The whole incident is full of significance. It is also full of perplexity. With whom are the Russian representatives dealing? For whom are the representatives of the Central Empires speaking? Are they speaking for the majorities of their respective parliaments or for the minority parties, that military and imperialistic minority which has so far dominated their whole policy and controlled the affairs of Turkey and of the Balkan states which have felt obliged to become their associates in this war? The Russian representatives have insisted, very justly, very wisely, and in true spirit of modern democracy, that the conferences they have been holding with the Teutonic and Turkish statesmen should be held within open, not closed, doors, and all the world has been audience, as was desired. To whom have we been listening, then? To those who speak the spirit and intention of the Resolutions of the German Reichstag of the ninth of July last, the spirit and intention of the liberal leaders and parties of Germany, or to those who resist and defy that spirit and intention and insist upon conquest and subjugation? Or are we listening, in fact, to both, unreconciled and in open and hopeless contradiction? These are very serious and pregnant questions. Upon the answer to them depends the peace of the world.

But, whatever the results of the parleys at Brest-Litovsk, whatever the confusions of counsel and of purpose in the utterances of the spokesmen of the Central Empires, they have again attempted to acquaint the world with their objects in the war and have again challenged their adversaries to say what their objects are and what sort of settlement they would deem just and satisfactory. There is no good reason why that challenge should not be responded to, and responded to with the utmost candor. We did not wait for it. Not once, but again and again, we have laid our whole thought and purpose before the world, not in general terms only, but each time with sufficient definition to make it clear what sort of definite terms of settlement must necessarily spring out of them. Within the last week Mr. Lloyd George has spoken with admirable candor and in admirable spirit for the people and Government of Great Britain. There is no confusion of counsel among the adversaries of the Central Powers, no uncertainty of principle, no vagueness of detail. The only secrecy of counsel, the only lack of fearless frankness, the only failure to make definite statement of the objects of the war, lies with Germany and her Allies. The issues of life and death hang upon these definitions. No statesman who has the least conception of his responsibility ought for a moment to permit himself to continue this tragical and appalling outpouring of blood and treasure unless he is sure beyond a peradventure that the objects of the vital sacrifice are part and parcel of the very life of Society and that people for whom he speaks think them right and imperative as he does.

There is, moreover, a voice calling for these definitions of principle and of purpose which is, it seems to me, more thrilling and more compelling than any of the many moving voices with which the troubled air of the world is filled. It is the voice of the Russian people. They are prostrate and all but helpless, it would seem, before the grim power of Germany, which has hitherto known no relenting and no pity. Their power, apparently, is shattered. And yet their soul is not subservient. They will not yield either in principle or in action. Their conception of what is right, of what it is humane and honorable for them to accept, has been stated with a frankness, a largeness of view, a generosity of spirit, and a universal human sympathy which must challenge the admiration of every friend of mankind; and they have refused to compound their ideals or desert others that they themselves may be safe. They call to us to say what it is that we desire, in what, if in anything, our purpose and our spirit differ from theirs; and I believe that the people of the United States would wish me to respond, with utter simplicity and frankness. Whether their present leaders believe it or not, it is our heartfelt desire and hope that some way be opened whereby we may be privileged to assist the people of Russia to attain their utmost hope of liberty and ordered peace.

It will be our wish and purpose that the processes of peace, when they are begun, shall be absolutely open and that they shall involve and permit henceforth no secret understandings of any kind. The day of conquest and aggrandizement is gone by; so is also the day of secret covenants entered into in the interest of particular governments and likely at some unlooked-for moment to upset the peace of the world. It is this happy fact, now clear to the view of every public man whose thoughts do not still linger in an age that is dead and gone, which makes it possible for every nation whose purposes are consistent with justice and the peace of the world to avow now or at any other time the objects it has in view.

We entered this war because violations of right had occurred which touched us to the quick and made the life of our own people impossible unless they were corrected and the world secured once for all against their recurrence. What we demand in this war, therefore, is nothing peculiar to ourselves. It is that the world be made fit and safe to live in; and particularly that it be made safe for every peace-loving nation which, like our own, wishes to live its own life, determine its own institutions, be assured of justice and fair dealing by other peoples of the world as against force and selfish aggression. All the peoples of the world are in effect partners in this interest, and for our own part we see very clearly that unless justice be done to others it will not be done to us. The program of the world's peace, therefore, is our program; and that program, the only possible program as we see it, is this:

I. Open covenants of peace, openly arrived at, after which there shall be no private international understandings of any kind but diplomacy shall proceed always frankly and in the public view.

II. Absolute freedom of navigation upon the seas, outside territorial waters, alike in peace and in war, except as the seas may be closed in whole or in part by international action for the enforcement of international covenants.

III. The removal, so far as possible, of all economic barriers and the establishment of an equality of trade conditions among all the nations consenting to the peace and associating themselves for its maintenance.

IV. Adequate guarantees given and taken that national armaments will be reduced to the lowest point consistent with domestic safety.

V. A free, open-minded, and absolutely impartial adjustment of all colonial claims, based upon a strict observance of the principle that in determining all such questions of sovereignty the interests of the populations concerned must have equal weight with the equitable claims of the government whose title is to be determined.

VI. The evacuation of all Russian territory and such a settlement of all questions affecting Russia as will secure the best and freest cooperation of the other nations of the world in obtaining for her an unhampered and unembarrassed opportunity for the independent determination of her own political development and national policy and assure her of a sincere welcome into the society of free nations under institutions of her own choosing; and, more than a welcome, assistance also of every kind that she may need and may herself desire. The treatment accorded Russia by her sister nations in the months to come will be the acid test of their good will, of their comprehension of her needs as distinguished from their own interests, and of their intelligent and unselfish sympathy.

VII. Belgium, the whole world will agree, must be evacuated and restored, without any attempt to limit the sovereignty which she enjoys in common with all other free nations. No other single act will serve as this will serve to restore confidence among the nations in the laws which they have themselves set and determined for the government of their relations with one another. Without this healing act the whole structure and validity of international law is forever impaired.

VIII. All French territory should be freed and the invaded portions restored, and the wrong done to France by Prussia in 1871 in the matter of Alsace-Lorraine, which has unsettled the peace of the world for nearly fifty years, should be righted, in order that peace may once more be made secure in the interest of all.

IX. A readjustment of the frontiers of Italy should be effected along clearly recognizable lines of nationality.

X. The peoples of Austria-Hungary, whose place among the nations we wish to see safeguarded and assured, should be accorded the freest opportunity of autonomous development.

XI. Rumania, Serbia, and Montenegro should be evacuated; occupied territories restored; Serbia accorded free and secure access to the sea; and the relations of the several Balkan states to one another determined by friendly counsel along historically established lines of allegiance and nationality; and international guarantees of the political and economic independence and territorial integrity of the several Balkan states should be entered into.

XII. The Turkish portions of the present Ottoman Empire should be assured a secure sovereignty, but the other nationalities which are now under the Turkish rule should be assured an undoubted security of life and an absolutely unmolested opportunity of autonomous development, and the Dardanelles should be permanently opened as a free passage to the ships and commerce of all nations under international guarantees.

XIII. An independent Polish state should be erected which should include the territories inhabited by indisputably Polish populations, which should be assured a free and secure access to the sea, and whose political and economic independence and territorial integrity should be guaranteed by international covenant.

XIV. A general association of nations must be formed under specific covenants for the purpose of affording mutual guarantees of political independence and territorial integrity to great and small states alike.

In regard to these essential rectifications of wrong and assertions of right we feel ourselves to be intimate partners of all the governments and peoples associated together against the Imperialists. We cannot be separated in interest or divided in purpose. We stand together until the end.

For such arrangements and covenants we are willing to fight and to continue to fight until they are achieved; but only because we wish the right to prevail and desire a just and stable peace such as can be secured only by removing the chief provocations to war, which this program does remove. We have no jealousy of German greatness, and there is nothing in this program that impairs it. We grudge her no achievement or distinction of learning or of pacific enterprise such as have made her record very bright and very enviable. We do not wish to injure her or to block in any way her legitimate influence or power. We do not wish to fight her either with arms or with hostile arrangements of trade if she is willing to associate herself with us and the other peace-loving nations of the world in covenants of justice and law and fair dealing. We wish her only to accept a place of equality among the peoples of the world,—the new world in which we now live,—instead of a place of mastery.

Neither do we presume to suggest to her any alteration or modification of her institutions. But it is necessary, we must frankly say, and necessary as a preliminary to any intelligent dealings with her on our part, that we should know whom her spokesmen speak for when they speak to us, whether for the Reichstag majority or for the military party and the men whose creed is imperial domination.

We have spoken now, surely, in terms too concrete to admit of any further doubt or question. An evident principle runs through the whole program I have outlined. It is the principle of justice to all peoples and nationalities, and their right to live on equal terms of liberty and safety with one another, whether they be strong or weak. Unless this principle be made its foundation no part of the structure of international justice can stand. The people of the United States could act upon no other principle; and to the vindication of this principle they are ready to devote their lives, their honor, and everything that they possess. The moral climax of this the culminating and final war for human liberty has come, and they are ready to put their own strength, their own highest purpose, their own integrity and devotion to the test.

Questions and Exercises

1. In what type of activities did Woodrow Wilson participate as a student?_____

_____

2. In what two capacities did he make his most significant contributions?_____

_____

3. Describe him as a speaker._____

_____

4. What conditions prevailed in the United States after April 6, 1917, and before Wilson gave his "Fourteen Points" speech?_____

_____

5. Who constituted the audience for his "Fourteen Points" speech?

_____

6. What was the main purpose of the speech?_____

7. Describe the organizational pattern._____

_____

_____

_____

8. Give an example of Wilson's use of the historical example._____

_____

9. What form does the conclusion take?_____

_____

_____

10. What were the immediate effects of the speech?_____

_____

_____

XIII *FOR THE LEAGUE OF NATIONS*

WOODROW WILSON
(1856-1924)

The Occasion

In June 1917 the American Expeditionary Force, under the command of General John J. Pershing, reached France. A little over a year later, some two million American soldiers were in France and another two million were in training at home. The influence of these new forces and a general decline of morale of the Central Powers resulted in the first German note of October 6, 1918, accepting the Fourteen Points and asking for an armistice. The armistice came the following month, on November 11, 1918.

Wilson, with his hand-picked delegates, set sail for Paris for the Peace Conference in December, 1918. When the conference got down to serious business, Wilson at once insisted on tying the Covenant of the League of Nations to the Treaty. Although this proposal received serious objections, Wilson finally prevailed and the Council of Ten voted favorably on his cherished Article X providing for a League of Nations. On February 14, 1919, after reading the final draft to the conference, Wilson declared "a living thing is born." But it was not yet born, as Wilson was to learn upon his return home.

During the two and one-half months that Wilson had been in

France, strong opposition had built up at home. The opposition gained force gradually. Wilson lost control of Congress in the election of November, 1918; he alienated the Congress by appointing a delegation to the Peace Conference that ignored representation from the Senate; he refused to compromise in the least on his terms for the Treaty. Local opinion favored that the Peace Conference should first make the treaty with Germany and leave the League for later deliberation. This issue became a long and bitter struggle between Wilson and the Senate.

Wilson decided to take his case directly to the people by means of a cross-country speaking tour of some forty speeches. His physician warned him against such a trip but he ignored the warning. He set out on September 3, 1919, and immediately encountered receptive audiences. As a result, he began to press harder and the strain began to take its toll. Following an especially strenuous speech in Pueblo, Colorado, on September 25, he was stricken and seven days later suffered a stroke of paralysis from which he never completely recovered.

Wilson's most significant message on the tour was made at Des Moines, Iowa, on September 6, 1919, when he delivered his famous speech "For the League of Nations." Planes dropped flowers on his train as it pulled into Des Moines; thousands of people lined the streets and cheered as he rode to the auditorium; and the coliseum was packed to capacity for his address. His audience was perhaps the most sympathetic that he ever addressed; many of them had lost sons in the war. The enthusiasm of the audience spurred him to new heights of oratory and caused him to drive himself even harder than usual.

The Speech

A comparison of Wilson's speech, "For the League of Nations," with his two speeches already discussed, reveals a paradox with each. His speech for the League is more of a "fighting" speech than his "War Message"; it contains a more fervent plea for principles than his "Fourteen Points" speech. The speech reveals a man pleading for a cause dearer to him than his own life. Many people may disagree with his ideas, but few will doubt his sincerity. The speech was voted the most famous of Wilson's messages although others were given on more momentous occasions.

In his introduction, Wilson referred to a statement by the chairman as striking the keynote of his speech. He went at once to the urgency of immediate action by the United States in ratifying the Treaty. "My fellow countrymen, the world is desperately in need of the settled conditions of peace, and it cannot wait much longer. It is waiting upon us." He traced briefly our struggle for freedom during the war and concluded, "Now we are free and what shall we do with our freedom?" He discussed in turn the necessity for our ratification as an example to other nations, the importance of our leadership, the importance of ratification to our business interests, and how the League would benefit all mankind. He then criticized those who sought to prevent the League and attempted to answer their objections. He concluded by stressing the importance of having a forum where men of all nations could talk their problems through. "This is a covenant of compulsory arbitration or discussion, and just so soon as you discuss matters, my fellow citizens, peace looks in at the window."

Wilson's "League of Nations" speech contains more direct persuasion than he usually employed. He spoke with a greater sense of urgency than usual. He used dialogue to good advantage and employed the example frequently, mostly examples of action. The speech contains a balance among logical, emotional, and ethical appeals. The style is direct and forceful, less academic than many of his previous speeches. The text is from Ray G. Baker, *The Public Papers of Woodrow Wilson,* Vol. 6 (New York: Harper & Bros., 1925-27), pp. 14-30.

MR. CHAIRMAN AND FELLOW COUNTRYMEN: You make my heart very warm with your generous welcome, and I want to express my unaffected gratitude to your chairman for having so truly struck the note of an occasion like this. He has used almost the very words that were in my thought, that the world is inflamed and profoundly disturbed, and we are met to discuss the measures by which its spirit can be quieted and its affairs turned to the right courses of human life. My fellow countrymen, the world is desperately in need of the settled conditions of peace, and it cannot wait much longer. It is waiting upon us.

That is the thought, that is the burdensome thought, upon my heart to-night, that the world is waiting for the verdict of the Nation to which it looked for leadership and which it thought would be the last that would ask the world to wait.

My fellow citizens, the world is not at peace. I suppose that it is difficult for one who has not had some touch of the hot passion of the other side of the sea to realize how all the passions that have been slumbering for ages have been uncovered and released by the tragedy of this war. We speak of the tragedy of this war, but the tragedy that lay back of it was greater than the war itself, because back of it lay long ages in which the legitimate freedom of men was suppressed. Back of it lay long ages of recurrent war in which little groups of men, closeted in capitals, determined whether the sons of the land over which they ruled should go out upon the field and shed their blood. For what? For liberty? No; not for liberty, but for the aggrandizement of those who ruled them. And this had been slumbering in the hearts of men. They had felt the suppression of it. They had felt the mastery of those whom they had not chosen as their masters. They had felt the oppression of laws which did not admit them to the equal exercise of human rights. Now, all of this is released and uncovered and men glare at one another and say, "Now we are free and what shall we do with our freedom?"

What happened in Russia was not a sudden and accidental thing. The people of Russia were maddened with the suppression of Czarism. When at last the chance came to throw off those chains, they threw them off, at first with hearts full of confidence and hope, and then they found out that they had been again deceived. There was no assembly chosen to frame a constitution for them, or, rather, there was an assembly chosen to choose a constitution for them and it was suppressed and dispersed, and a little group of men just as selfish, just as ruthless, just as pitiless, as the agents of the Czar himself, assumed control and exercised their power by terror and not by right. And in other parts of Europe the poison spread—the poison of disorder, the poison of revolt, the poison of chaos. And do you honestly think, my fellow citizens, that none of that poison has got in the veins of this free people? Do you not know that the world is all now one single whispering gallery? Those antennae of the wireless telegraph are the symbols of our age. All the impulses of mankind are thrown out upon the air and reach to the ends of the earth; quietly upon steamships, silently under the cover of the Postal Service, with the tongue of the wireless and the tongue of the telegraph, all the suggestions of disorder are spread through the world. Money coming from nobody knows where is deposited by the millions in capitals like Stockholm, to be used for the propaganda of disorder and discontent and dissolution throughout the world, and men look you calmly in the face in America and say they are for that sort of revolution, when that sort of revolution means government by terror, government by force, not government by vote. It is the negation of everything that is American; but it is spreading, and so long as disorder continues, so long as the world is kept waiting for the answer to the question, What kind of peace are we going to have and what kind of guarantees are there to be behind that peace, that poison will steadily spread more and more rapidly, spread until it may be that even this beloved land of ours will be distracted and distorted by it?

That is what is concerning me, my fellow countrymen. I know the splendid steadiness of the American people, but, my fellow citizens, the whole world needs that steadiness, and the American people are the make-weight in the fortunes of mankind. How long are we going to debate into which scale we will throw that magnificent equipoise that belongs to us? How long shall we be kept waiting for the answer whether the world may trust us or despise us? They have looked to us for leadership. They have looked to us for example. They have built their peace upon the basis of our suggestions. That great volume that contains the treaty of peace is drawn along the specifications laid down by the American Government, and now the world stands amazed because an authority in America hesitates whether it will indorse an American document or not.

You know what the necessity of peace is. Political liberty can exist only when there is peace. Social reform can take place only when there is peace. The settlement of every question that concerns our daily life waits for peace. I have been receiving delegations in Washington of men engaged in the service of the Government temporarily in the administration of the railways, and I have had to say to them, "My friends, I cannot tell what the railways can earn until commerce is restored to its normal courses. Until I can tell what the railroads can earn I cannot tell what the wages that the railroads can pay will be. I cannot suggest what the increase of freight and passenger rates will be to meet these increases in wages if the rates must be increased. I cannot tell yet whether it will be necessary to increase the rates or not, and I must ask you to wait." But they are not the only people that have come to see me. There are all sorts of adjustments necessary in this country. I have asked representatives of capital and labor to come to Washington next month and confer—confer about the fundamental thing of our life at present; that is to say, the conditions of labor. Do you realize, my fellow citizens, that all through the world the one central question of civilization is, "What shall be the conditions of labor?" The profound unrest in Europe is due to the doubt prevailing as to what shall be the conditions of labor, and I need not tell you that that unrest is spreading to America.

In the midst of the treaty of peace is a Magna Charta, a great guarantee for labor. It provides that labor shall have the counsels of the world devoted to the discussion of its conditions and of its betterment, and labor all over the world is waiting to know whether America is going to take part in those conferences or not. The confidence of the men who sat at Paris was such that they put it in the document that the first meeting of the labor conference under that part of the treaty should take place in Washington upon the invitation of the President of the United States. I am going to issue that invitation, whether we can attend the conference or not. But think of the mortification! Think of standing by in Washington itself and seeing the world take counsel upon the fundamental matter of civilization without us. The thing is inconceivable, but it is true. The world is waiting, waiting to see, not whether we will take part but whether we will serve and lead, for it has expected us to lead. I want to testify that the most touching and thrilling thing that has ever happened to me was what happened almost every day when I was in Paris. Delegations from all over the world came to me to solicit the friendship of America. They frankly told us that they were not sure they could trust anybody else, but that they did absolutely trust us to do them justice and to see that justice was done them. Why, some of them came from countries which I have, to my shame, to admit that I never heard of before, and I had to ask as privately as possible what language they spoke. Fortunately they always had an interpreter, but I always wanted to know at least what family of languages they were speaking. The touching thing was that from the ends of the earth, from little pocketed valleys, where I did not know that a separate people lived, there came men—men of dignity, men of intellectual parts, men entertaining in their thought and in their memories a great tradition, some of the oldest people of the world—and they came and sat at the feet of the youngest nation of the world and said, "Teach us the way to liberty."

That is the attitude of the world, and reflect, my fellow countrymen, upon the reaction, the reaction of despair, that would come if America said: "We do not want to lead you. You must do without our advice. You must shift without us." Now, are we going to bring about a peace, for which everything waits? We cannot bring it about by doing nothing. I have been very much amazed and very much amused, if I could be amused in such critical circumstances, to see that the statesmanship of some gentlemen consists in the very interesting proposition that we do nothing at all. I had heard of standing pat before, but I never had before heard of standpatism going to the length of saying it is none of our business and we do not care what happens to the rest of the world.

Your chairman made a profoundly true remark just now. The isolation of the United States is at an end, not because we chose to go into the politics of the world, but because by the sheer genius of this people and the growth of our power we have become a determining factor in the history of mankind, and after you have become a determining factor you cannot remain isolated, whether you want to or not. Isolation ended by the processes of history, not by the processes of our independent choice, and the processes of history merely fulfilled the prediction of the men who founded our Republic. Go back and read some of the immortal sentences of the men that assisted to frame this Government and see how they set up a standard to which they intended that the nations of the world should rally. They said to the people of the world, "Come to us; this is the home of liberty; this is the place where mankind can learn how to govern their own affairs and straighten out their own difficulties," and the world did come to us.

Look at your neighbor. Look at the statistics of the people of your State. Look at the statistics of the people of the United States. They have come, their hearts full of hope and confidence, from practically every nation in the world, to constitute a portion of our strength and of our hope and a contribution to our achievement. Sometimes I feel like taking off my hat to some of those immigrants. I was born an American. I could not help it, but they chose to be Americans. They were not born Americans. They saw this star in the west rising over the peoples of the world and they said, "That is the star of hope and the star of salvation. We will set our footsteps towards the west and join that great body of men whom God has blessed with the vision of liberty." I honor those men. I say, "You made a deliberate choice which showed that you saw what the drift and history of mankind was." I am very grateful, I may say in parentheses, that I did not have to make that choice. I am grateful that ever since I can remember I have breathed this blessed air of freedom. I am grateful that every instinct in me, every drop of blood in me remembers and stands up and shouts at the traditions of the United States. But some gentlemen are not shouting now about that. They are saying, "Yes; we made a great promise to mankind, but it will cost too much to redeem it." My fellow citizens, that is not the spirit of America, and you cannot have peace, you cannot have even your legitimate part in the business of the world unless you are partners with the rest. If you are going to say to the world, "We will stand off and see what we can get out of this," the world will see to it that you do not get anything out of it. If it is your deliberate choice that instead of being friends you will be rivals and antagonists, then you will get exactly what rivals and antagonists always get, just as little as can be grudgingly vouchsafed you.

Yet you must keep the world on its feet. Is there any business man here who would be willing to see the world go bankrupt and the business of the world stop? Is there any man here who does not know that America is the only nation left by the war in a position to see that the world does go on with its business? And is it your idea that if we lend our money, as we must, to men whom we have bitterly disappointed, that money will bring back to us the largess to which we are entitled? I do not like to argue this thing on this basis, but if you want to talk business, I am ready to talk business. If it is a matter of how much you are going to get from your money, I say you will not get half as much as antagonists as you will get as partners. Think that over, if you have none of that thing that is so lightly spoken of, known as altruism. And, believe me, my fellow countrymen, the only people in the world who are going to reap the harvest of the future are the people who can entertain ideals, who can follow ideals to the death.

I was saying to another audience to-day that one of the most beautiful stories I know is the story that we heard in France about the first effect of the American soldiers when they got over there. The French did not believe at first, the British did not believe, that we could finally get 2,000,000 men over there. The most that they hoped at first was that a few American soldiers would restore their morale, for let me say that their morale was gone. The beautiful story to which I referred is this, the testimony that all of them rendered that they got their morale back the minute they saw the eyes of those boys. Here were not only soldiers. There was no curtain in front of the retina of those eyes. They were American eyes. They were eyes that had seen visions. They were eyes the possessors of which had brought with them a great ardor for a supreme cause, and the reason those boys never stopped was that their eyes were lifted to the horizon. They saw a city not built with hands. They saw a citadel towards which their steps were bent where dwelt the oracles of God himself. And on the battlefield were found German orders to commanders here and there to see to it that the Americans did not get lodgment in particular places, because if they ever did you never could get them out. They had gone to Europe to go the whole way towards the realization of the teaching which their fathers had handed down to them. There never were crusaders that went to the Holy Land in the old ages that we read about that were more truly devoted to a holy cause than these gallant, incomparable sons of America.

My fellow citizens, you have got to make up your minds, because, after all, it is you who are going to make up the minds of this country. I do not owe a report or the slightest responsibility to anybody but you. I do not mean only you in this hall, though I am free to admit that this is just as good a sample of America as you can find anywhere, and the sample looks mighty good to me. I mean you and the millions besides you, thoughtful, responsible American men and women all over this country. They are my bosses, and I am mighty glad to be their servant. I have come out upon this journey not to fight anybody, but to report to you, and I am free to predict that if you credit the report there will be no fighting. It is not only necessary that we should make peace with Germany and make peace with Austria, and see that a reasonable peace is made with Turkey and Bulgaria—that is not only not all of it, but it is a very dangerous beginning if you do not add something to it. I said just now that the peace with Germany, and the same is true of the pending peace with Austria, was made upon American specifications, not unwillingly. Do not let me leave the impression on your mind that the representatives of America in Paris had to insist and force their principles upon the rest. That is not true. Those principles were accepted before we got over there, and the men I dealt with carried them out in absolute good faith; but they were our principles, and at the heart of them lay this, that there must be a free Poland, for example.

I wonder if you realize what that means. We had to collect the pieces of Poland. For a long time one piece had belonged to Russia, and we cannot get a clear title to that yet. Another part belonged to Austria. We got a title to that. Another part belonged to Germany and we have settled the title to that. But we found Germany also in possession of other pieces of territory occupied predominately or exclusively by patriotic Poles, and we said to Germany, "You will have to give that up, too; that belongs to Poland." Not because it is ground, but because those people there are Poles and want to be parts of Poland, and it is not our business to force any sovereignty upon anybody who does not want to live under it. When we had determined the boundaries of Poland we set it up and recognized it as an independent Republic. There is a minister, a diplomatic representative, of the United States at Warsaw right now in virtue of our formal recognition of the Republic of Poland.

But upon Poland center some of the dangers of the future. South of

Poland is Bohemia, which we cut away from the Austrian combination. Below Bohemia is Hungary, which can no longer rely upon the assistant strength of Austria, and below her is an enlarged Rumania. Alongside of Rumania is the new Slavic Kingdom, that never could have won its own independence, which had chafed under the chains of Austria-Hungary, but never could throw them off. We have said, "The fundamental wrongs of history center in these regions. These people have the right to govern their own Government and control their own fortunes." That is at the heart of the treaty, but, my fellow citizens, this is at the heart of the future: The business men of Germany did not want the war that we have passed through. The bankers and the manufacturers and the merchants knew that it was unspeakable folly. Why? Because Germany by her industrial genius was beginning to dominate the world economically, and all she had to do was to wait for about two more generations when her credit, her merchandise, her enterprise, would have covered all the parts of the world that the great fighting nations did not control. The formula of pan-Germanism, you remember, was Bremen to Bagdad—Bremen on the North Sea to Bagdad in Persia. These countries that we have set up as the new home of liberty lie right along that road. If we leave them there without the guarantee that the combined force of the world will assure their independence and their territorial integrity, we have only to wait a short generation when our recent experience will be repeated. We did not let Germany dominate the world this time. Are we then? If Germany had known then that all the other fighting nations of the world would combine to prevent her action, she never would have dreamed of attempting it. If Germany had known—this is the common verdict of every man familiar with the politics of Europe—if Germany had known that England would go in, she never would have started it. If she had known that America would come in, she never would have dreamed of it. And now the only way to make it certain that there never will be another world war like that is that we should assist in guaranteeing the peace and its settlement.

It is a very interesting circumstance, my fellow countrymen, that the League of Nations will contain all the nations of the world, great and small, except Germany, and Germany is merely put on probation. We have practically said to Germany, "If it turns out that you really have had a change of heart and have gotten nonsense out of your system; if it really does turn out that you have substituted a genuine self-governing Republic for a Kingdom where a few men on Wilhelmstrasse plotted the destiny of the world, then we will let you in as partners, because then you will be respectable." In the meantime, accepting the treaty, Germany's army is reduced to 100,000 men, and she has promised to give up all the war material over and above what is necessary for 100,000 men. For a nation of 60,000,000! She has surrendered to the world. She has said, "Our fate is in your hands. We are ready to do what you tell us to do." The rest of the world is combined, and the interesting circumstance is that the rest of the world, excluding us, will continue combined if we do not go into it. Some gentlemen seem to think they can break up this treaty and prevent this League by not going into it. Not at all.

I can give you an interesting circumstance. There is the settlement, which you have heard so much discussed, about that rich and ancient Province of Shantung in China. I do not like that settlement any better than you do, but these were the circumstances: In order to induce Japan to cooperate in the war and clear the Pacific of the German power England, and subsequently France, bound themselves without any qualification to see to it that Japan got anything in China that Germany had, and that Japan would take it away from her, upon the strength of which promise Japan proceeded to take Kiauchau and occupy the portions of Shantung Province, which had been ceded by China for a term of years to Germany. The most that could be got out of it was that, in view of the fact that America had nothing to do with it, the Japanese were ready to promise that they would give up every item of sovereignty which Germany would otherwise have enjoyed in Shantung Province and return it without restriction to China, and that they would retain in the Province only the economic concessions such as other nations already had elsewhere in China—though you do not hear anything about that—concessions in the railway and the mines which had become attached to the railway for operative purposes. But suppose that you say that is not enough. Very well, then, stay out of the treaty, and how will that accomplish anything? England and France are bound and cannot escape their obligation. Are you going to institute a war against Japan and France and England to get Shantung back for China? That is an enterprise which does not commend itself to the present generation.

I am putting it in brutal terms, my fellow citizens, but that is the fact. By disagreeing to that provision, we accomplish nothing for China. On the contrary, we stay out of the only combination of the counsels of nations in which we can be of service to China. With China as a member of the League of Nations, and Japan as a member of the League of Nations, and America as a member of the League of Nations, there confronts every one of them that now famous Article X, by which every member of the League agrees to respect and preserve the territorial integrity and existing political independence of all the other member States. Do not let anybody persuade you that you can take that article out and have a peaceful world. That cuts at the root of the German war. That cuts at the root of the outrage against Belgium. That cuts at the root of the outrage against France. That pulls that vile, unwholesome Upas tree of Pan-Germanism up by the roots, and it pulls all other "pans" up, too. Every land-grabbing nation is served notice: "Keep on your own territory. Mind your own business. That territory belongs to those people and they can do with it what they please, provided they do not invade other people's rights by the use they make of it." My fellow citizens, the thing is going to be done whether we are in it or not. If we are in it, then we are going to be the determining factor in the development of civilization. If we are out of it, we ourselves are going to watch every other nation with suspicion, and we will be justified, too; and we are going to be watched with suspicion. Every movement of trade, every relationship of manufacture, every question of raw materials, every matter that affects the intercourse of the world, will be impeded by the consciousness that America wants to hold off and get something which she is not willing to share with the rest of mankind. I am painting the picture for you, because I know that it is as tolerable to you as it is to me. But do not go away with the impression, I beg you, that I think there is any doubt about the issue. The only thing that can be accomplished is delay. The ultimate outcome will be the triumphant acceptance of the treaty and the League.

Let me pay the tribute which it is only just that I should pay to some of the men who have been, I believe, misunderstood in this business. It is only a handful of men, my fellow citizens, who are trying to defeat the treaty or to prevent the League. The great majority, in official bodies and out, are scrutinizing it, as it is perfectly legitimate that they should scrutinize it, to see if it is necessary that they should qualify it in any way, and my knowledge of their conscience, my knowledge of their public principle, makes me certain that they will sooner or later see that it is safest, since it is all expressed in the plainest English that the English dictionary affords, not to qualify it—to accept it as it is. I have been a student of the English language all my life and I do not see a single obscure sentence in the whole document. Some gentlemen either have not read it or do not understand the English language; but, fortunately, on the right-hand page it is printed in English and on the left-hand page it is printed in French. Now, if they do not understand English, I hope they will get a French dictionary and dig out the meaning on that side. The French is a very precise language, more precise than the English language, I am told. I am not on a speaking acquaintance with it, but I am told that it is the most precise language in Europe, and that any given phrase in French always means the same thing. That cannot be said of English. In order to satisfy themselves, I hope these gentlemen will master the French version and then be reassured that there are no lurking monsters in that document; that there are no sinister purposes; that everything is said in the frankest way.

For example, they have been very much worried at the phrase that nothing in the document shall be taken as impairing in any way the validity of such regional understandings as the Monroe Doctrine. They say: "Why put in 'such regional understandings as'? What other understandings are there? Have you got something up your sleeve? Is there going to be a Monroe Doctrine in Asia? Is there going to be a Monroe Doctrine in China?" Why, my fellow citizens, the phrase was written in perfect innocence. The men that I was associated with said, "It is not wise to put a specific thing that belongs only to one nation in a document like this. We do not know of any other regional understanding like it, we never heard of any other; we never expect to hear of any other, but there might some day be some other, and so we will say 'such regional understandings as the Monroe Doctrine,' " and their phrase was intended to give right of way to the Monroe Doctrine in the Western Hemisphere. I reminded the Committee on Foreign Relations of the Senate the other day that the conference I held with them was not the first conference I had held about the League of Nations. When I came back to this our own dear country in March last I held a conference at the White House with the Senate Committee on Foreign Relations, and they made various suggestions as to how the Covenant should be altered in phraseology. I carried those suggestions back to Paris, and every one of them was accepted. I think that is a sufficient guarantee that no mischief was intended. The whole document is of the same plain, practical, explicit sort, and it secures peace, my fellow citizens, in the only way in which peace can be secured.

I remember, if I may illustrate a very great thing with a very trivial thing, I had two acquaintances who were very much addicted to profanity. Their friends were distressed about it. It subordinated a rich vocabulary which they might otherwise have cultivated, and so we induced them to agree that they never would swear inside the corporate limits, that if they wanted to swear they would go out of town. The first time the passion of anger came upon them they rather sheepishly got in a street car and went out of town to swear, and by the time they got out of town they did not want to swear. That very homely illustration illustrates in my mind the value of discussion. Let me remind you that every fighting nation in the world is going to belong to this League, because we are going to belong to it, and they all make this solemn engagement with each other, that they will not resort to war in the case of any controversy until they have done one or other of two things, until they have either submitted the question at issue to arbitration, in which case they promise to abide by the verdict whatever it may be, or, if they do not want to submit it to arbitration, have submitted it to discussion by the council of the League.

They agree to give the council six months to discuss the matter, to supply the council with all the pertinent facts regarding it, and that, after the opinion of the council is rendered, they will not then go to war if they are dissatisfied with the opinion until three more months have elapsed. They give nine months in which to spread the whole

matter before the judgment of mankind, and if they violate this promise, if any one of them violates it, the Covenant prescribes that that
violation shall in itself constitute an act of war against the other members of the League. It does not provide that there shall be war. On the
contrary, it provides for something very much more effective than war.
It provides that that nation, that covenant-breaking nation, shall be
absolutely cut off from intercourse of every kind with the other nations
of the world; that no merchandise shall be shipped out of it or into it;
that no postal messages shall go into it or come out of it; that no tele-
graphic messages shall cross its borders; and that the citizens of the
other member States shall not be permitted to have any intercourse
or transactions whatever with its citizens or its citizens with them.
There is not a single nation in Europe that can stand that boycott for
six months. There is not a single nation in Europe that is self-sufficing
in its resources of food or anything else that can stand that for six
months. And in those circumstances we are told that this Covenant
is a covenant of war. It is the most drastic covenant of peace that was
ever conceived, and its processes are the processes of peace. The nation
that does not abide by its covenants is sent to coventry, is taboo, is put
out of the society of covenant-respecting nations.

This is a covenant of compulsory arbitration or discussion, and just
so soon as you discuss matters, my fellow citizens, peace looks in at the
window. Did you ever really sit down and discuss matters with your
neighbor when you had a difference and come away in the same temper
that you went in? One of the difficulties in our labor situation is that
there are some employers who will not meet their employees face to
face and talk with them. I have never known an instance in which such
a meeting and discussion took place that both sides did not come away
in a softened temper and with an access of respect for the other side.
The processes of frank discussion are the processes of peace not only,
but the processes of settlement, and those are the processes which are
set up for all the powerful nations of the world.

I want to say that this is an unparalleled achievement of thoughtful
civilization. To my dying day I shall esteem it the crowning privilege
of my life to have been permitted to put my name to a document like
that; and in my judgment, my fellow citizens, when passion is cooled

and men take a sober, second thought, they are all going to feel that the supreme thing that America did was to help bring this about and then put her shoulder to the great chariot of justice and of peace which was going to lead men along in that slow and toilsome march, toilsome and full of the kind of agony that brings bloody sweat, but nevertheless going up a slow incline to those distant heights upon which will shine at the last the serene light of justice, suffusing a whole world in blissful peace.

Questions and Exercises

1. Why did Woodrow Wilson make his cross-country speaking tour in the fall of 1919?_____

2. What personal calamity befell Wilson following his speech at Pueblo, Colorado, on September 25, 1919?_____

3. Where did he present his speech, "For the League of Nations"?
_____
When?_____

4. Who composed his audience?_____

5. What was the central idea of the speech?_____
_____
_____

6. Describe his organizational pattern._____
_____

7. Give one example of emotional appeal._____
_____

8. List the forms of support in order of their importance to the speech._____
_____
_____

9. What accounts for the forceful style of this speech?_____
_____

10. Why do you think this speech was voted Wilson's best?_____
_____
_____

XIV *FIRST INAUGURAL ADDRESS*

FRANKLIN D. ROOSEVELT
(1882-1945)

The Speaker

Franklin D. Roosevelt used speaking more extensively to carry out his program than any other President in history. His was literally "the voice heard around the world." His effective speaking carried him through four successful campaigns for the Presidency, enabled him to advance his New Deal program through hundreds of fireside chats over radio, and caused him to help shape the future of the United States by numerous speeches on momentous occasions.

Almost all lists of the great men in American history include our wartime Presidents—Washington, Lincoln, Wilson, and Roosevelt. They faced grave crises that helped shape their destiny. Perhaps other equally capable men did not encounter crises that brought forth their best efforts. Roosevelt attacked two such history-making problems— the economic depression and World War II. The two speeches by Roosevelt included in this anthology reveal him at his best in meeting both crises.

Franklin Delano Roosevelt was born on January 30, 1882, at Hyde Park, New York. He was the only child of James and Sara Delano Roosevelt—wealthy, aristocratic, highly respected citizens whose ancestors were among the early arrivals on this continent. Roosevelt's early training came from private tutors, from extensive travel abroad, and from his mother. He had all the advantages wealth and social position could offer. At fourteen he was enrolled in fashionable Groton School and four years later in Harvard College. After his graduation from Harvard in 1904, he enrolled in the School of Law of Columbia University. After being admitted to the bar in 1907, he left Columbia without graduating and joined the law firm of Carter, Ledyard, and Milburn. In 1905 he had married Anna Eleanor Roosevelt, who was his fifth cousin and a niece of President Theodore Roosevelt.

Roosevelt was a good, but not a brilliant, student. At Groton he made his best grades in foreign languages and mathematics, his poorest in English composition; his general average was B. When he took his entrance examinations for Harvard, however, he made the highest grade of any Groton student. Roosevelt showed unusual interest in both oral and written communication, as evidenced by his enthusiasm for debate and his editorship of *The Crimson*, the Harvard newspaper. His favorite courses at Harvard were history and government. He was especially interested and proficient in reading aloud. His education prepared him well for his chief political attribute—effective speech-making.

Roosevelt entered the race for the New York Senate in 1910 from his traditionally Republican home district. Since for twenty-eight years this district had voted Republican, Roosevelt was given little chance for victory. He won, however, by waging a vigorous campaign that included traveling throughout his district in a bright red automobile, a bold venture for that day.

Roosevelt attracted national attention in 1912 by vigorously supporting Woodrow Wilson for President against his distant cousin, Theodore Roosevelt. The following year he was appointed Assistant Secretary of the Navy, an important assignment because of the First World War. Roosevelt served the Navy well for seven years and was rewarded in 1920 by being nominated for the Vice-Presidency on the ticket with James M. Cox. The defeat of the Democratic ticket was a disappointment, but not nearly so severe a blow as when in August, 1921, he was stricken with poliomyelitis which caused a complete paralysis of both legs. His heroic struggle for recovery and his organization of the Warm Springs Foundation in Georgia were applauded by almost all Americans. Although his illness kept him from active participation in politics for the next seven years, the year 1928 witnessed his successful campaign for Governor of New York and his nomination of Alfred E. Smith for President at the National Democratic Convention held in Houston, Texas.

Roosevelt was re-elected Governor of New York in 1930 and was nominated for President on the Democratic ticket in 1932. He was elected President and was re-elected each term until his death on April 12, 1945, less than three months after he took office for a fourth term.

The Occasion

In the fall of 1929, when the country seemed at the peak of prosperity, the United States was suddenly plunged into the most devastating economic crisis in its history. On a single day, October 29, more than 16,000,000 shares of stock were dumped on the market of the New York Stock Exchange; prime stocks of major corporations fell an average of forty points. A major panic was on—banks and other business enterprises began to fail; the farmers' plight grew intolerable; factories and shops were closed; unemployment mounted to unbelievable proportions; hunger and ruin prevailed.

Leaders in business and government at first considered the conditions "just another panic," the result of our periodic economic depressions. President Hoover insisted that prosperity was "just around the corner," that the country would soon come out of the depression into another period of prosperity. As the depression continued, an attitude gradually arose that if capitalists could not conduct financial affairs to avoid periodic depressions and cope with the existing conditions, the government would have to assume the responsibility.

Contrary to popular opinion, Hoover took decisive action. He asked Congress to provide for a large-scale program of public works, established the Reconstruction Finance Corporation, created the Home Owners' Loan Corporation, and called upon the governors of the states for governmental controls. He was busily engaged in wrestling with problems of the depression as the presidential campaign of 1932 approached.

Paradoxically, the Democratic majority in the House of Representatives since 1930 had done little to cope with the depression. Neither did their presidential nominee, Franklin D. Roosevelt, indicate that he favored strong governmental controls. Roosevelt was known as a progressive, but not as an advocate of governmental regulation of business. Nevertheless, following a vigorous campaign, Roosevelt won the election handily—22,800,000 popular votes to 15,700,000 for Hoover and an electoral majority of 472 to 59.

Between the time of Roosevelt's election in November, 1932, and his inauguration in March, 1933, another panic plunged the country into greater financial despair. As Roosevelt approached his inauguration, some 13,000,000 people or more than one-fourth of the laboring forces were unemployed; business and industry were paralyzed; the farmer let his crops rot in the field because prices would not pay for the harvest; banks were closing throughout the country. The United States was in the depths of the depression.

Thus, as the time for Roosevelt's "First Inaugural Address" approached, an attitude of fear and loss of faith in our economic system prevailed. Although the attitude was perhaps more psychological than logical, economic despair had created unusual interest in Roosevelt's election. Some 500,000 people poured into Washington for the inauguration. More than 100,000 heard him over the public-address system and millions heard him over the radio networks, not only in the United States but in many foreign countries.

The Speech

Harry L. Hopkins, Roosevelt's close friend and adviser, wrote that he thought Roosevelt's "First Inaugural Address" was the best speech he ever made. The professors who selected the speeches in this anthology agree with Mr. Hopkins. They voted the speech as not only Roosevelt's best, but the best of the contemporary period.

The speech, given on March 4, 1933, required twenty minutes to deliver. The original draft was written by Roosevelt in his own handwriting on the evening of February 27, at his home in Hyde Park. After consulting with his Cabinet, he rewrote it on the evening before his inauguration and continued to make minor changes the next morning. Roosevelt explained that his principal purpose was to allay the fears which gripped the American people.

Roosevelt began by stating the necessity for facing economic conditions frankly and boldly—that there was no "need to shrink from honestly facing conditions. . . ." His next, and now famous, statement expressed the essence of his philosophy, ". . . let me assert my firm belief that the only thing we have to fear is fear itself. . . ."

The arrangement may be characterized as the problem-solution type. He reviewed the existing economic plight and then explained his proposals to remedy conditions. In one short paragraph he showed the seriousness of the problem as a whole; then he developed in detail the problem he considered the most serious—unemployment. He proposed six corrective measures: (1) encouraging direct governmental recruiting, (2) redistributing the population, (3) raising the value of agricultural products, (4) preventing foreclosures on homes and farms, (5) decreasing costs of governments, and (6) unifying relief activities. Next, he stated two safeguards—supervision of all banking and credits and prevention of speculation with other people's money. He then explained how he intended to effect his proposed changes and how the people of the country could help.

Roosevelt used little specific support. He relied on the prestige of his office and the general knowledge about prevailing economic conditions for acceptance of his contentions. Rather than arguing his points, he explained the process that he went through in reaching his conclusions. He seemed to sense that the people wanted a program of action, not arguments.

The speech shows the direct and forceful style for which Roosevelt became famous. His use of the telling phrase and his choice of colorful language permeate the speech. His choice of language corresponds with his direct, conversational, and communicative delivery.

The text that follows is from *Inaugural Addresses of the Presidents of the United States*, 87th Congress, 1st Session, House Document No. 218. (Washington, D.C.: United States Government Printing Office, 1961), pp. 235-239.

PRESIDENT HOOVER, MR. CHIEF JUSTICE, MY FRIENDS: This is a day of national consecration, and I am certain that my fellow-Americans expect that on my induction into the Presidency I will address them with a candor and a decision which the present situation of our nation impels.

This is pre-eminently the time to speak the truth, the whole truth, frankly and boldly. Nor need we shrink from honestly facing conditions in our country today. This great nation will endure as it has endured, will revive and will prosper.

So first of all let me assert my firm belief that the only thing we have to fear is fear itself—nameless, unreasoning, unjustified terror which paralyzes needed efforts to convert retreat into advance.

In every dark hour of our national life a leadership of frankness and vigor has met with that understanding and support of the people themselves which is essential to victory. I am convinced that you will again give that support to leadership in these critical days.

In such a spirit on my part and on yours we face our common difficulties. They concern, thank God, only material things. Values have shrunken to fantastic levels; taxes have risen; our ability to pay has fallen; government of all kinds is faced by serious curtailment of income; the means of exchange are frozen in the currents of trade; the withered leaves of industrial enterprise lie on every side; farmers find no markets for their produce; the savings of many years in thousands of families are gone.

More important, a host of unemployed citizens face the grim problem of existence, and an equally great number toil with little return. Only a foolish optimist can deny the dark realities of the moment.

Yet our distress comes from no failure of substance. We are stricken by no plague of locusts. Compared with the perils which our forefathers conquered because they believed and were not afraid, we have still much to be thankful for. Nature still offers her bounty and human efforts have multiplied it. Plenty is at our doorstep, but a generous use of it languishes in the very sight of the supply.

Primarily, this is because the rulers of the exchange of mankind's goods have failed through their own stubbornness and their own incompetence, have admitted their failure and abdicated. Practices of the unscrupulous money changers stand indicted in the court of public opinion, rejected by the hearts and minds of men.

True, they have tried, but their efforts have been cast in the pattern of an outworn tradition. Faced by failure of credit, they have proposed only the lending of more money.

Stripped of the lure of profit by which to induce our people to follow their false leadership, they have resorted to exhortations, pleading tearfully for restored confidence. They know only the rules of a generation of self-seekers.

They have no vision, and when there is no vision the people perish.

The money changers have fled from their high seats in the temple of our civilization. We may now restore that temple to the ancient truths.

The measure of the restoration lies in the extent to which we apply social values more noble than mere monetary profit.

Happiness lies not in the mere possession of money; it lies in the joy of achievement, in the thrill of creative effort.

The joy and moral stimulation of work no longer must be forgotten in the mad chase of evanescent profits. These dark days will be worth all they cost us if they teach us that our true destiny is not to be ministered unto but to minister to ourselves and to our fellow-men.

Recognition of the falsity of material wealth as the standard of success goes hand in hand with the abandonment of the false belief that public office and high political position are to be valued only by the standards of pride of place and personal profit; and there must be an end to a conduct in banking and in business which too often has given to a sacred trust the likeness of callous and selfish wrongdoing.

Small wonder that confidence languishes, for it thrives only on honesty, on honor, on the sacredness of obligations, on faithful protection, on unselfish performance. Without them it cannot live.

Restoration calls, however, not for changes in ethics alone. This nation asks for action, and action now.

Our greatest primary task is to put people to work. This is no unsolvable problem if we face it wisely and courageously.

It can be accomplished in part by direct recruiting by the government itself, treating the task as we would treat the emergency of a war, but at the same time, through this employment, accomplishing greatly needed projects to stimulate and reorganize the use of our natural resources.

Hand in hand with this, we must frankly recognize the over-balance of population in our industrial centers and, by engaging on a national scale in a redistribution, endeavor to provide a better use of the land for those best fitted for the land.

The task can be helped by definite efforts to raise the values of agricultural products and with this the power to purchase the output of our cities.

It can be helped by preventing realistically the tragedy of the growing loss, through foreclosure, of our small homes and our farms.

It can be helped by insistence that the Federal, State and local governments act forthwith on the demand that their cost be drastically reduced.

It can be helped by the unifying of relief activities which today are often scattered, uneconomical and unequal. It can be helped by national planning for and supervision of all forms of transportation and of communications and other utilities which have a definite public character.

There are many ways in which it can be helped, but it can never be helped merely by talking about it. We must act, and act quickly.

Finally, in our progress toward a resumption of work we require two safeguards against a return of the evils of the old order; there must be a strict supervision of all banking and credits and investments; there must be an end to speculation with other people's money, and there must be provision for an adequate but sound currency.

These are the lines of attack. I shall presently urge upon a new Congress in special session detailed measures for their fulfillment, and I shall seek the immediate assistance of the several States.

Through this program of action we address ourselves to putting our own national house in order and making income balance outgo.

Our international trade relations, though vastly important, are, in point of time and necessity, secondary to the establishment of a sound national economy.

I favor as a practical policy the putting of first things first. I shall spare no effort to restore world trade by international economic readjustment, but the emergency at home cannot wait on that accomplishment.

The basic thought that guides these specific means of national recovery is not narrowly nationalistic.

It is the insistence, as a first consideration, upon the interdependence of the various elements in, and parts of, the United States—a recognition of the old and permanently important manifestation of the American spirit of the pioneer.

It is the way to recovery. It is the immediate way. It is the strongest assurance that the recovery will endure.

In the field of world policy I would dedicate this nation to the policy of the good neighbor—the neighbor who resolutely respects himself and, because he does so, respects the rights of others—the neighbor who respects his obligations and respects the sanctity of his agreements in and with a world of neighbors.

If I read the temper of our people correctly, we now realize as we have never before, our interdependence on each other; that we cannot merely take, but we must give as well; that if we are to go forward we must move as a trained and loyal army willing to sacrifice for the good of a common discipline, because, without such discipline, no progress is made, no leadership becomes effective.

We are, I know, ready and willing to submit our lives and property to such discipline because it makes possible a leadership which aims at a larger good.

This I propose to offer, pledging that the larger purposes will bind upon us all as a sacred obligation with a unity of duty hitherto evoked only in time of armed strife.

With this pledge taken, I assume unhesitatingly the leadership of this great army of our people, dedicated to a disciplined attack upon our common problems.

Action in this image and to this end is feasible under the form of government which we have inherited from our ancestors.

Our Constitution is so simple and practical that it is possible always to meet extraordinary needs by changes in emphasis and arrangement without loss of essential form.

That is why our constitutional system has proved itself the most superbly enduring political mechanism the modern world has produced. It has met every stress of vast expansion of territory, of foreign wars, of bitter internal strife, of world relations.

It is to be hoped that the normal balance of executive and legislative authority may be wholly adequate to meet the unprecedented task before us. But it may be that an unprecedented demand and need for undelayed action may call for temporary departure from that normal balance of public procedure.

I am prepared under my constitutional duty to recommend the measures that a stricken nation in the midst of a stricken world may require.

These measures, or such other measures as the Congress may build out of its experience and wisdom, I shall seek, within my constitutional authority, to bring to speedy adoption.

But in the event that the Congress shall fail to take one of these two courses, and in the event that the national emergency is still critical, I shall not evade the clear course of duty that will then confront me.

I shall ask the Congress for the one remaining instrument to meet the crisis—broad executive power to wage a war against the emergency as great as the power that would be given me if we were in fact invaded by a foreign foe.

For the trust reposed in me I will return the courage and the devotion that befit the time. I can do no less.

We face the arduous days that lie before us in the warm courage of national unity; with the clear consciousness of seeking old and precious moral values; with the clean satisfaction that comes from the stern performance of duty by old and young alike.

We aim at the assurance of a rounded and permanent national life.

We do not distrust the future of essential democracy. The people of the United States have not failed. In their need they have registered a mandate that they want direct, vigorous action.

They have asked for discipline and direction under leadership. They have made me the present instrument of their wishes. In the spirit of the gift I take it.

In this dedication of a nation we humbly ask the blessing of God. May He protect each and every one of us! May He guide me in the days to come!

Questions and Exercises

1. Why was Franklin D. Roosevelt's termed "the voice heard around the world"?_____

_____

2. Describe his early education._____

_____

3. What colleges did he attend?_____

What was the highest degree he attained?_____

4. In what activities did he engage in college that influenced his development as a speaker?_____.

_____

5. What office did he seek in his first political campaign?_____

_____ What were the results?_____

6. Briefly describe the economic conditions that prevailed during his first campaign for the Presidency._____

_____

_____

7. What was the setting for his "First Inaugural Address"?_____

_____

_____

8. How did he prepare his inaugural address for delivery?_____

_____

9. What was the purpose of his address?_____

_____

10. Describe his forms of support._____

_____

_____

XV DECLARATION OF WAR AGAINST JAPAN

FRANKLIN D. ROOSEVELT
(1882-1945)

The Occasion

While the United States continued to wrestle with problems of the depression following Roosevelt's re-election in 1936, war clouds loomed over Europe and Asia. Adolph Hitler's National Socialists had taken over the German republic in 1933. Hitler suppressed civil liberties and persecuted the Jews, Social Democrats, and Communists. He announced his intentions to wage war against the neighbors of Germany in his book *Mein Kampf* and he began war preparations immediately. He aligned himself with Italy in a Rome-Berlin Axis and later with Japan in her war with China.

Great Britain, France, and other European countries at first refused to heed Hitler's warnings. They rejoiced in the Fascist suppression of the Communists in Italy and hoped that the full force of the Axis powers would be turned against the Communists in Russia. Although the popular sympathies in the United States were against Germany, Italy, and Japan, America resolved to stay out of war as indicated by a succession of neutrality acts. Roosevelt's first indication that neutrality might not be possible came in his speech at Chicago in October, 1937, when he denounced the existing reign of terror and international lawlessness. Early in 1938, he asked Congress for added military appropriations and indicated the imminence of war.

Germany launched war against Poland in the fall of 1939; Great Britain and France retaliated by declaring war on Germany; the United States repealed its embargo on the shipment of arms and munitions to England and France. Although "keeping out of war" was a major issue in the presidential campaign of 1940, both the Republican candidate Wendell Willkie and Roosevelt seemed to sense the improbability of avoiding war. Soon after his re-election, Roosevelt increased United States shipments of war materiel to the nations at war with Germany and Italy. A few months later, on March 11, 1941, his Lend-Lease Program went into effect.

While the attention of the American people was focused on troubles in Europe, conditions in Asia grew steadily worse. Roosevelt termed Japan's continued aggression against China a violation of existing treaties and international law. Japan countered by claiming that the United States had violated Japan's rights as a belligerent by giving financial aid and by shipping war materiel to China.

In an effort to avoid a two-front war, Great Britain tried conciliation with Japan by offering to close the Burma Road to shipments of arms and munitions to Chungking. The United States objected so strenuously that Great Britain refused to renew her agreement with Japan after the six-month expiration date. The United States began her shipments again and by November, 1941, tensions between the United States and Japan approached a climax.

An undeclared truce prevailed between Japan and the United States while diplomatic efforts continued in Washington. Even as President Roosevelt and Secretary of State Cordell Hull talked with the Japanese diplomats on December 7, 1941, Japanese planes suddenly attacked Pearl Harbor, Hawaii, destroying eight battleships, several smaller craft, numerous planes, and the airfields. Roosevelt called a special joint session of Congress for the following day to declare war on Japan. Without delay Great Britain also declared war on Japan and three days later Germany and Italy proclaimed war on the United States.

On December 8, 1941, Roosevelt addressed a joint session of Congress and members of the Supreme Court in the House chambers; spectators overflowed the gallery and millions of people from all over the world listened by radio. A standing ovation greeted the weary President as he entered the House chambers. Speaker Sam Rayburn quieted the audience and Roosevelt arose to make the most important speech of his life. The Senate withdrew to its own chambers immediately after the speech and quickly passed the war resolution by a unanimous vote. The House vote of 388 to 1 followed shortly. The United States was at war within two and one-half hours following Roosevelt's war message.

The Speech

Soon after the attack on Pearl Harbor, Roosevelt called his personal secretary into his office and dictated his war message in much the same form in which he later delivered it. Harry Hopkins suggested the addition of the next to the last sentence and the changing of one word in another sentence. The next morning Roosevelt added the sentence about the early-morning Japanese attack on Midway Island.

The speech lasted only six minutes. The chronological arrangement "past-present-future" characterizes the organizational pattern. Roosevelt started with "Yesterday, December 7, 1941—a date which will live in infamy. . . ." He briefly discussed the devastating effect of Japan's attack on Pearl Harbor and then cited six specific instances of other countries attacked by Japan. As a result of these attacks, he stated that ". . . I have directed that all measures be taken for our defense." He then looked to the future in expressing confidence in ultimate victory.

The speech consisted largely of explanation and specific instances. Although he discussed the United States' losses at Pearl Harbor, he gave no statistics to show the extent of the losses.

Ethical appeal resulted from references to his confidence in the American people, the justice of our position, and the guidance of a Higher Power; for example, "With confidence in our armed forces—with the unbounded determination of our people—we will gain the inevitable triumph—so help us God."

The speech abounds in pathos although apparently no attempt was made to play upon the emotional nature of the occasion. His choice of language evoked emotional appeal; for example, "deliberately attacked," "onslaught against us," "premeditated invasion," "righteous might," "form of treachery," and "grave danger." His style, although simple and direct, shows action and force.

The following text comes from the *Congressional Record*, 77th Congress, Vol. 87, December 8, 1941, pp. 9504-9595.

To the Congress of the United States: Yesterday, December 7, 1941—a date which will live in infamy—the United States of America was suddenly and deliberately attacked by naval and air forces of the Empire of Japan.

The United States was at peace with that nation and, at the solicitation of Japan, was still in conversation with its government and its Emperor looking toward the maintenance of peace in the Pacific. Indeed, one hour after Japanese air squadrons had commenced bombing in Oahu, the Japanese Ambassador to the United States and his colleague delivered to the Secretary of State a formal reply to a recent American message. While this reply stated that it seemed useless to continue the existing diplomatic negotiations, it contained no threat or hint of war or armed attack.

It will be recorded that the distance of Hawaii from Japan makes it obvious that the attack was deliberately planned many days or even weeks ago. During the intervening time the Japanese government had deliberately sought to deceive the United States by false statements and expressions of hope for continued peace.

The attack yesterday on the Hawaiian Islands has caused severe damage to American naval and military forces. Very many American lives have been lost. In addition American ships have been reported torpedoed on the high seas between San Francisco and Honolulu.

Yesterday the Japanese government also launched an attack against Malaya.

Last night Japanese forces attacked Hong Kong.

Last night Japanese forces attacked Guam.

Last night Japanese forces attacked the Philippine Islands.

Last night the Japanese attacked Wake Island.

This morning the Japanese attacked Midway Island.

Japan has, therefore, undertaken a surprise offensive extending throughout the Pacific area. The facts of yesterday speak for themselves. The people of the United States have already formed their opinions and well understand the implications to the very life and safety of our nation.

As Commander in Chief of the Army and Navy I have directed that all measures be taken for our defense.

Always will we remember the character of the onslaught against us.

No matter how long it may take us to overcome this premeditated invasion, the American people in their righteous might will win through to absolute victory.

I believe I interpret the will of the Congress and of the people when I assert that we will not only defend ourselves to the uttermost but will make very certain that this form of treachery shall never endanger us again.

Hostilities exist. There is no blinking at the fact that our people, our territory, and our interests are in grave danger.

With confidence in our armed forces—with the unbounded determination of our people—we will gain the inevitable triumph—so help us God.

I ask that the Congress declare that since the unprovoked and dastardly attack by Japan on Sunday, December 7, a state of war has existed between the United States and the Japanese Empire.

Questions and Exercises

1. List three important political positions that Franklin D. Roosevelt held prior to the Presidency. (1)_____
   (2)_____ (3)_____
2. For what political office was he defeated in 1920?_____
   _____
3. With what physical affliction was he stricken in 1921?_____

   What effect did his illness have on his political activities?_____
   _____
4. How many years did Roosevelt serve as President?_____
   When did he die?_____
5. What immediate event gave rise to Roosevelt's war message?_____

   _____
6. How did he prepare his war message for delivery?_____
   _____
7. Explain how his language evoked emotional appeal_____
   _____
   _____
8. Give an example of ethical appeal._____
   _____
   _____
9. What are the main forms of support?_____
   _____
10. What is the basic organizational pattern?_____
    inductive;_____deductive.

XVI ADDRESS BEFORE CONGRESS

DOUGLAS MACARTHUR
(1880-   )

The Speaker

General Douglas MacArthur is primarily a man of action rather than of words. Paradoxically, he made one speech that evoked perhaps more immediate emotional response than any other recent speech. It would be difficult to imagine a more emotionally charged audience than the forty-nine million people whom MacArthur addressed by radio and television on April 19, 1951. The same emotional feelings also pervaded the joint session of Congress, MacArthur's immediate audience.

For fifty-two years General MacArthur had served his country with distinction, having held most of the important posts in the military. He had just been relieved of his command in the Far East by President Harry S. Truman for failure to follow directives relative to the Korean War. Upon invitation from Congress, MacArthur addressed the joint session of Congress in an attempt to vindicate his position.

Douglas MacArthur was born in Little Rock, Arkansas, on January 26, 1880. He grew up in a military environment. His father, Lieutenant General Arthur MacArthur, had been a hero of the Civil War, a winner of the Congressional Medal of Honor, and later Military Governor of the Philippines. After graduating from West Texas Military Academy, Douglas MacArthur received an appointment to the United States Military Academy where he was graduated in 1903 at the head of his class. His four-year average of 98.14 was the highest ever attained at the Academy.

Immediately after graduation from West Point, MacArthur was sent to the Philippines with the engineering corps to help map the islands. This experience served him well forty years later during his command in World War II. In 1904, he returned to the United States where he served in various capacities prior to World War I. His first active service was in Mexico in 1914, during the occupation of Veracruz by American troops.

When the United States entered World War I in 1917, MacArthur was promoted to the rank of Colonel and to Chief of Staff of the famed Rainbow Division—a division composed of National Guard units from throughout the country. Thus, at thirty-seven, he became the youngest divisional commander in the American army. His courage under fire and brilliance of command in France brought official praise and promotion to Brigadier General and commander of an infantry brigade in 1918. From 1919 until 1922, MacArthur served as Superintendent of the United States Military Academy, the youngest man ever to hold the post. In 1922, he returned to the Philippines as commander of a division. He came back to the United States in 1925 and five years later became the youngest Chief of Staff in history. Upon resigning as Chief of Staff in 1934, he became director of defense organization in the Philippines and, in 1936, military adviser to the Philippines government. In 1937, at age fifty-seven, MacArthur retired from the United States Army but remained in the Philippines to help prepare the Islands against possible attack by Japan. Prior to World War II, MacArthur's distinguished war record consisted of many "firsts," but his greatest contributions were yet to come.

As conditions in the Far East grew worse in 1941, President Franklin D. Roosevelt recalled MacArthur to active service, named him commander of all United States forces in the Far East, and soon promoted him to four-star rank. When the Japanese attacked Pearl Harbor on December 7, MacArthur's forces were unable to withstand the attack and he withdrew them to the Bataan Peninsula on December 26. A few days later the Japanese captured Manila, but for three months the American forces on Bataan prevented the Japanese from making use of Manila Bay. In March, 1942, President Roosevelt ordered Mac-Arthur to leave his post in the Philippines for an important mission to Australia. Upon reaching Australia, he expressed his disappointment in having to leave his troops in the Philippines and made his famous promise, "I shall return."

Return he did; but the course was a rugged one. By late 1942, Mac-Arthur began a direct offensive against the Japanese which led eventually, on October 20, 1944, to his landing with his troops on Leyte Island. Six months later, the islands were free from Japanese control. MacArthur had made good his promise.

MacArthur was given the rank of General of the Army and made commander of all American forces in the Western Pacific early in 1945. On August 14, when the Japanese surrendered, President Truman appointed MacArthur Supreme Commander of the Allied Powers to receive the surrender and to rule Japan. When the Korean War broke out, MacArthur was appointed United Nations commander in Korea in addition to his occupational duties. He remained with these assignments until relieved of his command on April 11, 1951. Since 1951, MacArthur has served as adviser and chairman of the board of certain business enterprises. He resides in the Waldorf-Astoria Hotel in New York City.

The Occasion

MacArthur's famous speech before Congress grew out of his dismissal from his command in the Far East over differences between his policies and the United Nations-United States policies toward the war in Korea. Late in 1950, the Chinese Communists joined forces with North Korea. General MacArthur contended that such action necessitated a strong stand by the United Nations forces against China. The United Nations and the United States government believed his policy would increase the risks of another all-out war. MacArthur, through public statements and letters, criticized existing policies and pointedly derided certain prominent United Nations diplomats. In spite of indirect reprimands from Washington, MacArthur persisted in his criticisms and urged an aggressive war in Korea.

On April 11, 1951, President Harry S. Truman released a statement which said in part, "With deep regret I have concluded that General of the Army Douglas MacArthur is unable to give his whole-hearted support to the policies of the United States Government. . . . I have decided that I must make a change of command in the Far East. . . ." The reaction to President Truman's announcement was immediate and intense. Although almost all our allies approved, reactions within the United States were sharply divided. While a majority of the press supported the President's action, some strongly disapproved and demanded that the President be impeached. Reaction in Congress ran largely along partisan lines, but the mass of the American people reacted violently. More than 125,000 telegrams flooded Washington in the two days following MacArthur's dismissal. Over 500,000 people greeted him as he arrived in San Francisco and more than 7,500,000 turned out for his ticker-tape parade in New York City the day before his speech in Washington. MacArthur's homecoming was attended by the largest number of people in history, more than twice the number that witnessed General Eisenhower's return from Europe following World War II.

At 12:31 P.M. on April 19, 1951, MacArthur entered the House chambers escorted by a courtesy committee of Senators and Representatives. Dozens of floodlights were turned on as he entered; the radio and television broadcasters were ready for their largest combined audience in history. After an enthusiastic ovation, Speaker Sam Rayburn quieted the audience and presented the General.

Reactions to General MacArthur's speech were almost as divided as were reactions to his dismissal. They ranged all the way from minority Leader Joseph W. Martin, Jr.'s "The address . . . was a masterpiece of context and delivery, possibly the great address of our times" to journalist Richard H. Rovere's "MacArthur's speech seemed extremely weak to me . . . he never came to grips with the issues."*

---

* For an interesting symposium on MacArthur's speech, see Frederick W. Haberman, "General MacArthur's Speech: A Symposium of Critical Comment," *Quarterly Journal of Speech*, October 1951, pp. 321-331. Quotations used by permission.

The Speech

MacArthur's address required forty minutes to deliver, including some thirty pauses for applause. The introduction took only two minutes and consisted of a reference to the historic meeting place, his desire to be nonpartisan, and his wish for a fair hearing. The organizational pattern is basically deductive, each point tending to narrow the subject pointing toward his discussion of Korea. The speech consists of four basic parts: (1) world conditions—Communism as a global problem; (2) Asia's present—recent changes in her social and political institutions; (3) the Pacific area—its strategic potential as the nation's defense, and (4) Korea—the necessity for countering Red China's offensive. The fourth division constitutes the heart of the address. Here MacArthur explained his position on Red China's attack and answered some of the objections to his policies.

The forms of support consist largely of explanation and exposition. Rather than supporting his claims by evidence, he relied largely on ethical proof—his long years of experience and knowledge of Asia qualified him to speak with personal authority. He explained and asserted rather than argued except when refuting the charges against him. He used numerous specific instances but few statistics, comparisons, or testimonies. He dealt more in general terms than in specific proposals.

The emotional appeal lies more in the speaking situation than in what is said. Such references as "fighting sons in Korea," "growing bloodshed has caused me the deepest anguish and anxiety," and "old soldiers never die; they just fade away" tend to evoke emotional responses—sometimes of a conflicting nature. The conclusion constitutes the most controversial part of the speech. The critics have labeled it all the way from "sublime" to pure "corn."

The text that follows is reprinted with the permission of General Douglas MacArthur from the *Congressional Record*, 1st Session, 82nd Congress, April 19, 1951, pp. 4123-4125.

Mr. President, Mr. Speaker and distinguished members of Congress, I stand on this rostrum with a sense of deep humility and great pride

—humility in the weight of those great architects of our history who have stood here before me, pride in the reflection that this forum of legislative debate represents human liberty in the purest form yet devised. [*Applause.*]

Here are centered the hopes and aspirations and faith of the entire human race.

I do not stand here as advocate for any partisan cause, for the issues are fundamental and reach quite beyond the realm of partisan consideration. They must be resolved on the highest plane of national interest if our course is to prove sound and our future protected. I trust, therefore, that you will do me the justice of receiving that which I have to say as solely expressing the considered viewpoint of a fellow American. I address you with neither rancor nor bitterness in the fading twilight of life, with but one purpose in mind, to serve my country. [*Applause.*]

The issues are global, and so interlocked that to consider the problems of one sector oblivious to those of another is to court disaster for the whole.

While Asia is commonly referred to as the gateway to Europe, it is no less true that Europe is the gateway to Asia, and the broad influence of the one cannot fail to have its impact upon the other.

There are those who claim our strength is inadequate to protect on both fronts, that we cannot divide our effort. I can think of no greater expression of defeatism. [*Applause.*] If a potential enemy can divide his strength on two fronts, it is for us to counter his efforts.

The Communist threat is a global one. Its successful advance in one sector threatens the destruction of every other sector. You cannot appease or otherwise surrender to communism in Asia without simultaneously undermining our efforts to halt its advance in Europe. [*Applause.*]

Beyond pointing out these general truisms, I shall confine my discussion to the general areas of Asia. Before one may objectively assess the situation now existing there, he must comprehend something of Asia's past and the revolutionary changes which have marked her course up to the present. Long exploited by the so-called colonial powers, with little opportunity to achieve any degree of social justice, individual dignity or a higher standard of life such as guided our own noble administration in the Philippines, the peoples of Asia found their opportunity in the war just past to throw off the shackles of colonialism and now see the dawn of new opportunity, and heretofore unfelt dignity, and the self-respect of political freedom.

Mustering half of the earth's population, and sixty per cent of its natural resources, these people are rapidly consolidating a new force, both moral and material, with which to raise the living standard and erect adaptations of the design of modern progress to their own distinct cultural environments. Whether one adheres to the concept of colonization or not, this is the direction of Asian progress and it may not be stopped. It is a corollary to the shift of the world economic frontiers as the whole epicenter of world affairs rotates back toward the area whence it started. In this situation, it becomes vital that our own country orient its policies in consonance with this basic evolutionary condition rather than pursue a course blind to reality that the colonial era is now past and the Asian peoples covet the right to shape their own free destiny. What they seek now is friendly guidance, understanding and support, not imperious direction [*Applause*]; the dignity of equality and not the shame of subjugation. Their pre-war standard of life, pitifully low, is infinitely lower now in the devastation left in war's wake. World ideologies play little part in Asian thinking and are little understood. What the people strive for is the opportunity for a little more food in their stomachs, a little better clothing on their backs; a little firmer roof over their heads, and the realization of the normal nationalist urge for political freedom. These political-social conditions have but an indirect bearing upon our own national security, but do form a backdrop to contemporary planning which must be thoughtfully considered if we are to avoid the pitfalls of unrealism.

Of more direct and immediate bearing upon our national security are the changes wrought in the strategic potential of the Pacific Ocean in the course of the past war. Prior thereto, the western strategic frontier of the United States lay on the littoral line of the Americas with an exposed island salient extending out through Hawaii, Midway, and Guam to the Philippines. That salient proved not an outpost of strength but an avenue of weakness along which the enemy could and did attack. The Pacific was a potential area of advance for any predatory force intent upon striking at the bordering land areas.

All this was changed by our Pacific victory. Our strategic frontier then shifted to embrace the entire Pacific Ocean which became a vast moat to protect us as long as we held it. Indeed, it acts as a protective shield for all of the Americas and all free lands of the Pacific Ocean area. We control it to the shores of Asia by a chain of islands extending in an arc from the Aleutians to the Marianas held by us and our free allies.

From this island chain we can dominate with sea and air power every Asiatic port from Vladivostok to Singapore and prevent any hostile movement into the Pacific. Any predatory attack from Asia must be an amphibious effort. No amphibious force can be successful without control of the sea lanes and the air over those lanes in its avenue of advance. With naval and air supremacy and modest ground elements to defend bases, any major attack from continental Asia toward us or our friends of the Pacific would be doomed to failure. Under such conditions the Pacific no longer represents menacing avenues of approach for a prospective invader—it assumes instead the friendly aspect of a peaceful lake. Our line of defense is a natural one and can be maintained with a minimum of military effort and expense. It envisions no attack against anyone nor does it provide the bastions essential for offensive operations, but properly maintained would be an invincible defense against aggression.

The holding of this littoral defense line in the western Pacific is entirely dependent upon holding all segments thereof, for any major breach of that line by an unfriendly power would render vulnerable to determined attack every other major leader who will take exception. [*Applause.*]

For that reason I have strongly recommended in the past as a matter of military urgency that under no circumstances must Formosa fall under Communist control. [*Applause.*]

Such an eventuality would at once threaten the freedom of the Philippines and the loss of Japan, and might well force our western frontier back to the coasts of California, Oregon, and Washington.

To understand the changes which now appear upon the Chinese mainland, one must understand the changes in Chinese character and culture over the past fifty years. China up to fifty years ago was completely non-homogeneous, being compartmented into groups divided against each other. The war-making tendency was almost nonexistent, as they still followed the tenets of the Confucian ideal of pacifist culture. At the turn of the century, under the regime of Chan So Lin, efforts toward greater homogeneity produced the start of a nationalist urge. This was further and more successfully developed under the leadership of Chiang Kai-shek, but has been brought to its greatest fruition under the present regime, to the point that it now has taken on the character of a united nationalism of increasingly dominant aggressive tendencies. Through these past fifty years, the Chinese people have thus become militarized in their concepts and in their ideals. They now constitute excellent soldiers with competent staffs and commanders. This has produced a new and dominant power in Asia which for its own purposes is allied with Soviet Russia, but which in its own concepts and methods has become aggressively imperialistic with a lust for expansion and increased power normal to this type of imperialism. There is little of the ideological concept either one way or another in the Chinese make-up. The standard of living is so low and the capital accumulation has been so thoroughly dissipated by war that the masses are desperate and avid to follow any leadership which seems to promise the alleviation of local stringencies. I have from the beginning believed that the Chinese Communists' support of the North Koreans was the dominant one. Their interests are at present parallel to those of the Soviet, but I believe that the aggressiveness recently displayed not only in Korea, but also in Indochina and Tibet and pointing potentially toward the south, reflects predominantly the same lust for the expansion of power which has animated every would-be conqueror since the beginning of time. [*Applause.*]

The Japanese people since the war have undergone the greatest reformation recorded in modern history. With a commendable will, eagerness to learn, and marked capacity to understand, they have, from the ashes left in war's wake, erected in Japan an edifice dedicated to the primacy of individual liberty and personal dignity, and in the ensuing process there has been created a truly representative government, committed to the advance of political morality, freedom of economic enterprise and social justice. [*Applause.*] Politically, economically, and socially Japan is now abreast of many free nations of the earth and will not again fail the universal trust. That it may be counted upon to wield a profoundly beneficial influence over the course of events in Asia is attested by the magnificent manner in which the Japanese people have met the recent challenge of war, unrest, and confusion surrounding them from the outside, and checked communism within their own frontiers without the slightest slackening in their forward progress. I sent all four of our occupation divisions to the Korean battle front without the slightest qualms as to the effect of the resulting power vacuum upon Japan. The results fully justified my faith. [*Applause.*] I know of no nation more serene, orderly, and industrious—nor in which higher hopes can be entertained for future constructive service in the advance of the human race. [*Applause.*]

Of our former wards, the Philippines, we can look forward in confidence that the existing unrest will be corrected and a strong and healthy nation will grow in the longer aftermath of war's terrible destructiveness. We must be patient and understanding and never fail them, as in our hour of need they did not fail us. [*Applause.*] A Christian nation, the Philippines stand as a mighty bulwark of Christianity in the Far East, and its capacity for high moral leadership in Asia is unlimited.

On Formosa, the Government of the Republic of China has had the opportunity to refute by action much of the malicious gossip which so undermined the strength of its leadership on the Chinese mainland. [*Applause.*]

The Formosan people are receiving a just and enlightened administration with majority representation on the organs of government; and politically, economically, and socially appear to be advancing along sound and constructive lines.

With this brief insight into the surrounding areas I now turn to the Korean conflict. While I was not consulted prior to the President's decision to intervene in the support of the Republic of Korea, that decision from a military standpoint proved a sound one. [*Applause.*] As I say, a brief and sound one as we hurled back the invader and decimated his forces. Our victory was complete and our objectives within reach when Red China intervened with numerically superior ground forces. This created a new war and an entirely new situation, a situation not contemplated when our forces were committed against the North Korean invaders, a situation which called for new decisions in the diplomatic sphere to permit the realistic adjustment of military strategy. Such decisions have not been forthcoming. [*Applause.*]

While no man in his right mind would advocate sending our ground forces into continental China—and such was never given a thought—the new situation did urgently demand a drastic revision of strategic planning if our political aim was to defeat this new enemy as we had defeated the old. [*Applause.*]

Apart from the military need as I saw it to neutralize sanctuary, protection given to the enemy north of the Yalu, I felt the military necessity in the conduct of the war made necessary:

First, the intensification of our economic blockade against China;

Second, the imposition of a naval blockade against the China coast;

Third, removal of restrictions on air reconnaissance of China's coastal areas and of Manchuria [*Applause*];

Fourth, removal of restrictions on the forces of the Republic of China on Formosa with logistical support to contribute to their effective operation against the Chinese mainland. [*Applause.*]

For entertaining these views, all professionally designed to support our forces committed to Korea and bring hostilities to an end with the least possible delay and at a saving of countless American and Allied lives, I have been severely criticized in lay circles, principally abroad, despite my understanding that from a military standpoint the above views have been fully shared in the past by practically every military leader concerned with the Korean campaign, including our own Joint Chiefs of Staff. [*Applause, the Members rising.*]

I called for reinforcements, but was informed that reinforcements were not available. I made clear that if not permitted to utilize the friendly Chinese force of some 600,000 men of Formosa; if not permitted to blockade the China coast to prevent the Chinese Reds from getting succor from without; and if there were to be no hope for major reinforcements, the position of the command from the military standpoint forbade victory. We could hold in Korea by constant maneuver and at an approximate area where our supply line advantages were in balance with the supply line disadvantages of the enemy, but we could hope at best for only an indecisive campaign, with its terrible and constant attrition upon our forces if the enemy utilized his full military potential. I have constantly called for the new political decisions essential to a solution. Efforts have been made to distort my position. It has been said in effect that I was a warmonger. Nothing could be further from the truth. I know war as few other men now living know it, and nothing to me is more revolting. I have long advocated its complete abolition as its very destructiveness on both friend and foe has rendered it useless as a means of settling international disputes. Indeed, on the second of September 1945, just following the surrender of the Japanese Nation on the Battleship *Missouri*, I formally cautioned as follows:

"Men since the beginning of time have sought peace. Various methods through the ages have been attempted to devise an international process to prevent or settle disputes between nations. From the very start, workable methods were found insofar as individual citizens were concerned, but the mechanics of an instrumentality of larger international scope have never been successful. Military alliances, balances of power, leagues of nations, all in turn failed, leaving the only path to be by way of the crucible of war. The utter destructiveness of war now blots out this alternative. We have had our last chance. If we will not devise some greater and more equitable system, Armageddon will be at our door. The problem basically is theological and involves a spiritual recrudescence and improvement of human character that will synchronize with our almost matchless advances in science, art, literature, and all material and cultural developments of the past two thousand years. It must be of the spirit if we are to save the flesh." [*Applause.*]

But once war is forced upon us, there is no other alternative than to apply every available means to bring it to a swift end. War's very object is victory—not prolonged indecision. [*Applause.*] In war, indeed, there can be no substitute for victory. [*Applause.*]

There are some who for varying reasons would appease Red China. They are blind to history's clear lesson. For history teaches with unmistakable emphasis that appeasement but begets new and bloodier war. It points to no single instance where the end justified that means —where appeasement has led to more than a sham peace. Like blackmail, it lays the basis for new and successively greater demands, until, as in blackmail, violence becomes the only other alternative. Why, my soldiers asked of me, surrender military advantages to an enemy in the field? I could not answer. [*Applause.*] Some may say to avoid spread of the conflict into an all-out war with China; others, to avoid Soviet intervention. Neither explanation seems valid. For China is already engaging with the maximum power it can commit and the Soviet will not necessarily mesh its actions with our moves. Like a cobra, any new enemy will more likely strike whenever it feels that the relativity in military or other potential is in its favor on a world-wide basis.

The tragedy of Korea is further heightened by the fact that as military action is confined to its territorial limits, it condemns that nation, which it is our purpose to save, to suffer the devastating impact of full naval and air bombardment, while the enemy's sanctuaries are fully protected from such attack and devastation. Of the nations of the world, Korea alone, up to now, is the sole one which has risked its all against communism. The magnificence of the courage and fortitude of the Korean people defies description. [*Applause.*] They have chosen to risk death rather than slavery. Their last words to me were "Don't scuttle the Pacific." [*Applause.*]

I have just left your fighting sons in Korea. They have met all tests there and I can report to you without reservation they are splendid in every way. [*Applause.*] It was my constant effort to preserve them and end this savage conflict honorably and with the least loss of time and a minimum sacrifice of life. Its growing bloodshed has caused me the deepest anguish and anxiety. Those gallant men will remain often in my thoughts and in my prayers always. [*Applause.*]

I am closing my fifty-two years of military service. [*Applause.*] When I joined the Army even before the turn of the century, it was the fulfillment of all my boyish hopes and dreams. The world has turned over many times since I took the oath on the plain at West Point, and the hopes and dreams have long since vanished. But I still remember the refrain of one of the most popular barrack ballads of that day which proclaimed most proudly that—

"Old soldiers never die; they just fade away." And like the old soldier of that ballad, I now close my military career and just fade away—an old soldier, who tried to do his duty as God gave him the light to see that duty.

Good-by.

Questions and Exercises

1. Where was General Douglas MacArthur born?_____
   When?_____

2. What scholastic record did he make at the West Point Military
   Academy?_____ When did he return to the Academy
   as Superintendent?_____

3. What was the highest military rank that he attained?_____

4. What event led to MacArthur's invitation to address a joint session of Congress on April 19, 1951?_____

   _____

5. How did MacArthur's dismissal effect the emotional state of the
   American people?_____

   _____

6. What was the basic issue in the MacArthur-Truman controversy?

   _____

   _____

7. List the four divisions of the speech: (1)_____
   _____ (2)_____
   (3)_____ (4)_____

8. What forms of support did he use most?_____

   _____

9. Describe the style of the speech._____

   _____

   _____

10. What were some reactions to the speech?_____

    _____

    _____

XVII ACCEPTANCE ADDRESS—1952

ADLAI E. STEVENSON
(1900-   )

The Speaker

Adlai E. Stevenson talks sense, eloquently. If one accepts the premise that good oral communication consists of "having something to say and saying it well," few speakers in history have excelled Stevenson. His maturity of thought, his courage in speaking his convictions, his keen intellect, and his unusual facility in using the English language make him perhaps the most outstanding American speaker since Franklin D. Roosevelt. He has been termed a "Woodrow Wilson with warmth."

John Mason Brown, in writing of Stevenson's speech of welcome at the 1952 Democratic Convention, paid him an apt tribute: "He had convictions without dogmatism, and eloquence without demagoguery. . . . The Governor spoke as a man whose exceptional gift for phrasing was obviously the expression of a large spirit."* Matthew Arnold once wrote of "a man born out of date," that greatness depends upon the man and the moment being in happy conjunction. Stevenson exemplifies that principle. Many political observers believe that if Stevenson's opponent for the Presidency had been anyone but the popular

---

* John Mason Brown, *Through These Men* (New York: Harper & Row, Publishers, 1956), pp. 15-16.

and genial General Dwight D. Eisenhower, Stevenson would have been elected.

Adlai E. Stevenson was born in Los Angeles, California, on February 5, 1900. He was born with politics in his blood. His maternal great-grandfather, Jesse Fell, helped found the Republican party and was the first to suggest the famous Lincoln-Douglas debates; his grandfather, Adlai E. Stevenson I, was Vice-President under Grover Cleveland; his father, Lewis Green Stevenson, was a prominent leader of the Democratic party who served as secretary of state in Illinois. Soon after Adlai's birth, his father became associated with the Hearst newspapers in Los Angeles. When Adlai was six years old, the Stevensons moved back to Bloomington, Illinois, the home of their ancestors since 1857. Here Adlai entered the public schools. He was a sensitive, conscientious boy with an insatiable curiosity. When he was a child, his mother read aloud to him hour after hour from good literature. His wide knowledge indicates that he gained much from these early reading sessions.

After attending the public grammar schools, Adlai Stevenson was enrolled in the Metcalf Training School and later in University High School on the campus of Illinois Normal College. He attended these special-tuition schools largely because of family tradition. When Adlai's father became secretary of state for Illinois, the family moved to Springfield but they later returned to Bloomington where Adlai finished high school. After his graduation, he failed the entrance examinations to Princeton. He entered Choate School in Wallingford, Connecticut, where he made a good scholastic record, and was editor of the school newspaper, captain of the tennis team, and vice-president of the senior class. The following fall, he passed both his entrance examinations to Princeton and his Navy physical examination and became an apprentice seaman stationed at Princeton. At Princeton he continued his interests in extracurricular activities by working on the newspaper staff of *The Princetonian*, organizing a political club, and participating in athletic activities. He was graduated from Princeton in 1922.

The next fall he enrolled in the School of Law at Harvard University. During his second year, he withdrew to become managing editor of *The Panagraph*, a prominent newspaper of Bloomington in which his father acquired part ownership. In 1925, however, he resigned his position, enrolled in Northwestern University School of Law, and took his J.D. degree the following June.

For the next twenty-two years, Stevenson held a variety of positions —lawyer in Chicago, special counsel for the AAA in Washington, assistant to Secretary of the Navy, chief of an economic mission to Italy, War Department Mission to Europe, assistant to the Secretary of State, adviser to the United States Delegation on International Organization, and delegate to the General Assembly of the United Nations. These varied activities caused Stevenson to become well-known and respected in Washington but they gave him little opportunity for national recognition.

In 1928, Stevenson married Ellen Borden, the daughter of a wealthy lawyer and businessman of Chicago. Three sons were born: Adlai, Jr., Borden, and John Fell. The interests of Ellen and Adlai differed greatly; hers were centered in the creative arts and a settled life; his ran to the excitement of politics and travel. One of the disappointments in Stevenson's life is that the marriage ended in divorce in 1948 soon after he became Governor of Illinois.

Stevenson attracted national attention as Governor of Illinois. In 1948, the Democrats had two likely prospects to oppose Dwight Green's bid for a second term—Stevenson and Paul H. Douglas. Stevenson preferred to run for the United States Senate but the party decided that Stevenson should run for Governor and Douglas for the Senate. Although Stevenson waged a vigorous campaign, he approached election day with doubts about the outcome. His fears were unfounded, however; he won by the largest plurality in Illinois history —572,067 votes. Moreover, since President Harry S. Truman carried Illinois by only 33,612 in his bid for the Presidency, Stevenson was credited with carrying the state for him.

Stevenson's distinguished record as Governor of Illinois led to his nomination for President in 1952 and again in 1956. In spite of two defeats, he was prominently mentioned again at the 1960 Democratic Convention. The successful candidate, John F. Kennedy, appointed

Stevenson Ambassador to the United Nations, an ideal position that enables him to use his exceptional talents.

The Occasion

When the National Democratic Convention opened in the International Amphitheater in Chicago on July 21, 1952, uncertainty prevailed because no candidate could claim a clear-cut advantage. Since early January, repeated efforts had been made to induce Stevenson to become a candidate but he had steadfastly refused. He apparently preferred an almost certain re-election to the governorship of Illinois to the uncertainty of a presidential candidacy.

These conditions were in sharp contrast to those which had prevailed at the Republican Convention two weeks earlier. The Republican Convention witnessed an intense struggle between the Old Guard for Taft and the liberal wing for Eisenhower. Although the pro-Taft forces were in control of the convention machinery, they could not swing the nomination for Taft against so formidable an opponent as Eisenhower. The first ballot gave 595 votes to Eisenhower, 500 to Taft, and 111 to three other candidates. In short order the vote was made unanimous for Eisenhower. The lively struggle between two major candidates added interest to the convention.

As the Democratic Convention opened, the five avowed candidates were Senator Estes Kefauver of Tennessee, Senator Richard Russell of Georgia, Senator Robert Kerr of Oklahoma, W. Averell Harriman of New York, and Vice-President Alben Barkley. Only Kefauver had made a determined bid by entering several primaries; Barkley apparently had the blessings of President Truman but there was no unusual enthusiasm for any candidate and little rivalry among them. The convention lacked luster.

Only Stevenson's refusal to become a candidate and a heated struggle over the seating of contested Southern delegates added spark to the proceedings. Stevenson's speech of welcome at the opening session was heralded as a new era in convention speaking—a speech based on reason and open candor. A "draft" Stevenson movement started and interest mounted as the nomination speeches started on Thursday afternoon. By late afternoon the names of Senator J. W. Fulbright of Arkansas, Kerr, Kefauver, Russell, and Harriman had been placed in nomination. When Governor Henry F. Schricker of Indiana rose to nominate Stevenson, a demonstration resulted which left little doubt as to the convention's choice.

The balloting started on Friday afternoon. On the first ballot Kefauver led with 340 votes to Stevenson's 273. Kefauver continued to lead on the second ballot but his margin decreased. When the convention reconvened that evening, the crucial third ballot began. After many switches in votes, the tally showed Stevenson two and one-half votes short of nomination. Utah switched its twelve votes, the other major candidates yielded to him, and thus Stevenson became the nominee early in the morning of July 26.

Stevenson left soon to join President Truman in the Stockyard Inn for the short walk to the convention hall. Truman and Stevenson walked briskly to the rostrum where Truman gave one of the fighting speeches for which he had become famous. Then he presented Stevenson, who began with "I accept your nomination—and your program."

The Speech

Adlai Stevenson's speech was more than a perfunctory acceptance address. He used the occasion to set the keynote for the campaign to follow. "I hope and pray that we . . . can campaign . . . to educate and elevate a people. . . . Let's talk sense to the American people." These were words of no ordinary man signifying no ordinary political campaign.

In the introduction, after accepting the nomination and program, Stevenson engaged in a bit of self-depreciation characteristic of his personality. He emphasized that his reluctance to become a candidate did not lessen his appreciation of the nomination; he said, "You have summoned me to the highest mission within the gift of any people."

The body of the speech indicates four divisions: (1) He expressed appreciation to the losing candidates, to the manner in which the convention was conducted, and to the party platform. (2) He refuted criticisms of the party—that the two-party system was in danger, that the Democratic party had become fat and indolent, that a change was necessary, and that corruption in office threatened. (3) He indicated the spirit of the campaign to follow; for example, "What does concern me . . . is not just winning this election, but how it is won, how well we can . . . debate issues sensibly and soberly." (4) He called for unity and help from the party in conducting the campaign so that "We will justify our glorious past. . . . We will serve our great tradition greatly."

In the conclusion, after paying tribute to President Harry S. Truman, Stevenson stated that he would always try "to do justice, to love mercy and to walk humbly with my God."

The speech consists largely of explanation—a statement of aims and ideals. He called on authority once by quoting Charles Evans Hughes about corruption in office. He used an analogy, "If this cup may not pass from me, except I drink it, Thy will be done." He made excellent use of humor by labeling the Republican party as one with a hopeless case of political schizophrenia. About danger to the two-party system, he stated: "Certainly the Republican party looked brutally alive a couple of weeks ago, and I mean both Republican parties!" He evinced ethical appeal in his statements of principles and in his use of Biblical passages. The language is direct, colorful, and forceful. The text that follows is taken from Richard Harrity, ed., *Speeches of Adlai Stevenson* (New York: Random House, Inc., 1952), pp. 18-21. By permission of Adlai E. Stevenson.

Mr. President, Ladies and Gentlemen of the Convention, my Fellow Citizens:

I accept your nomination—and your program.

I should have preferred to hear those words uttered by a stronger, a wiser, a better man than myself. But after listening to the President's speech I even feel better about myself.

None of you, my friends, can wholly appreciate what is in my heart. I can only hope that you understand my words. They will be few.

I have not sought the honor you have done me. I could not seek it because I aspired to another office, which was the full measure of my ambition. And one does not treat the highest office within the gift of the people of Illinois as an alternative or as a consolation prize.

I would not seek your nomination for the presidency, because the burdens of that office stagger the imagination. Its potential for good or evil now and in the years of our lives smothers exultation and converts vanity to prayer.

I have asked the Merciful Father, the Father of us all, to let this cup pass from me. But from such dread responsibility one does not shrink in fear, in self-interest, or in false humility.

So, "If this cup may not pass from me, except I drink it, Thy will be done."

That my heart has been troubled, that I have not sought this nomination, that I could not seek it in good conscience, that I would not seek it in honest self-appraisal, it is not to say that I value it the less. Rather it is that I revere the office of the presidency of the United States.

And now, my friends, that you have made your decision I will fight to win that office with all my heart and my soul. And with your help, I have no doubt that we will win.

You have summoned me to the highest mission within the gift of any people. I could not be more proud. Better men than I were at hand for this mighty task, and I owe to you and to them every resource of mind and of strength that I possess to make your deed today a good one for our country and for our party. I am confident, too, that your selection of a candidate for Vice-President will strengthen me and our party immeasurably in the hard, the implacable work that lies ahead of all of us.

I know you join me in gratitude and in respect for the great Democrats and the leaders of our generation whose names you have considered here in this convention, whose vigor, whose character and devotion to the Republic we love so well have won the respect of countless Americans and enriched our party.

I shall need them, we shall need them, because I have not changed in any respect since yesterday. Your nomination, awesome as I find it, has not enlarged my capacities. So I am profoundly grateful and emboldened by their comradeship and their fealty. And I have been deeply moved by their expressions of goodwill and of support. And I cannot, my friends, resist the urge to take the one opportunity that has been afforded me to pay my humble respects to a very great and good American whom I am proud to call my kinsman—Alben Barkley of Kentucky.

Let me say, too, that I have been heartened by the conduct of this convention. You have argued and disagreed because as Democrats you care and you care deeply. But you have disagreed and argued without calling each other liars and thieves, without despoiling our best traditions in any naked struggles for power.

And you have written a platform that neither equivocates, contradicts nor evades.

You have restated our party's record, its principles and its purpose in language that none can mistake, and with a firm confidence in justice, freedom and peace on earth that will raise the hearts and the hopes of mankind for that distant day when no one rattles a saber and no one drags a chain.

For all these things I am grateful to you. But I feel no exultation, no sense of triumph. Our troubles are all ahead of us.

Some will call us appeasers; others will say that we are the war party.

Some will say we are reactionary; others will say that we stand for socialism.

There will be the invitable cries of "throw the rascals out"; "it's time for a change"; and so on and so on.

We'll hear all those things and many more besides. But we will hear nothing that we have not heard before. I am not too much concerned with partisan denunciation, with epithets and abuse, because the working man, the farmer, the thoughtful business man, all know that they are better off than ever before and they all know that the greatest danger to free enterprise in this country died with the great depression under the hammer blows of the Democratic party.

Nor am I afraid that the precious two-party system is in danger. Certainly the Republican party looked brutally alive a couple of weeks ago, and I mean both Republican parties!

Nor am I afraid that the Democratic party is old and fat and indolent. After 150 years it has been old for a long time; and it will never be indolent as long as it looks forward and not back, as long as it commands the allegiance of the young and the hopeful who dream the dreams and see the visions of a better America and a better world.

You will hear many sincere and thoughtful people express concern about the continuation of one party in power for twenty years. I don't belittle this attitude. But change for the sake of change has no absolute merit in itself.

If our greatest hazard is preservation of the values of Western civilization, in our self-interest alone, if you please, is it the part of wisdom to change for the sake of change to a party with a split personality; to a leader, whom we all respect, but who has been called upon to minister to a hopeless case of political schizophrenia?

If the fear is corruption in official position, do you believe with Charles Evans Hughes that guilt is personal and knows no party? Do you doubt the power of any political leader, if he has the will to do so, to set his own house in order without his neighbor's having to burn it down?

What does concern me, in common with thinking partisans of both parties, is not just winning this election, but how it is won, how well we can take advantage of this great quadrennial opportunity to debate issues sensibly and soberly.

I hope and pray that we Democrats, win or lose, can campaign not as a crusade to exterminate the opposing party, as our opponents seem to prefer, but as a great opportunity to educate and elevate a people whose destiny is leadership, not alone of a rich and prosperous, contented country as in the past, but of a world in ferment.

And, my friends, more important than winning the election is governing the nation. That is the test of a political party—the acid, final test. When the tumult and the shouting die, when the bands are gone and the lights are dimmed, there is the stark reality of responsibility in an hour of history haunted with those gaunt, grim specters of strife, dissension and materialism at home, and ruthless, inscrutable and hostile power abroad.

The ordeal of the twentieth century—the bloodiest, most turbulent era of the Christian age—is far from over. Sacrifice, patience, understanding and implacable purpose may be our lot for years to come.

Let's face it. Let's talk sense to the American people. Let's tell them the truth, that there are no gains without pains, that we are now on the eve of great decisions, not easy decisions, like resistance when you're attacked, but a long, patient, costly struggle which alone can assure triumph over the great enemies of man—war, poverty and tyranny—and the assaults upon human dignity which are the most grievous consequences of each.

Let's tell them that the victory to be won in the twentieth century, this portal to the golden age, mocks the pretensions of individual acumen and ingenuity. For it is a citadel guarded by thick walls of ignorance and of mistrust which do not fall before the trumpets' blast or the politicians' imprecations or even a general's baton. They are, my friends, walls that must be directly stormed by the hosts of courage, of morality and of vision, standing shoulder to shoulder, unafraid of ugly truth, contemptuous of lies, half truths, circuses and demagoguery.

The people are wise—wiser than the Republicans think. And the Democratic party is the people's party, not the labor party, not the farmers' party, not the employers' party—it is the party of no one because it is the party of everyone.

That, I think, is our ancient mission. Where we have deserted it we have failed. With your help there will be no desertion now. Better, we lose the election than mislead the people; and better we lose than misgovern the people.

Help me do the job in this autumn of conflict and of campaign; help me do the job in these years of darkness, of doubt and of crisis which stretch beyond the horizon of tonight's happy vision, and we will justify our glorious past and the loyalty of silent millions who look to us for compassion, for understanding and for honest purpose. Thus we will serve our great tradition greatly.

I ask of you all you have; I will give to you all I have, even as he who came here tonight and honored me, as he has honored you—the Democratic party—by a lifetime of service and bravery that will find him an imperishable page in the history of the Republic and of the Democratic party—President Harry S. Truman.

And finally, my friends, in the staggering task that you have assigned me, I shall always try "to do justly, to love mercy and to walk humbly with my God."

Questions and Exercises

1. In your opinion, what is the outstanding attribute of Adlai E. Stevenson's speaking?_____
   _____

2. Where was he born?_____ When?_____
   In what state was he elected governor?_____
3. Where did he receive his bachelor's degree?_____
   His law degree?_____
4. In what three professions did he engage? (1)_____
   (2)_____ (3)_____
5. How did he create uncertainty at the National Democratic Convention in 1952?_____
   _____

6. What was the setting for his "Acceptance Address"?_____
   _____

7. What is the central idea of the speech?_____
   _____
   _____

8. What are the main divisions of the speech?_____
   _____
   _____

9. Describe the language of the speech._____
   _____
   _____

10. Give an example of Stevenson's use of humor._____
    _____
    _____

XVIII *INAUGURAL ADDRESS*

JOHN F. KENNEDY
(1917-1963)

The Speaker

John F. Kennedy, the youngest man ever to be elected President of the United States, helped introduce a new medium to political campaigning—face-to-face television debates with his Republican opponent,Richard M. Nixon. Although Nixon was the more seasoned debater, Kennedy's confidence, courage, and strong ethical appeal came through to his advantage on the television screen. Since Nixon had served as Vice-President for eight years, his frequent public appearances had made him the better-known candidate. The television debates served to bring Kennedy before millions of American people whom he otherwise would not have reached. Because of the extreme closeness of the vote, many political observers attribute Kennedy's election to his ability at speechmaking.

John F. Kennedy was born May 29, 1917, in Brookline, Massachusetts, a suburb of Boston. He was the second of nine children born to Joseph P. and Rose Fitzgerald Kennedy. Joseph Kennedy, a self-made millionaire, served as United States Ambassador to Great Britain from 1937 to 1940 during the administration of Franklin D. Roosevelt. John Kennedy's mother came from a political environment; her father had served in the state senate, in the United States House of Representatives, and as Mayor of Boston. In spite of this political background, John gave little indication of becoming a politician. His older brother, Joseph, Jr., was considered the most likely politician in the family. Joseph was the sociable and outgoing type, whereas John was quiet and reserved. His family thought that John would become a writer or a teacher, but when Joseph was killed in World War II, John decided on a political career. Fourteen years after entering his first political race he attained the Presidency of the United States.

Kennedy attended elementary schools in Brookline, Massachusetts, and in Riverdale, New York. At age thirteen he entered Canterbury School in New Milford, Connecticut, but a year later transferred to Choate Academy in Wallingford from which he was graduated in 1935, at age eighteen. After studying in the London School of Economics during the summer of 1935, he enrolled in Princeton University that fall. He had to withdraw from Princeton at mid-year because of illness. He entered Harvard University in the fall of 1936, from which he was graduated with honors in 1940. During the spring and summer of 1939, Kennedy traveled in Europe to view first hand the conditions leading to war. From these observations and study, he wrote his senior thesis at Harvard the following year. His thesis, published under the title *Why England Slept,* became a best-seller. Upon graduation, Kennedy entered Stanford University Graduate School of Business but withdrew six months later because he did not like the study. A few months later he joined the United States Navy.

Kennedy was assigned to a PT squadron and was commissioned an ensign. He was assigned to patrol duty in the South Pacific off the Solomon Islands. On August 2, 1942, his boat was cut in two by a Japanese destroyer. Three crewmen were killed and the other ten, after clinging all night to the wreckage, swam to a nearby island. In spite of an injured back, Kennedy spent five hours towing a wounded crewman ashore. Five days later he and his crew were rescued. For his heroism, Kennedy received the Navy and Marine Corps medals as well as the Purple Heart.

Following the war, Kennedy served briefly as a reporter for the Hearst newspapers before deciding to run for the United States House of Representatives. In the campaign of 1946, he faced eight opponents for the Democratic nomination for the 11th Congressional District of Massachusetts. He won and then defeated his Republican opponent handily in the general election. Kennedy's family, except his father, took an active part in the campaign and were credited by Kennedy as a major factor in his election. His father has followed a consistent practice of remaining in the background in all his son's campaigns. He fears that his former isolationist and conservative views might hurt his son's chances.

Kennedy was re-elected Representative in 1948 and again in 1950. In 1952, Kennedy decided to run for the Senate. His formidable opponent, Henry Cabot Lodge, Jr., was considered too well-known and experienced an opponent for young Kennedy. After a particularly active campaign, Kennedy won by a narrow margin of 70,000 votes although the state gave Republican Dwight D. Eisenhower a majority of 209,000 votes for President. He was re-elected Senator in 1958 by a majority of 874,000 votes.

During the middle fifties, three events occurred which bear stressing. On September 12, 1953, Kennedy married Jacqueline "Jackie" Lee Bouvier, the attractive and accomplished daughter of a wealthy Wall Street broker. In 1954, while recovering from an operation on his back, Kennedy wrote a book about the courage of some United States Senators. The book, *Profiles in Courage*, won a Pulitzer Prize and became a best-seller. At the Democratic National Convention in 1956, Kennedy made a strong bid for the nomination for Vice-President, barely losing to Senator Estes Kefauver, of Tennessee. His strong showing paved the way for his election to the Presidency in 1960.

The Occasion

Kennedy started his bid for the nomination for President immediately after the 1956 Democratic Convention. He decided that his best chance lay in entering as many state primaries as possible. He entered seven and won them all. As a result, he went to the 1960 Democratic Convention in Los Angeles with a clear-cut advantage over such well-known opponents as Adlai E. Stevenson, Senator Stuart Symington, and Senator Lyndon B. Johnson. He won on the first ballot. Senator Lyndon B. Johnson of Texas was nominated for Vice-President.

The Republicans selected Vice-President Richard M. Nixon as their nominee for President and United Nations delegate Henry Cabot Lodge, Jr., Kennedy's old Massachusetts opponent, as Nixon's running mate. Both Kennedy and Nixon were young, aggressive campaigners and they ran a nip-and-tuck race to the finish.

Kennedy had several disadvantages to overcome; the most important was his religious affiliation. A Roman Catholic had never been elected President. Only Alfred E. Smith had ever been nominated and he was handily defeated by Herbert Hoover in 1928. One of the highlights of Kennedy's campaign was his meeting in Houston, Texas, with a delegation of Baptist ministers. So creditable was his showing before a national television audience that he largely overcame the religious issue. Other drawbacks were his youth, his father's conservatism, and his inexperience in international affairs. These drawbacks were offset by his handsome appearance, his attractive wife, a progressive program, his wealth, and a well-planned campaign. As previously noted, his television debates with Nixon tended to offset the initial advantage that Nixon had in being better known. More important, his vigorous "New Frontier" slogan exemplified a forward-looking, aggressive program which appealed to the people. Kennedy won by a narrow margin of approximately 120,000 popular votes and an electoral college majority of 303 to 219.

Inauguration day, January 20, 1961, was bitter cold but clear. A severe snowstorm the previous two days had seriously impeded travel into Washington and cut down on attendance at the open-air ceremony held on the Capitol steps. A smoldering fire, caused by the electrical wires inside the speaker's stand, marred the proceedings but millions viewed the program over national television networks and other millions heard it over the radio. Kennedy's well-planned inaugural address upheld the dignity of the occasion.

The Speech

Although Kennedy's "Inaugural Address" dealt with some controversial issues of the election, he dealt with them in a nonpartisan manner in keeping with the propriety of the ceremonial occasion. He spoke more slowly and deliberately than he did during the campaign, but his delivery showed restrained force and enthusiasm as well as dignity.

He began by referring to what the occasion signified, ". . . not a victory of party but a celebration of freedom . . . an end as well as a beginning . . . renewal as well as change." He struck the keynote early by stating, "The world is very different now. For man holds in his mortal hands the power to abolish all forms of human poverty and all forms of human life. . . . Let the word go forth from this time and place . . . that the torch has been passed to a new generation of Americans. . . ."

The organizational pattern is basically didactic. The main divisions consist of pledges to five different groups and a request for a sixth. The groups are identified first and then expanded: (1) To our old allies we ask for unity in cooperative adventure; (2) to our new allies we pledge our support to their freedom; (3) to those accustomed to mass misery we pledge our efforts to help them help themselves; (4) to the republics to the south we pledge new alliances for progress; and (5) to the United Nations we pledge our renewal of support. Turning to our adversaries, he requested that "both sides begin anew the quest for peace." Then he spelled out what both sides could do to promote a better world. He reached the climax with two statements most frequently quoted from the speech: "And so, my fellow Americans, ask not what your country can do for you: ask what you can do for your country. My fellow citizens of the world: ask not what America will do for you, but what together we can do for the freedom of man."

The forms of support consist primarily of explanation and reasoning. Two rhetorical questions near the end point up a challenge for cooperation toward a more fruitful life and serve as a transition to the conclusion. Ethical appeal comes from reference to high ideals, laudable aims, and the Bible. The speech appeals to basic motives of self-preservation, to freedom from want, to authority, and to justice in the pledges to the various groups. The sentence structure is balanced; the antithetical construction gives emphasis and rhythmic effect. The choice of words corresponds to the formal ceremonial occasion.

The text that follows is taken from *Inaugural Addresses of the*

Presidents of the United States, 87th Congress, 1st Session, House Document No. 218. (Washington, D.C.: United States Government Printing Office, 1961), pp. 267-270.

Mr. Chief Justice, President Eisenhower, Vice President Nixon, President Truman, reverend clergy, fellow citizens, we observe today not a victory of party, but a celebration of freedom—symbolizing an end, as well as a beginning—signifying renewal, as well as change. For I have sworn before you and Almighty God the same solemn oath our forebears prescribed nearly a century and three-quarters ago.

The world is very different now. For man holds in his mortal hands the power to abolish all forms of human poverty and all forms of human life. And yet the same revolutionary beliefs for which our forebears fought are still at issue around the globe—the belief that the rights of man come not from the generosity of the state, but from the hand of God.

We dare not forget today that we are the heirs of that first revolution. Let the word go forth from this time and place, to friend and foe alike, that the torch has been passed to a new generation of Americans—born in this century, tempered by war, disciplined by a hard and bitter peace, proud of our ancient heritage—and unwilling to witness or permit the slow undoing of those human rights to which this nation has always been committed, and to which we are committed today at home and around the world.

Let every nation know, whether it wishes us well or ill, that we shall pay any price, bear any burden, meet any hardship, support any friend, oppose any foe, in order to assure the survival and the success of liberty.

This much we pledge—and more.

To those old allies whose cultural and spiritual origins we share, we pledge the loyalty of faithful friends. United, there is little we cannot do in a host of cooperative ventures. Divided, there is little we can do—for we dare not meet a powerful challenge at odds and split asunder.

To those new states whom we welcome to the ranks of the free, we pledge our words that one form of colonial control shall not have passed away merely to be replaced by a far greater iron tyranny. We shall not always expect to find them supporting our view. But we shall always hope to find them strongly supporting their own freedom— and to remember that, in the past, those who foolishly sought power by riding the back of the tiger ended up inside.

To those peoples in the huts and villages across the globe struggling to break the bonds of mass misery, we pledge our best efforts to help them help themselves, for whatever period is required—not because the Communists may be doing it, not because we seek their votes, but because it is right. If a free society cannot help the many who are poor, it cannot save the few who are rich.

To our sister republics south of our border, we offer a special pledge —to convert our good words into good deeds, in a new alliance for progress, to assist free men and free governments in casting off the chains of poverty. But this peaceful revolution of hope cannot become the prey of hostile powers. Let all our neighbors know that we shall join with them to oppose aggression or subversion anywhere in the Americas. And let every other power know that this hemisphere intends to remain the master of its own house.

To that world assembly of sovereign states, the United Nations, our last best hope in an age where the instruments of war have far outpaced the instruments of peace, we renew our pledge of support—to prevent it from becoming merely a forum for invective—to strengthen its shield of the new and the weak—and to enlarge the area in which its writ may run.

Finally, to those nations who would make themselves our adversary, we offer not a pledge but a request: that both sides begin anew the quest for peace, before the dark powers of destruction unleashed by science engulf all humanity in planned or accidental self-destruction.

We dare not tempt them with weakness. For only when our arms are sufficient beyond doubt can we be certain beyond doubt that they will never be employed.

But neither can two great and powerful groups of nations take comfort from our present course—both sides overburdened by the cost of modern weapons, both rightly alarmed by the steady spread of the deadly atom, yet both racing to alter that uncertain balance of terror that stays the hand of mankind's final war.

So let us begin anew—remembering on both sides that civility is not a sign of weakness, and sincerity is always subject to proof. Let us never negotiate out of fear. But let us never fear to negotiate.

Let both sides explore what problems unite us instead of laboring those problems which divide us.

Let both sides, for the first time, formulate serious and precise proposals for the inspection and control of arms—and bring the absolute power to destroy other nations under the absolute control of all nations.

Let both sides seek to invoke the wonders of science instead of its terrors. Together let us explore the stars, conquer the deserts, eradicate disease, tap the ocean depths, and encourage the arts and commerce.

Let both sides unite to heed in all corners of the earth the command of Isaiah—to "undo the heavy burdens and to let the oppressed go free."

And if a beachhead of cooperation may push back the jungle of suspicion, let both sides join in creating a new endeavor, not a new balance of power, but a new world of law, where the strong are just and the weak secure and the peace preserved.

All this will not be finished in the first hundred days. Nor will it be finished in the first thousand days, nor in the life of this Administration, nor even perhaps in our lifetime on this planet. But let us begin.

In your hands, my fellow citizens, more than in mine, will rest the final success or failure of our course. Since this country was founded, each generation of Americans has been summoned to give testimony to its national loyalty. The graves of young Americans who answered the call to service are found around the globe.

Now the trumpet summons us again—not as a call to bear arms, though arms we need; not as a call to battle, though embattled we are; but a call to bear the burden of a long twilight struggle, year in, and year out, "rejoicing in hope, patient in tribulation"—a struggle against the common enemies of man: tyranny, poverty, disease, and war itself.

Can we forge against these enemies a grand and global alliance, north and south, east and west, that can assure a more fruitful life for all mankind? Will you join in that historic effort?

In the long history of the world, only a few generations have been granted the role of defending freedom in its hour of maximum danger. I do not shrink from this responsibility—I welcome it. I do not believe that any of us would exchange places with any other people or any other generation. The energy, the faith, the devotion which we bring to this endeavor will light our country and all who serve it—and the glow from that fire can truly light the world.

And so, my fellow Americans, ask not what your country can do for you: Ask what you can do for your country.

My fellow citizens of the world: Ask not what America will do for you, but what together we can do for the freedom of man.

Finally, whether you are citizens of America or citizens of the world, ask of us the same high standards of strength and sacrifice which we ask of you. With a good conscience our only sure reward, with history the final judge of our deeds, let us go forth to lead the land we love, asking His blessing and His help, but knowing that here on earth God's work must truly be our own.

Questions and Exercises

1. What were John F. Kennedy's principal assets as a presidential candidate in 1960?_____
_____

2. What were his principal disadvantages?_____
_____

3. What were the probable effects of his television debates with Richard M. Nixon during the campaign?_____
_____

4. List two books written by Kennedy that became best-sellers._____
_____

5. Describe the speaking occasion for his "Inaugural Address."_____
_____
_____

6. What is the basic organizational pattern?_____
_____

7. What are the principal forms of support?_____
_____

8. Give one example of the rhetorical question._____
_____
_____

9. To what basic motives does the speech appeal?_____
_____

10. What is the central idea of the speech?_____
_____
_____